Praise f...

"*Truth Without Fear* will change ... ...t being honest with the people who matter to them should buy this book. Foster's expertise offers a library's worth of experience and practical wisdom. This book is a pleasure to read; it's filled with wonderful stories of everyday people, and it's brilliant."
Mira Kirshenbaum, author of *Too Good to Leave, Too Bad to Stay*

"This book could untie tongues across the land. It will never be easy to tell a terrible truth, but Charles Foster's valuable advice on how to weigh what you need to say and how it will affect the listener can make the telling easier."
Rose DeWolf, author of *Woulda, Coulda, Shoulda* and *The 10 Dumbest Mistakes Smart People Make and How to Avoid Them*

"Business managers, professionals, teachers, administrators, Army and Naval officers—anyone responsible for managing others when faced with difficult, personal communications problems that need to be aired will greatly benefit from Charles Foster's new book. His system of conveying difficult truths to another makes it possible in such situations for fact and emotion to be combined without leaving hurtful feelings. His book is based not only on accepted research and personal experiences but on long-term records of an extremely wide variety of successful solutions in his clinic. Read this book carefully, and your problems with conveying difficult, truthful information to others in tough situations will markedly improve. So will your status. Skim Foster's book and his easy, fluid, conversational style will give you so many valuable tips, you'll read it again."
Thomas Dunn, Visiting Professor of Management, Carroll School of Management, Boston College

"Practical wisdom updated for the twenty-first century. A very useful book, indeed!"
William J. Richardson, Ph.D., Professor of Philosophy, Boston College

ALSO BY DR. CHARLES FOSTER

Parent/Teen Breakthrough
The Relationship Approach
(with Mira Kirshenbaum)

TRUTH
WITHOUT
FEAR

[How to Communicate Difficult News
in Tough Situations]

Formerly titled *There's Something I Have to Tell You*

Dr. Charles Foster

THREE RIVERS PRESS
New York

Published by Three Rivers Press, a division of Crown Publishers, Inc., 201 East 50th Street, New York, New York 10022.

Member of the Crown Publishing Group.

Random House, Inc. New York, Toronto, London, Sydney, Auckland

www.randomhouse.com

Originally published in hardcover by Harmony Books in 1997 as *There's Something I Have to Tell You.*

First paperback edition published in 1998.

Three Rivers Press is a trademark of Crown Publishers, Inc.

Printed in the United States of America

Design by Lynne Amft

Library of Congress Cataloging-in-Publication Data

Foster, Charles, 1946–

[There's something I have to tell you]

Truth without fear : how to communicate difficult news in tough

situations / Charles Foster. — 1st pbk. ed.

Originally published: There's something I have to tell you.

1st ed. New York : Harmony Books. © 1997.

1. Interpersonal communication.   2. Interpersonal relations.

3. Truthfulness and falsehood.   I. Title.

[BF637.C45F67   1998]

153.6—dc21   98-24968

ISBN 0-609-80199-6

10 9 8 7 6 5 4 3 2 1

First Paperback Edition

To my patients and all the people I've interviewed over the years.
Thank you for teaching me the life lessons it cost you so much to learn,
that can help other people so much.
To Rachel and Hannah. Thank you for your passion for the truth.
And to Mira. I still want to go with you wherever you're going.

CONTENTS

ACKNOWLEDGMENTS

IN A WORLD WHERE THE TRUTH SO OFTEN MAKES TROUBLE and yet where we're all so hungry for the truth, my partner, Mira Kirshenbaum, deserves a Nobel Peace Prize for her work at finding ways for all of us to have more honesty in our lives. This book would not have been possible without her contributions. Let me lay it on the line: Mira has been nothing less than my coauthor, a full and equal partner, fifty-fifty. Her brilliant, wide-ranging, and deep clinical experience and always amazing understanding of how people work inform every sentence of this book. We've been full partners in everything for thirty-one years, and thank God we've been partners here.

I owe deep gratitude to countless men and women whose stories have gone into this book. Many of these people, in effect, have sacrificed part of their lives to learn important lessons the hard way so that we can all benefit from their experience. I hope my ability to listen to the men and women whose lives and lessons have contributed to this book matches their awesome ability to tell the truth about what they've learned about telling the truth.

I want to thank Neil Simon for giving me the title of this book. He was the one who pointed out that there is no more dramatic moment than when one person leans toward another and says, "There's something I have to tell you."

It would take me countless pages to explain what I owe to all the people I'd like to thank. I wish I could do more here than list their names, but I hope they have a sense of what they've done to make possible the words you're holding in your hands. One way or another, these people—colleagues or teachers, heroes or friends—have given something specific to me personally or professionally that's made an enormous difference. To all these people I say thank you: Lisa Bankoff, William Barrett, Jon Bliss, Daniel Brown, Jim Callahan, June Comroe, Barry Dym, Paul Edwards, Milton Erikson, Dick Grossman, Elvin Jones, Ken Jones, Sidney Jourard, Larry Kessenich, Rabbi Harold Kushner, Dick Marek, Jon Matson, Amy Mintzer, Rev. Howard C. Olsen, Barbara Phillips, Elaine Pinderhughes, Adrienne Rich, Bill Richardson, S.J., Max Roach, David Slavin, Warren Sonbert, George Steiner, Paul Watzlawick, Elie Wiesel, Beth Winship.

There's one guy I gotta single out. Peter Murkett—artist, craftsman, historian, essayist, Renaissance man—has been an unbelievably good friend and source of support and guidance since we were crazy kids together. He knows what it's all about. Thanks, man.

Some people I must thank are no longer around to read these words, but my sense of gratitude demands I mention their names. Each in his or her own way has given me something precious: Bernard Berenson, Laurie Colwin, Gerry Conner, Alfred Conrad, Malcolm Forbes, Dody Giletti, Edwin Land, Robert Motherwell, Andy Warhol, Carl Whitaker.

Howard Morhaim, my friend and agent, knew what was needed to make this book go over and then he made it happen. His intelligence and support have been fantastic. And thanks to Kate Hengerer for being so unfailingly helpful.

Shaye Areheart is, to paraphrase the Bible, a pearl among editors. It's not just that she's responsible for a high proportion of this book's virtues, but she has the vision to make sure it reaches all the people who need what it contains. Beyond that, Shaye has provided strategic help from the beginning of my career—I don't know if any of this would have been possible if it weren't for her.

Thanks to Leslie Meredith for her all-important work on this book's behalf. Thanks to Dina Siciliano for being kind and together where it counts. Also I very much appreciate the efforts of Tina Constable and her talented staff.

I have to thank all the readers of my previous books for writing to tell me the difference my words made in their lives. You guys are the reason I'm here.

Everyone says, "How did you come to write this book?" I want to thank all my patients for giving me an answer to that question. I wrote this because you asked me to. One after another you showed how hungry you were for me to help you answer the question "But how do I tell him?" or "How can I possibly tell her that?" Too often you came to me only after you'd broken a long silence by blurting out some truth in a way that did terrible damage. By taking the risk of sharing your pain and hunger for help with me, by bringing to me the people you cared most about to join you in the search for truth, you taught me lessons I had to share with others.

"IS THIS BOOK FOR ME?"

WE'VE ALL BEEN THERE. You want to tell someone how you feel or what you need or what's going on for you. But how do you tell *this* truth to *that* person without causing pain or without making a mess? How do you decide whether it's best to tell that truth in the first place?

Based on what countless men and women who've faced this challenge have shared with me, our dilemma is this:

On the one hand, we love and respect the truth. We dream of being able to talk from the heart to everyone we care about. We long to feel free and unafraid to let ourselves be completely honest. We remember when we were growing up and saw what seemed to us to be a world of secrecy, lies, and hypocrisy, and we vowed to be as honest as we could every moment of our lives, particularly with the people who mattered to us.

But we've all had too much experience with the delicate nature of relationships. We've all seen how shooting from the lip, even if the words come straight from the heart, has a bad effect on people. Instead of applauding our honesty, they get hurt, sad, or angry. Instead of more closeness or a better working relationship, there's suspicion and distance. There are fights, long silences, broken-off relationships.

And because this has happened one too many times, we've gotten gunshy. We're so afraid of conflict that we start watching our words. Better to say nothing, we think, better to tell a white lie, better to be "diplomatic," than to blurt out honest words that will just make a mess.

But—and this is how our dilemma keeps us circling round and round—the very tactics we use to preserve the peace and keep things running smoothly make us feel something's missing from our relationships. We find it's hard to be ourselves. We hate not feeling free to speak the truth.

In the end, we're torn between our sense of ourselves as honest people and our fear of the terrible messes that get made when some truths are spoken, between our sense that to be responsible you must tell the truth and our feeling that it may not be responsible to tell a particular truth.

I wrote *Truth Without Fear* to help you

- Get the confidence that comes from knowing the right way to tell the truth.

- See when it's best to tell the truth and when it isn't.
- Find relief from guilt and fear, because your truth will no longer make a mess or force you to remain silent.
- Recover the self-respect you know you deserve as someone who valiantly struggles to uphold the standards of honesty and of harmony at the same time.

And I wrote this book to offer you a new chance at happiness. Silence can be miserable, but being able to break through the silence is wonderful. Conflict and confusion are awful, but being able to prevent them by seeing how to tell the truth responsibly is exhilarating. The happiest people in the world are those who feel free to tell the truth and can do so without hurting *anyone,* and I wrote this book to show you how easy it is to achieve this kind of happiness.

You're probably a good communicator already, but some things are hard for almost anyone to say. And when there's something that's hard to say to someone who's important to us, most of us fall into one of two groups. Your problem might be that you think you should be able to just speak your mind and be yourself, except that when you do there are too often hurt feelings and strained relationships. Or your problem might be that you usually try to get away with saying nothing, hoping that the need to say this difficult thing will pass, except that silence feels bad and in the end you discover you've made a bigger mess by keeping quiet than if you'd spoken in the first place.

No matter which it is, and for some of us it's both, this book will help you find a way to speak the truth without hurting anyone, including yourself.

And this book will help you if you're looking for a way to speak the truth in *any* of your relationships. For example:

- Perhaps you've had too many experiences where you thought you could be completely honest with someone you were intimate with but then you had something to say that was hard for her to hear and you blurted it out and it damaged or even destroyed your relationship. Yet love can turn sour when the other person makes you feel you have to hold back the truth too often.
- Perhaps you've seen too many situations at work where you were sure

honesty was the best policy, but when you carried out that policy and told the truth, it was a catastrophe. And so the comfort you need to feel with your colleagues and associates is tainted by the half-truths and deceptions you use to stay away from danger.

- Perhaps you've had too many friendships that seemed possible only because you bit your tongue, and at the same time too many friendships that you lost because you failed to bite your tongue. The fun and freedom we want to have with our friends is spoiled by our sense that there are huge areas where it's not safe to tell the truth.

And this book is for you no matter what your truth is. The fact is that any truth you've ever wanted to tell someone, or ever will want to tell someone, falls into one of six categories. And you'll learn to tell your truth effectively no matter which category it falls into:

1. You want to *tell someone how you really feel*.
   - A woman wanted to tell her son that she felt disappointed in who he'd turned into.
   - A man wanted to open up to his best buddy about his long-held-back feelings of resentment and jealousy.
   - A woman wanted to tell her husband she felt bitter about what she'd given up to help him succeed.
   - A man wanted to tell the woman he was getting romantically involved with that he'd thought he loved her but now he wasn't so sure.

   What we're hoping is that the other person will simply hear our feelings without judging us or feeling judged by us. We want to feel closer to the other person or at least feel accepted for who we are. Instead, what keeps happening is that the other person ends up feeling threatened, you both get upset, and there's a big fight.
2. You want to *give someone needed criticism*.
   - A man wanted to tell his sister that she was leading a trashy, empty life with her husband.
   - A woman wanted to tell a roommate that she smelled bad.
   - A man wanted to tell a colleague that no one in the office liked his stupid jokes.
   - A woman wanted to tell a friend she was acting like a slut.

What we're hoping is that this criticism will ultimately benefit everyone. Instead, what keeps happening is that people hear what we think of as "helpful feedback" as a put-down or an attack, and they respond by getting upset or angry or defensive. The truth gets lost.

3. You want to *ask for something that's hard to ask for* but that's important to you. Even if your need isn't a big deal in itself, it may be a big deal that you're saying that you have a need like this.

   • A woman wanted to tell her partner how much she wanted him to perform oral sex.
   • A man wanted to ask his adult son to move out of the house.
   • A woman wanted to ask her boss to cut her some slack for the next couple of years because she had increased family responsibilities.
   • A man wanted to borrow money from a brother with whom he'd had a strained relationship.

   You'd be surprised at some of the things that are requests even if we don't think of them that way.

   "Every time my boss asks me to do something, I can't say no." But *saying no is a request.* You're requesting the option of saying no to the other person's demand.

   "I've done a couple of things to hurt my girlfriend and everyone tells me I have to apologize, but I find it hard to ask her to forgive me." *An apology is a request too.* You're asking someone to forgive you.

   Whatever it is, of course you'd like the other person to agree to your request, but you're hoping that if he can't give you what you want, you'll at least feel there's still a sense of respect and comfort between you. Instead, what keeps happening is that not only do you not get what you want but your request makes trouble and the other person seems to think less of you for needing what you do.

4. You want to *confess a guilty secret* without your confession blowing up in your face.

   • A woman wanted to tell her business partner that a year ago she'd had a series of conversations with someone about selling her share of the business to him.

- A man wanted to tell his spouse that he'd had an affair with his old girl-friend.
- A man wanted to tell his mother that over the past years he'd lost a lot of her money in bad investments.
- A woman wanted to tell her best friend that she'd lied about someone the friend was seeing because she didn't want her to get involved with him.

What we're hoping is that confessing our secret will relieve us of guilt and fear; that bringing the secret out into the open will enable us to solve some problem we've not known how to solve. What keeps happening is that the other person is first shocked by what you've told them and then feels deeply suspicious because you haven't told them sooner. Instead of clearing the air, you've muddied the water.

5. You want to *disclose sensitive personal information*.
   - A woman wanted to tell her boss that she was going through menopause.
   - A man wanted to tell his wife that years before they met there was a period when he was gay.
   - A woman wanted to tell her liberal husband that she'd turned conservative.
   - A man wanted to tell his friend that his father was not dead as he'd claimed but was serving a life sentence for murder.

   What we're hoping is that indeed honesty is the best policy. Instead, what keeps happening is that the other person is disturbed or shocked and changes how she feels about you for the worse.

6. You want to *report bad news* without getting blamed *and* without the other person's being devastated.
   - A man wanted to tell a friend that he'd accidentally broken his friend's snowblower.
   - A woman wanted to tell her spouse that she'd been fired.
   - A woman wanted to tell her close friend at work that many rumors were going around that this friend was sleeping with the boss.
   - A man wanted to tell his colleagues that the software application he'd been developing probably wasn't going to work out.

• A woman had to tell her brother that he couldn't come to live with her after his divorce.

What you're looking for is a way to convey the bad news that will minimize recriminations and keep the focus on what the two of you can do to make things better. Instead, what keeps happening is that bringing bad news creates shock waves of disappointment and distrust that destroy whatever healing power the truth might have.

And whichever category your truth falls into, it can be about any issue at all, such as

• *Money:* asking for a loan from a relative or friend, or telling someone who deserves to know how much money you have, or anything else having to do with money.

• *Health:* telling someone you have cancer or AIDS or that you can't have a child, or asking someone to take care of you while you're sick, or any other health issue.

• *Sex:* confessing that you've had an affair, or asking your lover to do something kinky in bed, or telling your partner that the things she does in bed no longer arouse you, or any other sexual issue.

The things that are hard for us to say can touch on matters of religion, crime, politics . . . anything you do, anything you believe, anything you feel, anything that happens to you.

Unless you can say these difficult things to the person you want or need to say them to, you live in a world of walls, not bridges. Unless you can say them effectively, you live in a world where your bridges keep collapsing.

I wrote this book to bring you the hope that you can be both a completely honest and a thoroughly caring person in all your important relationships. You *can* say the difficult things that need to be said. You *can* get the truth out and heal things at the same time. You *can* satisfy the part of yourself that's committed to honesty as well as the part of yourself that's learned how some truths, when they're handled poorly, can blow up in your face. Truth, safety, and harmony *can* go hand in hand, and you will learn how.

PART I

EXPLORATIONS

Happiness consists of being able to tell the truth
without hurting anyone.

FEDERICO FELLINI, *8 1/2*

1   Bombshells: A Personal Introduction

• LEARNING HOW TO DO IT RIGHT

WHAT'S TRUE FOR YOU IS TRUE FOR ME. I wasn't born with a silver tongue in my mouth; what I know, I've learned through hard experience. Whatever fears you've had, I've probably had too. If you'll do anything to avoid conflict, I'm probably just as much a conflict-phobe as you are. The mistakes you've made are probably the mistakes I've made.

To understand the journey I've taken, you need to hear a story about how ignorant I was and how much damage my ignorance caused in my personal life when a long time ago I had a truth to tell the most important person in my life. After all, I'd be a hypocrite if I didn't share a personal truth of my own in my book on sharing truths.

So let's go back about eighteen years. Since I was already a therapist—a guy licensed by the state to deal with difficult truths—you'd think I'd have known better. But dealing with my own personal bombshell, I screwed up in every way you can imagine. I kept it hidden far too long. Then I revealed it in the worst possible way. And I dealt with the other person's response as blindly and stupidly as anyone could possibly have done. My story is a mini-encyclopedia of mistakes. But as I tell you about my mistakes, each one gives me the opportunity now to point out the kinds of help we all need and that you'll get in this book.

True Confessions

There are many kinds of difficult truths. Mine happened to be a guilty secret. Like most of the truths we find hard to say, mine would never have made the news. It was a big deal only to my wife and me.

It came up during a period in which the busy lives we were leading were driving us apart. At a university where I was working I became close friends with a woman to whom I was attracted. We had long personal conversations. A simple way to describe what happened is to say that I fell in "like" with this woman.

That was the secret I was keeping from my wife, the whole thing: I'd become close and attracted to a woman I worked with. It wasn't a physical affair—no sexual or romantic touching—but it was a kind of emotional affair.

It wasn't a tabloid-size secret, but I caused as much damage with the way I told my wife my stupid little secret as other people have caused with much juicier ones. While some might say that my secret was almost nothing, I'm sure you'll understand how if not handled properly it could be deeply upsetting to someone you're married to.

Let me tell you how I turned what could've been a simple marriage-healing sharing of information into a near marriage-destroying catastrophe.

The silence of the clams

I let months go by without saying anything—the ever-attractive "don't tell" option. This is what most of us who hate conflict do. We feel committed to the truth, but when we think of the shouts and tears and struggles that come with telling the truth, we just clam up. I guess I thought that my secret would simply melt away into that place we all hope our secrets disappear to. It's as if we feel that our silence contains a kind of magical solvent that if given enough time will make a difficult truth go away.

Of course, the opposite happened. By letting weeks and weeks go by before the truth came out, I made it seem as if I were in a major conspiracy and so turned a minor situation into a disaster. Later my wife saw every day I was silent as evidence that something huge had been going on. Why, she kept asking after I spilled the beans, would I hide the truth for so long if I weren't guilty? Didn't my silence mean that something was going on that was far worse than I was claiming?

I probably knew I was going to tell at some point because we had, and have, one of those marriages where you both try to live up to the ideal of being completely open and honest with each other. But while I gave myself credit for honesty by telling myself I would reveal my secret at some point, like the coward I was, I kept putting it off. People with difficult truths to tell live by the code of mañana. We will tell, but not today, only tomorrow.

A naked Mighty Mouse

I didn't prepare myself for revealing the truth. You'll learn how to prepare, but I didn't know how eighteen years ago. As it is for so many of us with a hot truth, telling for me happened in a haphazard moment that took me as much by surprise as it took my wife.

It's often an unexpected event that spurs us into blurting out the truth. In my case it was seeing *Kramer vs. Kramer*. You know, Dustin Hoffman and Meryl Streep going through a bitter divorce with a horrible custody battle. I felt scared leaving the movie theater because it gave me a vision of where my wife and I could end up if we didn't deal with the growing distance between us. So I had the impulse to play the hero we all imagine ourselves to be when we tell our truths. I'd be like Mighty Mouse saying, "Here I come to save the day," except that I'd be Naked Truth Guy showing up to save the day.

So I didn't think about how to tell my truth or what were the best words to use or what I wanted to get out of telling it. I didn't plan for how my wife would respond or what my disclosure would mean to her or what would happen to my disclosure when it entered the transforming vortex of her emotions and turned into something quite different. Like an idiot, I just winged it. I sat her down on our bed and said what everyone always says: "There's something I have to tell you. I don't know how to say this, so I'll just come right out with it." And I did.

I now know that just as it's possible to walk and chew gum at the same time, it would've been equally possible for me to have maintained my self-image as an honest guy while at the same time thinking about exactly what I wanted to tell her and how my telling might affect her. The problem was that back then I didn't know any of the basic principles of making difficult truths easier to tell and easier to hear. You're luckier. You will.

Messy beans

I couldn't have done a worse job of telling my secret. I've blocked from memory the exact words I used as I went on and on, blah blah blah, telling my wife a vague and messed-up version of what had happened. But it must've looked awfully suspicious to her for me to have a full-blown case of confession sweats over what I was claiming was a tiny little confession. I just know that what came across was something like, "Aren't I wonderful for confessing I was attracted to another woman. It may seem like a huge thing because I'm so obviously uncomfortable about it all, but you should think of it as a tiny, meaningless thing because that's how I'd like you to think of it. And now that I've spilled the beans, I'd like you to forget about this so we can get back to things as they were."

Every word I spoke reeked of egotism and defensiveness. My "confession" was all about how wonderful I was for making it and how her only possible response should be instant and complete understanding and acceptance. To show how wonderfully honest I was, I threw in the detail that this woman and I had once hugged good-bye in a stairwell, when that detail could illuminate nothing important but would be sure to fuel suspicions.

Wobbling weasels

And I didn't even tell the actual truth. Without intending to, I deepened and prolonged the damage to my wife and to me and to our marriage by telling her a confused and distorted version of my little secret. I actually made my relationship with that other woman seem more intense than it was.

I left out a lot of details that I told my wife later on because when I was leaving them out, I thought, well, it'll be easier this way. I now know that what I did was typical: people distort and minimize whatever's difficult in what they have to say. But I didn't realize then what you'll come to see: you must be crystal clear about what the actual truth is.

In my headlong desire to protect myself (what an irony!) I did other things guaranteed to maximize the trouble I got into. So, for example, in my attempt to minimize what happened, I neglected to apologize to my wife for hurting her. I was thinking something stupid like, "Now, if I don't apologize for anything, she'll understand that nothing happened for which an apology is necessary. I'll get credit for initiating this truth telling without being blamed for anything bad actually having happened." By misunderstanding what my wife needed, if I thought about what she needed at all, I virtually guaranteed that I'd make her as miserable as possible.

Building bombshells

Mine are the mistakes I've discovered people consistently make when they have something that's difficult for them to say. If I'd done nothing more than just avoid these mistakes, as you'll learn how to do, I'd have prevented half the trouble I got into.

But you can do much better than that. You can go the whole distance and get all the good things it's possible to get when you tell your truth in the right way. I didn't know any better then, but I now know simple techniques that work like magic to allow the healing you want to happen, guaranteeing you'll avoid the worst pitfalls.

For example, I was so consumed by how this beautiful moment of truth telling was supposed to play out that I didn't think about how my wife would feel. She naturally enough said that she felt betrayed by me, that I'd violated our intimacy, that she could no longer trust me. How did I respond? Instead of being there for her and understanding her needs, I got mad. She was not calmly swallowing my confession the way I wanted her to, so I made her the bad guy. Our mutual disappointment and anger escalated. But I was the one who had turned a simple truth into a bombshell.

A long nightmare

I ended up looking like a cheating, lying bastard, and my wife ended up looking like an unforgiving, crazy bitch, and that's not who we were. It's who my clumsy truth telling turned us into. It took over a year to clean up the mess I made by the way I told my secret. We came out of it fine, but it took too long for our relationship to recover from damage that should never have occurred in the first place.

For a long time I was convinced that my biggest mistake was telling the truth at all. If only I'd kept my big mouth shut, I thought, my "relationship," or whatever you want to call it, with that woman would have faded into nothingness without my wife and I having to go through any of the pain.

Now, older but wiser, I see that if I'd known then what you'll know once you read this book, telling the truth in an effective way would've been the right thing to do in my circumstances, although not for other people in other circumstances. And you'll learn how to identify the exact circumstances in which telling makes sense.

Telling without telling

I've since discovered that I had another alternative that never even occurred to me back then. What do you do when you want to tell the truth but the truth is simply too hot to handle?

Well, you have an option, an alternative to both hiding and telling. I call this the *virtual disclosure* option, and later you'll learn how to use it and when it's appropriate to use it. Everything that's difficult for you to say to someone is a kind of egg hiding a yolk of truth about an important issue between you and that person. Remember I said my wife and I had been going through a period of difficulty. Within the egg of my secret were issues vital to the health of our relationship, which my secret brought to a head.

I could have employed virtual disclosure to confess not the who, what, when, where, and how of my little secret, but the feelings, needs, and concerns I had, such as how lonely I'd felt with the growing distance between us. I didn't have the option of saying nothing. That would have been stupid. But I did have the option of telling a truth that focused on the important issues we needed to deal with.

FINDING THE TRUTH ABOUT TELLING THE TRUTH

I've come a long way since then. I now know that telling the truth can almost always be a positive experience, no matter how difficult you're afraid the truth will be for the other person to hear. How did I come so far? I have to give the credit to my patients and all the people who were so eager to share their lives and stories with me. Without exception they passionately wanted to help me discover the truth about telling the truth, because they knew firsthand the suffering that's caused by not knowing how to tell the truth in the right way.

I'm here because I can listen, not because I can talk. This book is the product of years spent helping everyday men and women find a way to have more truth and more harmony in their relationships. Some of these men and women were my patients, some worked for organizations I consulted with, and some were people who agreed to participate in the research for this book. The answers you'll find came from listening to their problems and, more important, to their solutions.

Back when I was first starting out in the shrink business, I learned that if I could help people solve the problems they had with other people in their current lives, I'd not only remove toxic elements from their social environment that were making them miserable, but I'd be giving them the very skills they needed to finish with therapy in the shortest time possible.

"But How Can I Tell Him That?"

No other problem came up more often than people wanting to tell someone something and worrying about how to tell it and inevitably having to clean up the mess that occurred after telling it. Tell what? The truths my patients wanted to tell someone important to them didn't have to be all that dramatic to be a psychological burden that created havoc in their lives. They were the most common truths you and I agonize over whether to tell and how to tell, as well as some unusual ones.

Truths like these were so all-pervasive that at some point in our work together virtually every person would ask me at least once, "Should I tell this truth to this person? How should I tell him?"

The Raw Truth Shall Set You Free

At first, I'm sorry to say, I wasn't very helpful. I automatically believed what most people believe when they're young, that the sheer naked truth is all anyone needs. And like most people in my profession I subscribed to the belief that the raw truth was an imperative of mental health. So with few exceptions my advice was "You've simply got to tell, and the best way to do it is to just come right out with it."

Of course a week later I'd hear about what happens when you drop an explosive truth into a delicate relationship between two people, each with a history of hurts and fears. Friendships were destroyed, marriages damaged, families torn apart, work environments filled with stress and confusion.

Alongside people's deep desire to tell went a profound dread of telling. Everyone knows how much easier it is to just not say anything today, and tomorrow, and then to just *stay* silent. And some of us are more afraid of making a mess than others.

The Name for Our Fears

The reason we don't just blurt out every truth that comes up is that hard-earned experience has made us afraid. And the first step in overcoming fear is to give it a name. *Algolalophobia* is the name for the fear of saying something difficult. It literally means "fear of painful talking." It's pronounced *al-go-LAY-lo-phobia*. Everything we're afraid of when we have something that's hard to say falls under the umbrella of algolalophobia.

If you're someone who says, "I hate conflict and confrontations," and you do everything you can to avoid them, then you're an algolalophobic.

But a big messy confrontation where you get yelled at and put on the spot is only one of the things algolalophobics are afraid of. You might be afraid of the other person's crying. You might be afraid of the other's despising you for what you've said. You might be afraid of the other's breaking off your relationship. You might be afraid of being laughed at.

All you know is that you're about to open your mouth and tell the truth, and you're scared. It's crucial to overcome algolalophobia because more often than not your fear leads you to make things worse for yourself. Here's an example.

Ron's story

Ron, thirty-eight, had worked for a large consumer-products company for eleven years. Shortly after New Year's, a round of promotions was announced, but the promotion Ron had expected to divisional manager wasn't on the list. Ron waited until after five and then casually wandered into his boss's office. After chatting about this and that, Ron offhandedly mentioned his not getting the promotion. That's when he learned he was simply no longer being considered a candidate for senior management, period. "Ron, you're off the fast track" was how his boss put it. Ron's skills as a lawyer would still be needed by the company but only in staff positions.

Ron knew he should tell his wife, Tracey, about this. But some things are hard to say indeed, and this was one of them. After all, if his own future now looked less rosy, her future looked less rosy too. How do you tell something like that to your wife?

If Ron hadn't been so afraid of how she'd respond, he would probably have just come home and told Tracey what happened straight out. But Ron hated conflict and he knew how upset Tracey got when she heard anything unpleasant. She could dissolve in a torrent of tears. She could take off in a whirlwind of blame. She could shut down in icy silence. His experiences with the ways Tracey had responded before made him afraid of how she'd respond now.

The say-nothing option

So Ron looked at his situation from the other angle, asking himself what would happen if instead of telling her he kept silent. And it was soon clear to Ron that he might get away with never telling his bad news to Tracey. There'd be no way she'd find out in the near future, because who'd tell her? Obviously by the time he hit sixty-five she'd see he wasn't CEO, but in the meantime all she'd see, dimly at first and not for a while, was that he wasn't rising as fast as she'd hoped. And so what? They both knew how tough it was to make it. She wouldn't know for years that he'd been derailed; she'd just think he had been given slow signals on the fast track.

So what would be the harm, Ron wondered, if twenty years from now Tracey began to see that Ron wasn't going to get the top jobs? Silence now seemed less scary than her possible reaction, even though he knew he'd have to face the truth at some distant point.

The cost of silence

Not telling seemed like an easy decision at first, but it soon started taking a huge toll on Ron psychologically. Because staying silent felt like what only a weak man would do, Ron's self-esteem headed south. Because he felt bad about himself, he fell prey to depression, sleeplessness, and anxiety. Because he'd always relied on Tracey for support, with her now being in the dark he was denied her support.

But these problems didn't push him to reveal the truth at first. What happened to Ron is what happens to so many of us when we find ourselves in this kind of situation. The worse we feel about ourselves for not coming out with the truth, the more scared we feel about what will happen if we *do* tell the truth.

There's something paradoxical about fear. It's an emotion that evolved to help us protect ourselves, and yet it so often leads us to do things that hurt us. As with so many people, Ron's algolalophobia ultimately led him to do the worst possible thing: he kept silent for too long and then blurted out his truth at the worst time and in the worst way.

Ron said nothing for many months. His silence lost him all possibility of getting credit from Tracey for being open and honest. And notice how our silence traps us: since he didn't tell Tracey what had happened the same day he heard it, it seemed so easy to wait another day, and after waiting a week, why not wait another week, and then a month?

Shattering the silence

Silence has a way of growing heavier with time. So one day in the middle of a fight about whether to buy a sofa, Tracey accused Ron of being stingy. That's when he blurted out his bad news in an angry, blaming way, as if to tear from his shoulders the mantle of guilt he'd been carrying. "I have to be careful with money, but I'm always worrying about your wild spending. I'm not CEO, you know, and I'm never going to be. What do you think it's like for me having to be with someone who can't face facts?" And he went on to tell her the truth he'd been hiding.

As you can imagine, Tracey had all kinds of feelings about Ron's bad news. But like most people she was transfixed by *how* he told her—the words he used, his timing, his lack of openness, his failure to take into account any of her needs. How could she begin to respond? But since the way he told her seemed designed to make her feel guilty, that's how Tracey responded. And what do we do when we try to ward off guilt? We blame. Tracey expressed such hostile and vehement disappointment in Ron that a terrible breach was opened between them that has yet to heal.

This breach was not about Ron's bad news. Ron and Tracey's marriage isn't in trouble because he was taken off the fast track at work. It's in trouble because Ron's algolalophobia prevented him from considering the possibility that he could tell her his news without a disaster. And with the typical mixture of silence and blurting, he created the very disaster he'd been trying to avoid.

From understanding comes relief

Ron's story is not unique. In fact, it's the rule rather than the exception. It's what happens to most of us when we let our fears govern the way we handle the truths we need to tell.

I want to reassure you that this book offers relief from algolalophobia. Up until now your fears have been realistic. Most people don't know how to tell difficult truths without making a mess. When you learn how to tell the truth effectively, there will be nothing left to be afraid of.

Silent Poison

I eventually saw one thing clearly. The silence that's so comfortable when we're afraid to speak the truth can easily cause as much damage as the raw truth itself. Poison is just as deadly as gunpowder. The following story illustrates the trouble we get into when it's hard for us to tell the truth.

Karen's story

Five years ago Karen went into business with Larry, a friend of hers from work, to develop and manufacture educational software. With their combination of skills you'd have thought they were the perfect team. But in fact

Karen had specific goals that weren't compatible with Larry's. In a fast-paced industry, Karen wanted to grow the business as quickly as possible and then sell it to a large company as soon as possible. Karen was in it to make money, not because she was a do-gooder. Larry wanted to spend more time on research, more time soliciting grants to develop content, more time focusing on the needs of underserved kids.

Karen never told Larry the truth about her goals because she kept thinking that their differences would work themselves out.

But the two of them got increasingly frustrated with each other. Larry was disappointed in what he thought of as Karen's crass commercialism. Karen was annoyed with the way Larry kept slowing them down. They each kept silent because they had a large emotional and financial investment they didn't want to jeopardize by facing facts.

Finally the inevitable, messy breakup happened. What Karen said to me is crucial: "I only wish I'd told Larry five years ago what I told him today. It would've saved both of us five years of pain and frustration. It would've prevented us from wasting five years of our lives. The mess I hoped to avoid by keeping silent only grew larger until it overwhelmed us."

In the Truth Chamber

It was countless stories like Karen's and Ron's that kept reminding me that silence is almost never a good option. I started to encourage people who wanted to tell someone a difficult truth to bring that person into my office and drop the bombshell while I was in the room to help.

The old idea that the truth shall set you free proved true. You had to tell the truth effectively and it had to be a truth that *should* be told, but if both of these criteria were in place, telling the truth could make all the difference.

Anna's story

When I first started seeing Anna and her family, she was thirty-nine. Although she was a talented artist, her work was almost completely unappreciated and she'd never been able to support herself through her work, even though it was both brilliant and commercial. Her problem was fear of speaking a certain kind of truth: the truth of what she needed. She was utterly unable to ask anyone for anything.

Anna was born in Holland immediately following the Nazi occupation. Throughout her mother's pregnancy there'd been a severe food shortage, which gave her mother the guilty feeling that Anna was being malnourished inside her womb.

Because of this experience, Anna's parents constantly feared that they wouldn't have enough to give their children. As Anna grew up, anytime she asked for something beyond what was given her, it would throw her parents into an uproar. They seemed to think that by discouraging her from asking for things, they would protect her from having needs that could be threatened by shortages. Like a lab animal who receives a shock every time it does something, Anna learned to expect an uproar whenever she asked for something.

A learned disability

Not only was Anna made fearful of asking for things, but she never became skilled at asking. And that's exactly what happens to all of us who hate confrontations: our fears keep us away from anything likely to provoke a confrontation, and so we never get skilled at dealing with those situations. This meant, in Anna's case, that it was all the more likely that she'd ask for things ineffectively, which meant she wouldn't get them, which deepened her fear of making requests still more.

Progress through understanding

Anna made progress almost as soon as she understood that her inability to ask for things was a fear, a fear she'd learned through a special set of circumstances. Anna realized that it wasn't anything about making requests in itself that was necessarily crisis-creating, but that her fear was exclusively based on distorted lessons she'd learned while growing up.

A whole new set of possibilities opened up for her. As Anna developed the capacity to ask for things, she was able to start making things happen in her career. Gallery owners started paying attention to her work. Influential critics started hearing about her and from her. People she'd sold paintings to years ago heard from her again and were asked by her for referrals to other potential buyers.

Actually the change in her professional life, dramatic as it was, wasn't the biggest surprise that resulted from Anna's being able to speak the truth of her needs. The biggest surprise was what happened in her marriage. She'd spent ten years feeling deprived by her husband and furious with him because she never got what she wanted. It had seemed to her as though only his needs counted. But once she felt safe enough to start asking for things and learned to ask for them effectively, Anna's husband astounded her by meeting needs she thought would never be satisfied.

To take just one example, she'd thought Joe was a selfish lover when they did have sex and that he didn't want to have sex more than once every few weeks. Once she was able to speak the truth of her needs, she was amazed to find out how willing Joe was to have sex more often and to do things in bed for her and with her that she'd only dreamed about.

Learning to do it right

The good news was that helping people tell difficult truths in my presence made things better, because I could create some healing of the damage that occurred by how they told their truth. Anna told Joe the "truth" of her sexual needs by saying he was a lousy lover, and it took too much time and pain to work through the hurt that caused. It soon became clear to me that I was healing damage that didn't have to occur in the first place.

I started catching glimmers of how to do it right. Instead of saying to the people I worked with, well, just bring your sister or husband or mother or friend or colleague into my office and tell them your truth here, I'd say, well, bring them in, but first let's figure out together the best way of saying the truth so that all of its healing goodness comes through with a minimum of destructive side effects.

I found that the more time I spent coaching people *how* to tell *before* they told, the less time we'd have to spend cleaning up the mess afterward. But my work wasn't done. I needed to learn more in order to help people tell the truth effectively.

Putting It All Together

So I did some research. I basically talked to men and women who had a difficult truth to tell and followed what happened over the next several months. I also asked people to tell me about those times when someone told them a difficult truth.

For example, I asked people what it was like to be on the receiving end when someone confessed a guilty secret. What was it like when someone shoved a hefty slice of negative feedback in your face? What was it like when someone asked you for something that put you in a terrible position? What was it like to be a parent and have your thirty-one-year-old son suddenly tell you he's gay? What was it like to hear your sister tell you all the angry feelings she's harbored toward you over the years?

The end result of all that research and all my clinical work is this book you're holding in your hands. It contains everything you need to be able to tell any truth, however difficult, so that the truth actually gets through while at the same time you're furthering your goals and preserving your relationship with the person who's hearing your truth.

WORDS CREATE WORLDS

Having the Right Attitude

The truth is never naked. It's always clothed in *some* words. And words create worlds. That's why people have concluded that the pen is mightier than the sword. Words create worlds in the sense that what a parent says to a child, and the way it's said, can create a life-long foundation of hope and self-esteem in that child. If the same truth is said in other words, a parent can cripple the child emotionally.

The principle that words create worlds applies to adults as well. Anyone who's longed for someone they care about to say "I love you" understands how words create worlds. Anyone who's been devastated by cruel criticisms understands it. Anyone who's suddenly gotten a new sense of a brighter future through some words of encouragement understands this.

So it matters very much what words we use to speak the truth. And the more important *what* we have to say is, the more it matters *how* we say it.

Bad Attitudes

Some people with a naive view don't want to pay attention to the consequences of their words. They think that bluntly speaking the naked truth protects them against the charge that they've said things clumsily, cruelly, insensitively, ineffectively. Listen for the word *just:* "I was just telling the truth." "I was just saying what was on my mind." "I was just reporting the facts." They say this the way someone might say, "It was just a bag of trash. Why are you making a big deal about my throwing it out the car window?" Their attitude is just say it and let the chips fall where they may.

Meanwhile, other people think that some truths are so hard to say or so hard to hear that it doesn't matter how you say them, and so it's better *not* to say them at all. Just *don't* say it and hope that silence protects you. But words do make a difference, and they're a much better alternative than silence.

The fact that words can facilitate truth telling while at the same time protect us from unintended but toxic side effects means that you no longer need to feel torn between troublemaking truths and guilty silence. You can live every day in every one of the relationships that are important to you as the fully honest, fully authentic truth teller you'd like to be without any of the destruction or difficulties you've experienced in the past. You can harness the truth so that it retains its power for good and yet is completely safe. You can become a responsible truth teller.

2 To Tell or Not to Tell? That Is the Question

You don't always have to tell the truth. But not telling should be an option you choose responsibly, not one you fall into just because you're afraid of making a mess. It's wonderful to be liberated from silence, but it's also wonderful to be liberated from the sense that you always have to tell every truth.

So you have to be smart about telling the truth. As long as you think of the truth as sacred, there's no basis for determining whether to tell or not. You just tell, or you feel guilty. But the "Should I tell?" decision is a practical matter that can have far-reaching consequences for your life.

The Truth Investment

For the purposes of making the "Should I tell?" decision, I'd like you to think of the truth as a kind of investment. I'd like you to think of *investing* in the truth. That's what it means to tell a difficult truth to someone who's important to you. It's hard to say, but because of who this person is to you and the future you're looking forward to sharing together and what you're hoping will come from sharing this truth, it makes sense to tell it anyway. There are costs now, but there will be benefits in the future.

Weighing the Costs and Benefits

This means that you can approach the tell/don't-tell decision by weighing the hassles and heartaches against all the possible payoffs. As a practical matter, why would you tell if telling resulted in all costs and no benefits?

For example, if someone comes into your office to work as a temp for one day only, and she doesn't do such a great job, it's likely you won't tell her the truth about her performance, because what's the point? You'll pay the price of a painful scene, but you won't get anything for it. But if you have a permanent assistant, you have an investment in his doing the best possible job. It might feel hard to tell him the truth about his poor performance, but because he's permanent, it's worth it.

If you have a first date with someone, it's not likely you'll tell him your deepest feelings or share your most important needs. Why invest in someone when you have no future with him yet? But the minute you fall in love or there's the possibility of a commitment, then suddenly many things that are difficult to say you want to say because investing in the truth will pay off in the future.

Deciding whether to tell a particular truth to a particular person is connected to a whole range of moral, psychological, and practical issues. But thinking about the truth as an investment is the best way to begin sorting through these issues to come to the best decision.

Not Knowing How Is No Excuse

One of the biggest reasons people have for not telling is that they don't know how. This book takes away that reason. There might be other reasons for not telling, but not knowing how to tell will no longer be one of them.

What does this mean for you? It means that the question is no longer "To tell or not to tell?" The question now is "To tell in the best possible way or not to tell?"

The morality of happiness

I think that when it comes to telling the truth, one great moral principle operates:

Do what's best for everyone in the long run. Generally that means telling the truth. But the basic principle here isn't some abstract notion of honesty as an absolute good in itself or as a moral law given by God. I'm more interested in a quite practical calculation of what makes everyone happiest.

My moral position is more happiness and less pain. Do everything you can to create more happiness for yourself and everyone around you in the short run. And lay the groundwork for more happiness in the long run. And do everything to prevent pain in the short run and to lay the groundwork for preventing pain in the long run. The truth fits in as a way of creating happiness and preventing pain when you take the broadest, deepest view of things.

In other words, you tell the truth because it makes people's lives better, and *only* when it makes people's lives better. The bottom line for me is dealing with people kindly and helpfully and intelligently and in a way that makes their lives better.

Some people believe that morality is a series of rules that you must follow strictly, and that "Tell the truth" is one of these rules. But the morality of an act must be gauged by including the consequences of that act as part of a moral whole. The morality of telling a particular truth has to include not only what's best for everyone in the short run but the consequences in the long run of telling that particular truth.

Truth and psychology

People thrive on hope and knowledge. We all need as much as possible of both. We need knowledge so we can figure out the best thing to do. And we need hope so we can believe that the best is possible.

Our need for knowledge demands the truth at all times. But our need for hope makes things more complicated. Studies have shown that mildly depressed people—people with less hope—have a more accurate view of reality than the typical optimistic person. This means that psychologically there is a trade-off, whether we like it or not, between being hopeful and being realistic. Our need for hope requires that the truth be shaded in rosy hues. Deciding to tell or not to tell means understanding what knowledge of the truth will do to a person's hope. It doesn't make sense to devastate hope in exchange for a tiny increase in useless knowledge.

What does all this add up to? Simply this. The truth is good and useful (to use the language of Socrates), but our ultimate goal is what's best for everyone. We serve the truth only as a way of serving our fellow human beings.

DECIDING TO TELL: QUESTIONS AND ANSWERS

To help you decide whether it's best for you to tell your specific truth or not, we're going to go through a series of questions and answers. Ultimately this is a matter of practicalities. It involves weighing pros and cons.

Truth? What truth?

At this point some people have only a general or vague idea of what their truth actually is. If you had asked me eighteen years ago when I was thinking of telling my wife about my relationship with another woman what my secret really was, I wouldn't have known what to say. I hadn't thought about it. What details would I mention? What would I emphasize? What would I say was the point of this confession?

So before you decide whether it's best for you to tell or not, you need to write down specifically what your truth is that you're thinking of telling. And I do mean specifically. For example, if you're thinking of telling your boss how you feel about the way he's been treating you recently, write down how you actually feel and how you're going to describe to him how you feel. Then outline what you're going to say about the way he's been treating you and why that's made you feel the way you do.

In the same way, write down here what you would actually say to the other person *if* you decided to say it:

_____

_____

_____

_____

_____

Now let's figure out if you should decide to say it.

Question #1. What are you trying to accomplish from telling this truth to the other person and what difference will your telling it actually make?

I've learned through long and painful experience that every time someone speaks a difficult truth before he's figured out *why* he wants to tell it, it's a disaster. Every time someone says something that's hard for him to say without knowing what he wants to get out of saying it, it's a disaster. Every time someone speaks an emotionally charged truth for no other reason than that you're supposed to speak the truth, it's a disaster.

So the principle is very firm: You've got to understand why you want to tell before you decide whether to tell. Unless you understand your motives and needs for telling, you won't be in the position to decide whether it's best to tell or not. And the reason is this. The truth makes a difference. Things are different after you tell a difficult truth from the way they were before. What you do when you tell the truth is make things different. Only when you understand why you want to tell can you decide whether the way things *will* be different after you tell your truth is the way you *want* things to be.

Let's say you "borrowed" some money from petty cash at work and then replaced it, but now you're burning to confess your crime to your boss. Telling him just because you feel guilty is not a reason to tell unless you're clear about the difference your telling will make. Will you actually feel less guilty afterward? Do you want your boss to trust you? If so, will telling him create more trust?

The point is to think through your real goals and then ask yourself how telling will accomplish your goals. Here's an illustration of this.

Derek's story

There was something bothering Derek about his wife, Mimi, and it bothered him a lot. She was flat chested. He loved her and he felt she was a wonderful person, but Derek had been one of those guys who liked big-breasted women. He'd gotten together with Mimi because she was smart and funny and beautiful, and he'd told himself he shouldn't care so much about big breasts. But now they were married and he did care. Should he tell Mimi the truth about his feelings about her chest size?

Well, the first question to focus on was what difference telling her would make, so he could decide whether he wanted things to be different in that way.

At first Derek claimed it would make a big difference to him. The difference was that he'd explode if he didn't tell Mimi. He's not alone in this belief. A lot of people believe that an unspoken truth is a kind of nitroglycerin of the soul, or else they believe that an unspoken truth will give you cancer if you don't clean it out of your system.

In truth, unspoken feelings or other truths when kept on the shelf usually fade in urgency over time. Twenty years ago, let's say, you desperately wanted to date your best friend's boyfriend. But you didn't and you never told your friend, even though you worried that you should. For 98 percent of people, problems and desires such as these fade to nothing.

When I asked Derek if he could avoid exploding if he didn't tell, he said he thought he could. But he still wanted to tell Mimi.

But what about Mimi? What difference will this make to Mimi, I asked Derek, beyond making her feel you're not attracted to her and making her feel bad about her body?

She'll know how I feel, he said. Well, obviously, I said, she'll know how you feel if you tell her how you feel, but when I say what difference will it make, what changes will there be when she knows you have those particular feelings? For example, will knowing how you feel about her small breasts make her feel closer to you?

No. Derek thought it would make Mimi feel more distant. Will it make Mimi feel she can trust you to be honest? No. Derek thought he already had a reputation for being a direct, open guy.

Well, what other difference will this make to Mimi? I asked. For example, do you want her to do something to make it up to you, like acting more sexy in bed or wearing sexy underwear? This was an attractive thought for a moment, but the more Derek considered it, the more he realized that Mimi was giving him all he needed, and anything else would probably seem to her as if she was paying some kind of penalty for not having big breasts, and that felt awful to him.

I was running out of ideas for what difference his telling her might make. Finally I asked Derek if he wanted Mimi to get breast implants. But Derek was a health-food-eating kind of guy who was suspicious of artificial remedies of any sort, and he was filled with a sense of unease over the health risks of breast implants.

Nothing good will come of it

So, I said to Derek, let's see if we can get to the bottom line on this for you. Other than Mimi's knowing that you're unhappy with her breasts as they are, her knowing this truth will make no positive difference whatsoever to either of you. It won't make anything better in any way. Neither of you will do anything different. The only clear impact will be Mimi's feeling bad about herself and feeling you don't find her attractive.

Will what happens when you tell Mimi the truth achieve any of your goals?

I asked Derek to think about this for a week. When he came back, he said, "You know, I fantasized about a day when we'd both be old and Mimi would tell me about how she was always grateful to me for telling her that I didn't like her being flat chested because that had made her feel I'd always tell her the truth. But the more I thought about that fantasy, the more I realized it was bullshit."

The moral of this story is that you've got to focus on the real difference telling your truth will make and not get caught up in phony, empty, illusory reasons for telling. The truth is our servant. If you can understand why it's better for Derek not to tell Mimi, then you can understand why you have to feel clear about your own reasons for telling and why they have to make a lot of sense to you before you tell. Not just that you agree with these reasons for telling, but that you believe they'll actually come to pass.

Derek avoided making a mistake. Let me help you do on your own what I was able to do with Derek. Write down the three main things you want to happen when you tell:

1. _____

2. _____

3. _____

Ask yourself if these things you want to happen are actually likely to happen. If the things you want to happen aren't likely to happen, *then you shouldn't tell.* But if the things you want to happen are likely to happen, *then that's a reason to tell.*

Finally, write down the three things you most want *not* to happen when you tell:

1. _____

2. _____

3. _____

Ask yourself if these things you don't want to happen are likely to happen anyway. If the things you don't want to happen are likely to happen anyway, *then you shouldn't tell.* But if the things you don't want to happen are not likely to happen, *then that's a reason to tell.*

Telling a difficult truth is like getting a baby animal. Those of us who've been through it know that you don't just get a kitten, you also get a future cat. You get everything that will happen after you take your kitten home.

You should get a kitten only if you've thought about the whole future package and decided you want that. I have a cat now and I would certainly take home a kitten in the future. Baby elephants are cute too. But I would never buy a baby elephant. What is your truth as it plays out over time? A cat? Or an elephant?

Question #2. How likely is it that what you're thinking of telling is going to come out anyway?

No matter what your answer to the previous question was, if the other person is going to find out anyway, you're better off telling him yourself as soon as possible. That's true even if it looks as if bad things will happen if you tell and that's making you think you shouldn't. If the other person *will* find out, then you should do the telling.

After all, you're saying something that's hard for you to say because of your commitment to the truth and because of your commitment to working things out between you and the other person. If the other person finds out before you tell, you'll lose all credit for both of these commitments. And that would be a tragedy. There's a much greater likelihood of your working things out if you're seen as being committed both to the truth and to the relationship.

I realize that it's easy for me to say, "Tell if it's likely the other person will find out." Where it gets sticky is figuring out how likely is likely. What makes something like your truth "likely" to come out or not?

The big mistake people make is confusing their wishes with reality. The fact that you hope the other person won't find out doesn't mean he won't find out. You might think that you could get away with not telling your boss that you're involved in an extensive and elaborate search for a better job. But there you are making endless copies of your résumé, putting calls in all over the place, taking time off to go for interviews, and mentioning your boss as a reference but asking people not to contact him until you're ready. What could possibly go wrong? Only everything.

"Will he ever find out?"

Here are some questions that might help you see how likely it is the other person will find out.

Is the truth you're thinking of telling something you want to tell? Or is it just a fact that you have no desire to tell? This makes a big difference. If there's no other way the other person will find out and you have no desire to tell him, he probably won't find out. But it's a funny thing about people. It's almost impossible for us to hold back telling something we're dying to tell. If you want to tell badly enough, you will tell eventually.

And you might be surprised at how many of our truths we really want to tell. People who've had affairs often have a strong desire to confess this to their partners, for example. Grievances and feelings of resentment, whether expressed as feelings or as needs or as feedback, often seem to have a life of their own—no matter how many years go by, we still want to tell them. Don't confuse your fear and reluctance to tell a particular truth with your not wanting, at the same time, to tell that truth. Often we both want and don't want to tell the same truth, and if we really want to, we will. So if you really want to, you'd better tell sooner rather than later.

Is the truth you're thinking of telling something known by other people who know both of you? If people who know both of you know your truth, you've got to tell it. Think of it like this. If you've been talking about leaving your job to anyone who happens to know someone who knows your boss, then you've got to figure your boss will find out. You might have a brief period when your secret will hold. But you'd better prepare sooner rather than later to tell your boss before he finds out from someone else.

Is the truth you're thinking of telling something that the circumstances of your life will bring out whether you want it to come out or not? A lot of human tragedy grows out of people not facing up to this question. For example, take friendships that are lost. There was something you thought of saying to your friend, some criticism or confession such as that you were sick of her complaining, and you didn't really want to tell her and no one else knew about it. But the reality of it was that you couldn't help yourself acting on this truth. You avoided your friend. You stopped calling her back. You cut short your conversations.

But your friend wasn't stupid. She knew you were distancing yourself. So she wanted to know why and she bugged you to tell her. The only way you could avoid telling her was to distance yourself even further.

And the tragedy was that you liked this friend. You didn't like her complaining, but you liked everything else about her. And what you needed to see was that your truth would come out through your breaking off your friendship even if you didn't want it to come out at all. This was a truth you should have told because the circumstances of your life would have brought it out anyway.

Familiarity breeds knowledge

The rule of thumb I'd like you to follow is that the closer you are to someone, the more likely it is that she will find out your truth. I don't just mean emotionally close. Even if you have a business relationship with someone, if your relationship forces you to work together closely, that increases the likelihood that she will find out. So the question you have to ask yourself is *not* whether you can prevent yourself from telling, but whether you can prevent the other person from eventually finding out even if you don't tell.

This is particularly applicable when your truth is a feeling. Suppose you've been in a romantic relationship with someone for a long time, but the truth is that now you feel bored by him. You love him, but he bores you. It's not that there's something that you want to do—such as go out more often—that he won't do; it's that who he is makes you feel bored.

Do you tell or not? Well, the question here is, will he find out or not? This is where a lot of people make a big mistake. They assume that the only way the other person would find out is if they tell him. They assume that since it's easy not to tell him tomorrow and even the day after, that it's easy not to tell him forever. But it doesn't work that way, particularly when it comes to feelings. Intense feelings ultimately intrude.

The pebble test

The best way I know how to be absolutely clear about this is with the pebble analogy. Any feeling that bothers you is either like a pebble in your shoe or it isn't. If it's just a transient pain, like a muscle twinge that goes away, then you obviously don't need to say anything. But if it's a pebble, then no matter how small it is and no matter how much you try to ignore it, it will either make you scream or it will cripple you.

The circumstances of life are bound to bring out every truth and feeling that's real and permanent and solid enough to make itself felt over time.

Doesn't this mean that Derek should have told Mimi that he was unhappy with her small breasts? No, because it failed the pebble test. It wasn't as if Mimi had bad breath that made physical intimacy unpleasant. He was attracted to her and sex was good. Derek guessed, correctly as it turned out, that his truth would diminish in importance over time.

Question #3. How much benefit will there be from telling your truth?

Remember, the truth exists to make our lives better, not the other way around. If telling the truth makes no one's life better and makes everyone miserable, why tell it just to serve an abstract principle? You would never tell an aged relative who was reminiscing about how she was beautiful as a young woman that you'd seen pictures of her and she was actually pretty ugly even then. A remark like this would cause pain to your relative without accomplishing anything worthwhile for anyone.

So we're in agreement: your decision about whether to tell or not has to do with whether there will be any benefit from telling. Obviously, if there's a real benefit, you should tell, and if there's no real benefit for anyone, that's a reason not to tell. But here's where a lot of people get into trouble. They make two mistakes. They think someone's going to benefit when there's no benefit. And they think there's no benefit when there really is a benefit.

So my job here is to help you see overlooked benefits and to help you look past unrealistic expectations. Here's a story that might help you sort through these different kinds of benefits.

Brett and Mattie's story

They had one of those problems so many couples face. Seven years of knowing each other all too well, the stress of daily life, and a hundred and one petty annoyances had made Brett and Mattie's relationship stale, distant, and uncomfortable. And this was sad for both of them because their first few years together working in the Peace Corps in Bolivia had been wonderful. And they both still deeply loved each other.

These days Brett was busy working as a lawyer for the city and Mattie worked as a cost estimator for an architectural firm. Pierce, one of the architects Mattie worked with, started pursuing her and she encouraged him. Finally, Mattie agreed to go to a hotel with Pierce, but she felt bad about her decision. They had sex but it was awful for Mattie, and she said she wouldn't sleep with him again. Interestingly, this didn't destroy her relationship with Pierce, but rather they developed one of those relationships that are all the more intimate and romantic because there's no sex. Pierce wanted to sleep with her again but Mattie kept saying no.

One day Mattie met for lunch with a friend who was getting married. As her friend talked about everything she was looking forward to, Mattie realized that she was living out all the good parts of her marriage with Pierce and saving all the bad parts for her husband, Brett. It struck her how silly and destructive this was. But what should she do? Should she tell Brett about Pierce?

Mattie was highly organized. So she made a list of what she hoped to get out of telling Brett. There were two benefits she looked forward to. One was feeling closer to Brett. The other was that things would be better between them simply because Brett would know about Pierce.

A full year after Mattie told Brett, when there'd been plenty of time for the two of them to digest the impact of her revelation, Mattie told me that if I ever wrote a book about this, I should make a point to enlighten people about the benefits she got that she'd overlooked and about the unrealistic expectations she'd had. Here's what Mattie wished she'd known back then, plus what I've learned since.

Some Benefits from Telling the Truth That People Overlook

Closeness

Feelings follow actions. This is a long-established psychological principle. When you don't tell someone who's important to you something, you're acting distant and then you feel distant. Telling difficult truths is an act of intimacy, and it can create a sense of closeness throughout your relationship. And I'm not just talking about personal relationships. Business relationships can be distant and uncomfortable too. The things you reveal about yourself can make them feel closer.

A better-functioning relationship

Information is the fuel of relationships. Silence, secrecy, and lies kill relationships the way a blocked fuel line will kill your car's engine. When the truth comes out, it often supplies crucial information the relationship needs to function better. For example, the truth Mattie had to tell Brett was about the real needs she had for warmth and friendliness that she'd gone outside of their marriage to satisfy. By telling her story to Brett she was able to show how important these needs were to her as well as make Brett realize that he could lose her. Brett started treating Mattie much better, and in response to this Mattie started treating Brett much better.

More trust

Many times we find something hard to say because it puts us in a bad light. We screwed up. We went back on an agreement. We need to reveal something unflattering about ourselves. And it seems to us that by saying this we're giving the other person less reason to trust us. But seeing it this way is the result of misunderstanding what trust is. You don't trust me because I'm perfect. You know that I'm fallible, and you trust me because I'm honest about my mistakes and weaknesses. Mattie was amazed that Brett—after some initial anger and suspicion—actually seemed to trust her more after she confessed her involvement with Pierce.

A new solution to old problems

With everyone who's important to you there's probably some area where you've just given up on being able to make things better. You love your sister, but she's unreliable. Your father's a great guy, but he'll never talk about himself. Your boss will never tell you how he wants you to do a job until after you screw up. Not always, but surprisingly often, telling a difficult truth throws something brand new into your relationship that solves these old problems. Boring sex had been an old problem for Brett and Mattie. The truth Mattie told Brett not only opened his eyes to their need for intimacy but taught him something about how to make it happen. They both started talking about what they wanted, and they both stopped being such lazy lovers. Their sex life got better.

Less loneliness

Loneliness is not being able to talk about stuff. It might be hard to admit this sometimes, or even see it, but what I've noticed is that people can be lonely to some extent in virtually every one of their important relationships. Even bosses talk about feeling lonely on the job. That's because in every relationship there are huge areas you just don't talk about. Like a lot of people, Brett and Mattie had gotten in the habit of talking about little but who was supposed to do which chore. Mattie's revelation opened up a whole new personal area of things for them to talk about, and they were both amazed at how much less lonely they felt afterward.

Giving the other person a chance to surprise you

Most of us find incredible safety in feeling we "know" the other people in our lives: it protects us against disappointment. But it also prevents us from doing anything new that would give them the opportunity to show us that they're better than we think they are. That's why taking the risk of sharing a difficult truth gives the other person the chance to pleasantly surprise you. When Mattie told Brett about what had happened between her and Pierce, Brett surprised her by acknowledging how little he gave to her and how she deserved a partner who was more affectionate than he'd been.

More energy

You're about to meet a new client for lunch, and a colleague has told you that no matter what, you must absolutely avoid mentioning marriage because the client has just gone through a harrowing divorce and he's a nut on the subject. So you're likely to use up a lot of energy trying to stay away from anything that would remotely touch on marriage or divorce or relationships. It's the same way when there's something you want to say to someone who's important to you. Even if you've gotten used to not saying it, most people report being surprised by how freed up they feel once they've gotten it off their chest.

More respect

When someone tells the truth, we think he's a strong, courageous person with integrity. And that's who we respect. It takes those qualities to say something that makes things hard for you or puts you in a bad light. Let's not kid ourselves, though. If you have something to say that will be hard for the other person to deal with, his response will be all about that aspect of what you're saying. But over time, your honesty will pay off in respect, *if* your honesty is a sign of respect in the first place. If you're honest because the other person is too unimportant for you to have to think about how you're saying things to him, you're going to cultivate resentment.

Adding up the benefits

What do these benefits from telling the truth add up to? A larger, freer, smoother, better-functioning life. We're so afraid of confrontations that we all overlook how much a difficult truth well told opens things up and makes them better.

Some Unrealistic Expectations from Telling the Truth

In deciding whether to tell or not, people commonly look forward to some benefits that they keep not getting. Based on my experience, it's unrealistic to expect them. It doesn't mean it's better not to tell. It does mean that if telling depends on getting this benefit, then you might want to rethink your decision.

Being praised for your honesty

Yes, honesty does earn you respect. But that respect, while real, is often invisible. We respect people for being honest but we also expect them to be honest. And you don't praise someone for doing what's expected. My father worked with Admiral Rickover, the founder of the U.S. nuclear-submarine program. Rickover was a tough guy. At one meeting a hapless executive was stupid enough to begin a sentence, "Well, frankly . . ." Rickover smashed his fist down on the table, making the glasses shake, and shouted, "Damn it, I expect you to be frank."

That's exactly the kind of thing that happens when we tell someone something that's hard for us to say. We keep hoping that the other person's gratitude for our honesty will all by itself smooth away whatever difficulties arise from what we've said. But honesty is like air: its absence is a huge problem, but its presence is taken for granted. Don't expect that gratitude or joy over your honesty will help you through whatever difficulties your truth brings up.

Things will be better just because the other person knows the truth

The idea that merely telling your truth will make things better is like thinking a cake will get made merely because you have the ingredients. Besides telling the truth, it's essential that you help the other person understand what to do with your truth.

When Mattie told Brett about her involvement with Pierce, they wasted three weeks because Brett's understanding was that he just wasn't able to meet Mattie's needs. He thought Mattie was telling him he simply wasn't good enough. Mattie was waiting for Brett to start delivering, and Brett was thinking she was saying he couldn't *ever* deliver. Any truth, all truths, point to problems and require certain actions. What problems? What actions? You have to make it clear. If you can't work through whatever follows from your truth, the truth itself won't do your work for you.

Things will get better fast

Suppose you hadn't told your partner that you were tired of the way the furniture in your living room was arranged. Just because you finally did say something wouldn't mean that the furniture would rearrange itself. You'd have to get up and move things around and experiment with arrangements that might turn out to be worse than what you had before. You might even find that you need to buy something new you hadn't planned on buying.

Only when you're truly finished rearranging the furniture in a satisfactory way will the room look better. That's what it's really like when you tell the truth. Let's say that some things have to be "rearranged" in your relationship with your coworker. She's bossy about stuff she's not really good at. You tell the truth, as you see it, and then the two of you have got to go through a difficult process of moving from the old order to some new order. And that means that you and the other person will be in unfamiliar territory and make mistakes and step on each other's toes. If a truth is worth telling, it will make things better eventually. But the more important that truth is, the more stuff needs to be rearranged before things get better.

The other person wants to know your particular truth

People often say to us that they welcome our feedback, that they're eager for us to share our feelings, that if there's any bad news at all, they can't wait for us to disclose it, that if there's anything we want at all, they'd love for us to ask for it. You'd think that with all that eagerness no one would have any trouble saying a difficult truth.

But we human beings are contradictory creatures. One part of us wants the truth, period. The other part of us wants the truth only as long as it's good news. The same person who said he's eager for your feedback might be dismayed when you actually criticize him. Often, precisely because a truth is so difficult for us to say, we desperately need the other person to welcome our truth. If your truth is not going to be welcome and you need it to be, then it might be better for you to rethink your decision to tell.

Guilt reduction

One of the most frequently mentioned reasons people give for telling a difficult truth is "because I'll feel less guilty." Mattie felt guilty for getting involved with Pierce, then she felt a whole new sense of guilt for not telling Brett about it. The expectation she had was that guilt is like a bad smell in a closed room and it will disappear when you open the windows of honesty.

The reason this expectation is so often unrealistic is that we don't understand how guilt really works. Suppose you feel guilty for not telling someone something, but then he feels worse after you tell him. Why wouldn't you feel more guilty, not less? Suppose you want to be forgiven for what you did but the other person can't forgive you. Wouldn't you feel more guilty, not less? This happened to Mattie.

The rule of thumb here is to decide whether it's best to tell and let the guilt take care of itself. Generally, if it is best to tell, you will feel better, whatever happens with your guilt in the short run. If it's not best to tell, feeling less guilty shouldn't tip the balance in favor of telling.

Question #4. How painful will it be for the other person to hear what you have to say?

Of course, one of the things that makes something difficult to say is our fear of a confrontation. In other words, how painful will it be *for us* when the person we're addressing hears what we have to say? But the question that really needs to be addressed first is how much pain is involved for the other person?

The issue is clear. The less real pain for the other person, the more that weighs on the side of your telling. The more your truth will cause the other person pain, the more you need an awfully good reason to tell that truth. It had better be a reason that makes the pain worthwhile.

So that's what I want to look at here—real pain—because it's important to separate this from the ruckus people raise sometimes when you tell them something they don't want to hear. What I'd like to do is give you a way to determine how much real pain your words might cause. We've gotten used to thinking that everyone's different and that people's reactions are completely subjective. But there is a way to get a handle on the amount of pain your words might cause.

How to measure pain

Emotional pain is all about loss. When you tell someone he's fired, for example, there's a loss of income, prestige, and future prospects. It's losses that cause the pain of getting fired. You can have a good sense of how much loss there is when you fire somebody by looking at his age, the job market for someone with his skills and background, the overall economy, and other factors. You would expect a just-fired fifty-five-year-old marketing executive to feel more emotional pain than a just-fired thirty-year-old software engineer, because he's lost more.

Actual loss is the best way to measure subjective pain. I think you'll be amazed at how accurately you can assess the pain your words might cause if you ask yourself what the actual loss is this person will face.

Suppose you want to tell someone how you feel. For example, your father has been asking you to do things for him and you want to tell him that you've always been angry with him for the way he bullied you when you were a kid. But you're afraid it will be too painful for him to hear this. To determine how painful it will be for him to hear this, ask yourself what he'll lose, now and in the future.

In this case it's probably not much. You're not saying that you won't have anything to do with him. You're not even saying you won't do things for him anymore. You just want him to know what you're feeling. The only loss to him is the sense that you feel as wonderful about him as he'd thought. As for the future, there's more gain than loss because there's a chance for the two of you to work things out.

On the other hand, if the only thing that still gives him a shred of self-esteem is his sense that he was a good father and he has no skills for talking things out, then there'd be a lot of unmitigated loss and you'd have to wonder if the pain was worth it.

On the job

Giving feedback on the job often causes more pain than we think it will. When you tell a subordinate that her reports are poorly researched and poorly thought out, for example, from your point of view you're just trying to get her to do better reports because you need her reports to be good. But for her a huge black cloud has now formed over her sense of who she is and what kind of future she can expect with your company or maybe any company. A vision of future promotions has died in her heart. A sense of herself as smart and competent has been lost. Understanding her pain might not make it possible for you to avoid telling her the truth, but it might make you rethink exactly what you plan to say and how to say it.

In general, it's in giving feedback that we tend to most underestimate the pain our words will cause, since we're focused on getting someone to change and so we miss *their* focus on what they've lost.

The end of a mystery

Other people's emotional pain no longer needs to be a complete mystery to you. You can gain a somewhat accurate sense of it by asking yourself what their loss is in the present and what they'll be afraid of losing in the future. Just the way you can imagine the loss that comes from hearing "You're fired," you can imagine the loss that comes from hearing anything *you* might have to say. That's where the emotional pain comes from and that's what you can weigh in the balance when deciding whether your truth is worth telling or not.

If you remember Derek and Mimi, he decided not to tell her how he felt about her having small breasts precisely because he could imagine her emotional pain as she was figuring out her loss. And her pain wasn't worth it.

Question #5. Do you and the other person have a future together?

This question gets at the seeming mystery of why we're polite to strangers and yet have big messy fights with the people we're closest to. We're polite to strangers because there's no point in struggling over anything with someone you'll never see again. What will you get for it?

The point of this question is that you don't just decide whether you should tell this truth to this person; you're also deciding whether you want to have a future with this person, and how connected you want to be in this future.

The rule of thumb is clear. The more you want to have a future with the other person, the more weight there is on the side of telling. The closer you want to be to the other person in the future, the more weight there is on the side of telling.

You might think this is obvious. But those of us who are afraid of confrontations and of bringing up painful feelings, no matter how sophisticated we are, act as if the opposite were true. The closer someone is to us, the more eager we are to keep difficulties out of the relationship because that's where we're most vulnerable to a confrontation. We'll talk to everyone else we know about our feelings or problems instead of telling the person who's close to us, who needs to hear it. This always feels as if it makes things easier in the short run, but these are the same relationships where years later we wonder where all the accumulated resentment and unsolved problems came from—why we're so distant from each other and why it's so hard to communicate.

Cliff's story

Cliff, a popular local TV sports reporter, had the same agent for ten years. Like so many people, Cliff dreaded conflicts with anybody, but particularly with someone as tough talking as his agent, Dick. So he didn't tell Dick that he was unhappy with the way Dick seemed to cave at the last minute in salary negotiations or how intimidated he felt by the way Dick made him feel like an idiot for thinking that he got anything other than the best possible deal. He didn't tell Dick how much he wanted to move out of the area, or about a nodule doctors found on his throat that turned out to be benign.

Cliff handled things this way because he believed it would be better. Or at least smoother. But he destroyed their relationship. One day Cliff heard about a new young agent who was supposed to be really good, and he went over to her. I happen to know that she turned out to be far less satisfactory than Dick had been, but by then it was too late. You can imagine for yourself the painful conversation Cliff had with Dick when they ended things. Cliff tried to keep things general. "I just thought it would be best" was the reason he first gave. But as you might predict, Dick pushed and Cliff's real grievances started pouring out.

"Why didn't you tell me sooner?" Dick said with each new grievance of Cliff's. "We could have worked things out."

In general, all else being equal, if you have a future with someone, you tell him the truth.

Question #6. Do you have personal reasons for wanting to tell this truth that might be destructive or that might be satisfied in a better way?

We began this chapter by saying that if you're deciding whether to tell the truth or not, you decide to tell because you realize telling will make things better. You don't tell if it will make things worse.

This becomes all the more important when you examine all the instances where people just wanted to "be themselves" and share what was in their hearts, convinced it was the right thing to do, and it created a disaster, even when they didn't make things worse by the way they told. I've discovered that in many of these instances the person who did the telling had dark motives and didn't realize it. Take revenge.

Sally's story

Sally and Claire had been best friends since childhood. The big difference between them growing up was that Sally's father was a disabled veteran and she grew up very poor, while Claire's father was a partner in a downtown law firm, with all the prosperity and privilege that came with that. By the time the two women were in their late twenties, things had equaled out between them. Claire was struggling to establish a pottery business and Sally was scraping by as a lawyer in the public defender's office.

They'd talk about their career difficulties the way old, close friends do, but Sally became almost obsessed with wanting to tell Claire that she'd been spoiled, that she had no right to complain, that she'd always had it easy, and that with a rich father there was always a cushion behind her that she could fall back on.

Sally told me in passionate words that "I cannot be myself with Claire anymore unless I tell her what's in my heart. I've got to be open with her, otherwise our entire relationship is a complete lie. If she doesn't know this truth about my feelings, then she doesn't know me. And if I can't tell her this, then maybe we shouldn't be friends." And Sally said all this in spite of the fact that otherwise their relationship was warm and close and satisfying.

I talked to Sally about this and tried to get at what she wanted to make happen besides simply letting Claire know the truth of her feelings. And that's when I tapped into the resentment Sally felt for all the privileges Claire had had in high school and all the worries Sally'd been burdened with because she hadn't had these privileges and how the demands of their relationship had forced Sally to keep her worries to herself. It was clear to me that she wanted to punish Claire and make her suffer and that the desire for revenge was the piece of unfinished business that brought urgency to her truth.

You can't hide dark motives

I tried to make it clear to Sally that when revenge is the motive, you're investing not in the truth but in destruction. But she insisted that this was simply about "being myself."

It was a disaster. We can hide our dark motives from ourselves more easily than we can hide them from people who bear the brunt of them. When Claire realized Sally's desire for revenge, she suddenly didn't know this person she'd thought was her best friend. Had Sally really been this angry woman waiting years to vent her resentment? And how could Claire ever be herself with Sally again if every expression of hope or pleasure would be interpreted as evidence of privilege?

Their twenty-five-year friendship ended, needlessly. Sally could have worked through her feelings about her difficult childhood in therapy. She could even have talked about her own childhood to Claire without making Claire feel in the wrong. "You've always had it easy" was not a truth that needed to be told.

The moral of this story is that dark motives are always a reason not to tell. Any negative feeling can be a dark motive and that means you must make sure there's some constructive reason to tell your truth beyond this dark motive. And I'm not talking about an abstract reason either. You've got to have an actual plan for how your truth will make things better.

Question #7. Does the other person have a right to know?

This question shines a light on a fascinating aspect of all of our relationships. Imagine that who you are and everything about you is a large house with many rooms. Imagine that every truth, every secret, is a separate room. Every time you knew someone was coming into your house, you'd run around closing some doors and opening others. The more intimate you were with someone, the more doors you'd open. Strangely enough, though, you might open some doors to someone you were less intimate with that you'd close to someone you were more intimate with.

For example, women who have a close and open relationship with their husbands will still not tell them things that they talk about with even relatively casual women friends.

In general, the other person has a right to know the kind of thing you'd normally tell him given the kind of relationship you have. A spouse has the right to know something that spouses in general have the right to know. A client has the right to know something that clients in general know. Using our analogy, if the door to a particular room is open to that person at other times, then it should be open to that person all the time.

Take sex. When a couple gets married, they are saying that their bed is their sexual universe. Whatever happens about sex for them will happen with each other. That means each has a right to know whatever's happening about sex with the other.

Now you see why we generally feel an obligation to confess our extra-marital affairs. When you have sex with someone outside the relationship, you still feel your partner has a right to know, and your partner for sure feels he or she has a right to know, because sexual issues belong to both of you.

But if you buy supplies from one company and start talking to another company about buying supplies from them because they offer a better price, you don't feel the first company has a right to know that you're looking for a better deal. It's business, even if you and the first supplier have drinks together from time to time.

The point is that thinking about telling a difficult truth to someone means thinking about who they are to you. If you're of retirement age, your adult son may have a right to know about your finances because he's not only your son but your heir. But he still has no right to know about your sex life. A man with whom you're going on a first date has no right to know your sexual history, but a man with whom you're about to be sexually intimate does have a right to know about anything in your sexual history that could put him physically at risk.

This brings up the other part of the story. A person's right to know isn't only based on who he is to you. It's also based on what not knowing will do to him. That takes us to the next question.

Question #8. What will it cost the other person not to know?

You tell someone with whom you're about to sleep that you might have been exposed to a sexually transmitted disease. Why? Because otherwise he'd be deprived of the possibility of deciding whether to wear a condom or not to engage in sex at all.

The importance of this question can clearly be seen by going back to the example of the guy who was thinking of signing up with a new supplier for his business. We said it's just business. If you get a better price, you change suppliers. The guy who sells you paper clips doesn't have a right to know that you're planning to stop doing business with him.

But suppose you're the supplier's main customer. That happens more often than you might think. Many large- and medium-size corporations buy goods and services from companies that have virtually no other business, or that would certainly go under if they lost their largest account. Because of the nature of business relationships, strictly speaking these companies might not have a right to know if their customer is thinking of dropping them. But when you assess the damage they are about to sustain, the cost of not telling them would be enormous. They wouldn't have a chance to meet their potential competitor's price. They wouldn't have a chance to offer other inducements to stay. They wouldn't have a chance to line up new business or obtain credit before you pulled out.

A moral obligation

It's still just business. But the fact that it will cost the other person a lot not to know means there is a significant moral obligation weighing on the side of telling. But you have to calculate the cost in the right way. Suppose you're thinking of telling your spouse you are not eager to have a child. You might be afraid that saying this would cause so many shock waves you'd be better off not saying anything. And to cap it off, you might think, "Well, I can't see how it would cost her anything not to know that I don't want to be a father."

You're probably right, if your feeling is just transitory. But if it's serious and important and, most of all, probably permanent, then there's a real chance that the cost of not telling could be enormous.

Suppose that by not feeling you can say this to your wife you resent her for the rest of your lives. Suppose your not saying how you feel now means saddling your children with a halfhearted father and saddling your wife with far more than her share of parenting responsibilities. Run the clock ahead forty years. With all the history that's accumulated between you, don't you think that there's a good chance she'd say, "I wish you'd told me how you felt"? Don't you think there's a good chance she'd say that it cost her a lot not to know the truth?

Long-term effects

It can be hard to figure out the long-term effects of a decision not to tell someone something. There's an image I use that helps me see what's best. It's an image of the difference between dropping a pebble into a pond and dropping an alien weed into that pond. With the pebble there are ripples, but the ripples die down fast. The effects of dropping in the alien weed get bigger, not smaller, with time. In the end, it can take over the entire pond, choking out every other form of life. You've got to ask yourself whether the truth you're thinking of telling is like the pebble whose ripples will quickly die down or like the weed that if not dealt with can grow larger and more destructive with time.

A number of years ago I got a call from a patient at two o'clock in the morning of the day she was to be married. Patrice, twenty-four, had just slept with a guy she'd known from college. Should she tell Bob, the man who in ten hours would become her husband? There was so much to think about. We focused on what it would cost Bob not to know. I said, "You have to be honest with yourself, Patrice. Is this event merely a last fling, a unique occurrence with no long-term implications? In other words, is it something that's *not* a sign of danger? *Or* is your sleeping with this guy the beginning of a pattern of infidelity or a sign of something really missing in your relation-ship? In other words, is it a sign that Bob's going to be in for trouble?"

Patrice was silent for what seemed like a long time at two o'clock in the morning. Finally she said, "Bob makes me very happy. I can't imagine I'd be unfaithful to him once we're married. It's just that I'd never slept with a man before and I didn't want to spend my life with Bob being the only guy I'd ever had sex with. I think it would cause Bob a lot of pain to know about this, but I don't think it means anything that would make him wish I'd told him thirty years from now."

It was a tough call because clearly this was the kind of thing that Bob had a right to know about. But it was her decision to make. And the issue was whether this event had implications for Bob. Patrice was convinced that what she'd done was really all about her past, about clearing the slate, and it had no implications for the future that Bob needed to know about.

Like all of us trying to figure out whether or not to tell a truth, Patrice would be playing God either way, telling or not telling, and I asked her to be sure that she was at least acting like a wise and kind God with her decision. Because she'd shown a significant degree of self-awareness and freedom from self-deception, I accepted her decision not to tell Bob as a good-faith attempt to do what was best for everyone.

But suppose *you're* in the position that Patrice was and that you also decide it's best not to tell.

Question #9. Can you tell this truth later if you don't tell it now?

I told Patrice that I could understand her decision, but I didn't think she could ever tell Bob in the future if she didn't tell him now. Deciding not to tell now meant deciding not to tell forever. Why? Because timing made a big difference. If Bob knew before the wedding, he could decide not to go through with it. But if he learned about it a year later, on top of needless pain would be the feeling that he'd been had.

And yet sometimes it is possible to wait before you tell your truth. In fact, sometimes it's better to wait. How can you tell which is which?

It's *always* a matter of timing. Patrice would have made things worse by telling later because a real decision of Bob's was involved: whether or not to go through with the wedding. If she wouldn't tell him in time for him to make that decision, then telling him later would literally be adding insult to injury.

I realize that timing is a difficult matter for everyone from comedians to statesmen. I think what helps us most is to remember to think about the other person. We're reluctant to tell our truth in the first place, so we're going to be biased toward thinking that waiting is better, just the way we tend to put off doing anything that's unpleasant. But the real issue is whether waiting is better for the other person, not whether it's better for us.

The simplest way to determine this is to imagine a little scene being played out. Suppose you don't tell now but instead you wait. After you've told later on, is it easy for you to imagine the other person saying, "I'm glad you waited to tell me"? Or is it easier for you to imagine the other person saying, "Why didn't you tell me this sooner?"

If you sincerely predict that the other person would say the latter— "Why didn't you tell me?"—then, as they say at weddings, speak now or forever hold your peace.

Question #10. What are the wider repercussions of telling your truth outside of this particular relationship?

We've left something out of the discussion so far. I might have made it sound as though your telling your truth to a particular person had no impact on anyone else besides you and that person. But in fact other people are often involved. Sometimes other people are the most important consideration.

Emily's story

One of my patients had a disease called neurofibromatosis (NF), a degenerative disease of the nerves in the skin that often caused painful and disfiguring boil-like bumps. People at work had occasionally asked Emily about it, and she'd brushed off their questions by saying it was nothing. But she had a best friend at work she wanted to tell. It's lonely to be sick and not have anyone you can talk to about it. But part of the problem was that NF is often incorrectly referred to as the Elephant Man's disease because of the possibility that the Elephant Man had NF.

Emily had learned that people at work often can't keep secrets. If you tell one person, other people will know. Even though she was sure her friend at work would be supportive, did she really want to risk working in an environment where everyone saw her as the Elephant Woman? Because of the possible repercussions, she decided not to tell.

Fran's story

In other cases, you might be leaning toward not telling, but when you look at the effect of not telling on other people, you realize it's best to tell. Fran had almost decided not to confront her father with how she felt about his being one hundred pounds overweight. Why provoke his anger? Why set the stage for future battles between them? Why force him to hide his overeating from her when it was unlikely that he'd lose weight anyway?

Then she thought about her mother. A dead father meant a widowed mother. A fight to get her father to lose weight was hard, but it might mean her mother would have her husband with her for ten years longer. Fran decided to tell because of what not telling might cost her mother.

Ed's story

One young man, the adoptive son of parents who loved him and whom he loved, decided to find his birth mother, as many adopted kids do. Without telling anyone, Ed conducted a search and discovered that his birth mother had been a pregnant teenager who'd given him to an agency for adoption and was now the wife of their small town's most prominent businessman.

He wanted to tell her who he was. He had a sense, although he couldn't be sure, that she'd want to know who he was. Then he thought about his adoptive parents (who'd always had to struggle to earn a living), and how they'd feel about his discovering a rich birth mother, and how her husband and family would feel about his coming forward. Ed started to add up all the people whose lives would be affected by his revelation, besides himself and his birth mother, and he came to the grand total of twenty-seven people.

Fortunately in this situation there was no particular cost to waiting to tell. Ed still hasn't figured out what all the repercussions add up to, but you can't make a responsible decision until you look at the effects on everybody.

Question #11. Do you actually have a solid truth to tell that won't get distorted in leaving your mouth and entering the other person's ear?

Don't tell unless you know what the truth is that you're confessing. That way what you confess won't be misunderstood.

My own story illustrates this. There I was, virtually confessing that I'd had an affair, just because I'd become friends with a woman at work. That happens all the time. I was attracted to her. *That* happens all the time.

I felt guilty, but most of that guilt was fueled by my fear and sadness about the growing distance between my wife and me. The biggest, most difficult truth I had to tell had to do with my thoughts and feelings and needs about my wife. By introducing the theme of the "other woman" I created the likelihood of enormous distortion, where the focus would be put on damage, not healing.

The farmer's tale

Here's another illustration of a "truth" that turns out not to be a truth. A farmer friend of mine almost fell off the roof of his barn. Wind had knocked a branch down onto the roof and he climbed up to pull the branch off. Not being as careful as he should've been, he tugged on the heavy branch and it lurched unpredictably. A piece of it whipped around and hit him a glancing blow to the head. He almost fell, and if he'd fallen off the roof, he might've seriously hurt himself. His wife was unemployed. Without his being available to earn a living, there'd be no income.

He agonized over whether to tell his wife what had happened until he realized there was nothing to tell.

Was this a story of his falling into some new state of carelessness that meant that all their calculations of his reliability would have to be revised? No.

Was this a story about how precarious their lives together were, how thin the ice was on which they were skating? But there was no news here. The family finances were an open book to both of them, and it had always been clear that they were one mishap away from disaster.

Was this a story about the kind of thing a guy tells his wife if they have a relationship in which he tells her everything? After all, he told me, as his friend. But if you have a relationship where you tell the other person everything, do you tell them things that serve no function except to scare them?

The way these things work is that if my friend had thought this was a big enough deal to tell his wife about, she would've concluded that it was a big deal indeed, because otherwise why would he have told her? She would've overreacted and they would've had strain and conflict that neither of them needed and that would've been based on nothing really having happened.

The moral of these examples is that before you decide to tell your truth, you have to make sure there's a real truth to tell.

Question #12. What's happened in the past when you've told or failed to tell this person something like this?

Let's say you've got some piece of feedback you'd like to share with your mother, and in the past she's responded poorly to the slightest hint of criticism. In this case, deciding whether to tell her or not means factoring in the likelihood that she won't respond well this time, either.

If all you've done in the past is blurt out your truths with minimal care and planning, then you have to give the other person the opportunity to respond differently this time once you've figured out how to do it right. It may be that it's not criticism itself that she responds to poorly but the way you give criticism, perhaps because you've always said it in a way that sounds disrespectful. But if you help her out and take away the disrespect as you're offering the criticism, then there's a good chance that the future will be different from the past.

The point is that you shouldn't give up on someone's ability to *hear* difficult truths until you've maximized your own ability to *tell* difficult truths. But what then? How can you tell when poor reactions in the past make future efforts pointless?

Predicting the future

There are three things I look for. The most obvious is the one most often overlooked. You can *look for people to tell you their wishes directly.* People will often tell you, if you listen carefully, that they just don't want to be criticized or they don't want to hear bad news or they don't want to hear your guilty secrets.

One woman tried to kill herself after her husband confessed he'd had an affair. It turns out that this was her second marriage and she had told him near the beginning of their relationship that she didn't want him ever to cheat on her, but if he ever did, she didn't want to know about it.

If the person doesn't tell you his or her preferences about criticism and confession, you can always ask. You can say, for example, "Do you want me to never criticize you?"

The second thing I look for is what I call *no delayed benefits.* Often, when you tell a person something difficult, the response is bad in the short run but good in the long run. A lot of teenagers are like this. They respond badly if you ask them to do something, but if you're patient, they'll get around to doing it. It's almost as if they're responding to the command to behave well and they just want a chance to be their own person. But if you don't get a good reaction in the present and the way the other person acts in the future is just as bad, then that's really telling you there are no benefits from telling.

The third thing I look for is *being attacked.* There are bad reactions and there are *bad* reactions. It's one thing for the other person to get upset and miserable, but if you feel there's been an attack on you that in some sense draws blood, such as being denied a promotion at work or being bad-mouthed to your friends, then this is a substantial attack and it's a sign that the costs of telling this person a truth are real and very high.

One more word about being attacked if you're someone who's a con-frontation-phobic. You need to look at instances where you feel attacked to see if there's anything real behind it. Instead of failing to realize that the at-tack is serious, you may be failing to realize that what seems like a serious attack is just words that pass.

The past is the best predictor of the future. If you've not known how to tell a difficult truth effectively, then the person deserves another chance. But if the other person hasn't responded well even when you've done your best, then you're dealing with someone who will most likely give you trou-ble in the future.

These twelve questions will show you whether it's best for you to tell or not tell your difficult truth to a particular person. To get experience with them, let's put the questions through their paces. Let's look at the classic test case of whether or not to confess you've had an affair. Obviously this will be important to you if you're in this situation right now. But even if this particular situation does not apply to you, you will need this general expe-rience of working through all the issues involved.

Should You Confess You've Had an Affair?

The first thing you have to ask yourself is what you're trying to accomplish from telling your truth to the other person and *what difference it will actually make*. He or she will probably be upset in the short run, but in the long run will there be more trust and respect because you were honest or will there be more suspicion and anger because you had an affair? Will there be more of a desire to heal the relationship or more of a desire for punishment? And is this what you want?

Suppose that what you're trying to accomplish is feeling better because you've confessed. Well, if you tell, you'll certainly have confessed, but will you actually feel better? The only way you can gauge that is by being honest about the actual difference your telling will make. You won't feel better *just* because you've confessed if your bald confession makes the other person so angry and miserable that your life becomes a hell.

Next you have to ask yourself, *how likely is it that your affair is going to come out anyway?* If your partner is going to find out, you should be the one to tell her. Based on my experience, I am now convinced that relationships that were destroyed when one partner discovered the truth could have been saved if the guilty partner had confessed first.

And it's important not to deceive yourself. If you're having a big, messy, complicated affair right now with all kinds of intrigues going on, your partner will probably find out. If you're having an affair with someone your partner knows or with someone your partner's friends know, your partner will probably find out. If you're having an affair with someone who doesn't have boundaries—who's crazy or irresponsible—your partner will probably find out. If you're not a genius at keeping secrets, your partner will probably find out.

Next you have to ask yourself *how much benefit there will be from telling your truth*. Not illusory benefit, but real benefit. For example, it might already be obvious to you and your partner that your marriage has a lot of problems. Confessing that you've *ended* an affair might serve not only as solid evidence that you take it seriously as a warning sign but that you're serious about working on your marriage.

How painful will it be for the other person to hear what you have to say? It's not that people have trouble answering this question; it's that they forget to ask it. They're so busy following the Boy Scout rule about always telling the truth and are so full of their need to unburden themselves of guilt that they just don't think about the other person's pain. In my research, people who regretted telling pointed to "not realizing how much it would hurt my partner" as their biggest mistake. You've got to think about who your partner really is before you inflict this pain; and you've got to be clear that the benefits are worth it.

Do you and the other person have a future together? This next question is more important than you might think. It points to the need for dealing with things for the sake of your future relationship. If you're committed to someone, then you have a future relationship. The goal is to make that future relationship as good as possible. That's why you endure the short-term discomfort that can arise when you tell your truth. But be careful. That you have an ongoing relationship may be a reason to tell, but the possibility that your telling might destroy that ongoing relationship is a reason not to tell.

Do you have reasons for wanting to tell this truth that might be destructive or that might be satisfied in a better way? The most common reasons people give for wanting to confess an affair are relieving guilt, obtaining forgiveness, putting honesty back into the marriage, and solving particular problems in the relationship. If you're thinking of confessing an affair, you must ask yourself whether some of these reasons can't be satisfied outside the marriage. For example, confessing to a clergyman or close friend might relieve you of guilt as well.

And other reasons for telling can be satisfied by not telling. For example, the two of you can be more honest about how you feel and what you need even though you've spared yourself the destructive consequences that follow when you confess an affair. You can solve your problems, you can even go into therapy, without confessing.

Confessing an affair is a big deal, like putting a man on the moon. Teflon was a by-product of the space program, but you don't go to the moon so that you can invent Teflon. And you don't confess your affair just to get stuff you can get without confessing your affair.

Does the other person have a right to know? Of course your partner has a right to know. And that weighs heavily on the side of telling. For some people that tilts the balance. But let's look at the next question.

What will it cost the other person not to know? Your partner also has a right to be saved from pain. If your affair is part of a pattern, that too weighs on the side of telling, because then the pain comes from not knowing. But if your affair is an isolated incident, then where's the pain from not knowing? What does it cost you not to know an isolated event from history that has no bearing on the present?

Can you tell this truth later if you don't tell it now? This is the ever-tempting put-it-off-until-tomorrow option. Or until twenty years from now. Here's what I've found. We're all tempted by the proposition that confessing an affair you've had "a long time ago" is easier because at some point the past is encased in a bubble that prevents it from leaking into the present.

But one of the main reasons *for* confessing an affair is that it's a thermonuclear wake-up call to problems in the relationship. And that's a reason for telling now, when the problems can be solved, if indeed you need that wake-up call to solve those problems. But if you wait a long time, then those problems will have remained unsolved for a long time. What if your long-delayed confession only makes your partner realize that you lived for years with unmet needs for love and affection and that you deprived your partner of the chance to satisfy those needs? Then waiting to tell means there's a double loss. And that's a reason to tell now or not at all.

What are the wider repercussions of telling your truth outside of this particular relationship? First, there's the issue of who else will know. You have to assume that there's a sizable probability that your partner will tell the people she talks to. She might tell your kids. She might tell your mother. She might tell the woman in the couple the two of you are best friends with. She might tell someone you're close to at work. I'm not saying she will tell. But you can't count on her not telling.

Second, there's the issue of who will be affected if things go badly. A confession that leads to the breakup of your marriage might have a disastrous effect on your kids or your career.

The point is that you've got to assume that your confession will probably become known in your circle and that the effects of your confession will certainly ripple through that circle. Do you want those repercussions?

Do you know what the truth is that you're confessing so that what you confess won't be misunderstood? If you've had an affair with someone, you've got to get absolutely clear about what actually happened and what it actually meant. Was it a romance that led to sex? Was it just being close to someone on a business trip that led to sex? Was it alcohol that led to sex? And was it good sex or bad sex, or was it a kind of sex that was very different from what you've experienced with your partner? And did this affair happen because you were falling in love with the other person or falling out of love with your partner, or did it have nothing to do with love?

You have to know the answers to questions like these because when you realize what it is that you actually have to say, you may change your decision about whether to say it. If the truth, for example, is that your affair was part of a big romance, then you might be kidding yourself if you think you can get away with confessing that it was "just sex." The romantic part of it will come out anyway, and then you'll not only have made a devastating confession but you'll look like a liar in the process. It's not a question of whether you want to confess what you've been thinking of confessing. It's a question of whether you want to confess what you're going to end up confessing.

Finally, *what's happened in the past when you've told or failed to tell this person something like this?* You've probably never told your partner something like this before. After all, what's "something like" an affair? But have you screwed up big time in the past in other ways? If so, has he exhibited extreme jealousy and possessiveness? Has he shown a capacity to forgive? Even if it's never come up before, there are signs like these that will help you predict how your partner will react now.

Real Responsibility

What all these questions and answers have to do with is being a responsible truth teller. The mistake people make is to tell the truth simply to be able to "be myself." Or because it's simply "the right" thing to do in absolute moral terms. Or because it's supposed to necessarily have some automatic healthful property that always makes things better.

On the other side, people make the mistake of not telling the truth simply because they're scared or because it's easier not to tell.

The point I'm trying to illustrate by using confessing an affair as a way of running through the twelve questions is that deciding to tell or not isn't about abstract moral principles nor is it about psychological theory. It's a practical decision involving real people in the real world. It involves real goals and real needs. It has everything to do with how your partner will really respond and what the real outcome will be.

Real responsibility means that you don't merely choose to take a first step. When you choose to take a first step, you're actually choosing all the steps that follow from the circumstance you find yourself in after you take that first step. You can't say it's better to tell the truth or not until you've decided whether all the things that follow from telling the truth will probably be better than all the things that follow from not telling the truth.

You're not choosing between two actions, you're choosing between two bundles of consequences. Which consequences do you want? The ones that follow from your telling your truth? Or the ones that follow from staying silent? Answering these questions honestly is what it means to make a really responsible decision about whether to tell or not.

But we have to be aware of our own psychology. Most of us are afraid of confrontations. Silence feels smoother and safer to us. So as we weigh the reasons for telling, we have to remember not to press our thumb on the scale. That means we have to remember the absolute value of a climate of openness and honesty. On the other side of whatever difficulties result from telling the truth is a relationship that's filled with greater trust and a freer exchange of information in the long run.

PART II

SOLUTIONS

3 The One Thing You Need to Tell the Truth

• WHAT PUTS THE BOMB IN THE BOMBSHELL

IF YOU WANT TO UNDERSTAND HOW TO SAY SOMETHING DIFFICULT, you have to understand what makes some things *easy* to say.

It's easy to say something you know will be *welcome:* "I like your new suit" or "The package you were waiting for just came." Even something you might think would be hard to say—"You've got goo in the corner of your eye"—is easy to say to someone you're comfortable with who is perhaps going out on a date and would be horrified if you didn't tell her.

And it's easy to say something that confirms the other person's hope that everything is okay: "I just called to see how you're doing" (reaction: good, we're still friends) or "I look forward to working with you" (reaction: good, he's not threatened by my joining the team). This is why friends call each other even when they have nothing to say: it reestablishes the feeling that everything is okay between them.

Most of us talk all day, and a huge proportion—about 95 percent—of the things we have to say to other people are easy because they're welcome or they're routine or they confirm the sense that everything is okay.

When the Truth Is Trouble

It's the other 5 percent that gives us trouble. It's the other 5 percent that we spend 100 percent of our time worrying about. That's when we say things that are true but are not welcome or not routine or don't confirm the sense that everything is okay.

Here's a good example because, as you'll see, it captures so many of the ingredients of what makes something hard to say.

Postponing the wedding

Suppose you were planning to marry somebody and the two of you had tentatively set a date and things seemed to be going along okay. But gradually you realized that you weren't sure, that you wanted to work through some of your doubts first. So you started thinking that you wanted to postpone the wedding for six months. How would you feel about telling your future spouse that difficult truth?

Well, it's certainly not an easy thing to say. On the contrary. The news that you want a postponement will probably make your future spouse mad. And who among us wants to deal with someone who's angry at us? And since we're not sadists, who likes to hurt someone's feelings? Most of us hate confrontations. Who likes to precipitate a big, messy struggle?

You tell me. What are *you* afraid of having happen when a truth is hard for you to tell?

Awkwardness, struggle, painful feelings. All the normal reactions we have when we hear something unpleasant that turns our world upside down. *This* is what makes some truths hard to say. It's what makes it hard for honest people to be themselves. It's what challenges the abilities of even the best communicators. These are the kinds of truths that make well-intentioned people feel they don't know how to speak.

It's hard not to say

Notice something else about a difficult truth. It's not so easy *not* to say it either. Once you realize that you want to postpone the wedding, you have to deal with this truth somehow. How can you say nothing when the whole point is that you want to find out if you're sure about getting married before it's too late? Silence, while it's incredibly tempting, is usually not the best option. Too often it's not an option at all.

So you have to deal with your truth by saying something. But what? And how? We all know how easy it is to say something the wrong way and have the whole situation blow up in our face. That's why it's called a *bombshell*. I've seen a case where the guy waited until the very last minute to talk about postponing the wedding, and the bride, veil in place, had a nervous breakdown. I've seen another case where a woman said so pugnaciously that she wanted to postpone the wedding that her fiancé, whom she loved, said, "Screw you, let's just cancel the whole thing."

HOW TO TELL A DIFFICULT TRUTH WITHOUT MAKING TROUBLE

But you can turn something this hard into something easy. Life is complicated and our relationships are complicated and the truth is complicated. When you're scared, you need something clear and simple to hold on to. So if I had to boil down into one sentence everything important about telling the truth effectively, what would that one sentence be? And how would you apply it to your life? Read on.

How to Be Responsible

Deep down we all want the same thing: to be *responsible truth tellers*. That's what unites us in this task we're working on together, the task of trying to be people who can say the things that need to be said, feel good about ourselves for saying them, and make good things happen when we say them. We have the right goals, but we don't know how to achieve them.

Being a responsible truth teller means figuring out how to be both a savvy and a moral human being. That means balancing a number of different, even conflicting, duties:

- *Honesty:* there's your duty to honesty itself as a basic moral principle.
- *Self-interest:* there's your duty to protect yourself as well as the people whom you need.

- *Kindness:* there's your duty to spare others pain and harm.
- *Fairness:* there's your duty to give others the full information they need so they're not operating in the dark.

The reason we find it so psychologically challenging to tell a difficult truth is that we don't know how to satisfy all these duties at the same time (and you can see how easily they might conflict).

Suppose you want to reveal a guilty secret to someone: your duty to be honest might conflict with your duty to protect yourself if a confession like this will get you into hot water.

Suppose you want to criticize someone: your duty to be kind might tell you to keep your mouth shut, while your duty to be fair might point to your letting the truth out of the bag. Balancing all these duties that we feel so keenly is part of what makes it difficult to tell a difficult truth.

This entire book is based on a simple principle that can help people navigate among all their duties. It's the Principle of Responsible Honesty:

> Something is hard to say because *it creates needs* in you and in the other person. You tell the truth most responsibly and effectively when the way you tell takes into account the needs your truth creates and goes some distance toward meeting those needs.

This is the principle for how to tell a difficult truth so that the truth gets through without causing pain and damage to anyone or to your relationship.

You can sum up the Principle of Responsible Honesty in seven words:

> Tell the truth but meet the need.

These seven words are the key that will enable you to tell every difficult truth you've longed to tell and be much more effective than you've ever dreamed possible. This is not an abstract principle either. It is primarily a guide to action. I want you to be able to say what a client of mine once said:

"People can be difficult and the truth can be a hard thing, but with this principle I always knew what to do."

Going astray

It's in not following the principle that people go wrong. When they blurt out the truth, they're acting as if hearing the truth is the only need anyone has. When they keep quiet, they're acting as if hiding the truth is the only way to take care of people's needs. But none of this meets anyone's real needs. And so none of this makes it easier to tell the truth.

The Principle in Action

Let me show you how those seven words—Tell the truth but meet the need—make all the difference. Suppose that the truth you want to tell is that you'd like your fiancée to postpone the wedding. But you don't know how to say this.

These seven words show you what to do. Your fiancée already has needs and will have other needs when you've told her the truth. What are those needs? It's easy. If you're not sure, guess. If you don't want to guess, then go with what's most obvious. Then when you tell her that you want to postpone the wedding, say what you have to say so that at every point—before you tell, while you're telling, and afterward—you're focusing on doing something to satisfy her most important needs.

People who deal with the public use the principle all the time. Let's say you've just had a nice meal in a restaurant and order the chocolate mousse for dessert. A couple of minutes later the waiter comes out and says, "I'm sorry, sir. We're out of the mousse, but we have a lovely chocolate torte." He knows you'll be disappointed and figures that you need to know there's an alternative to pacify your chocoholism. It's not your first choice, but you still feel taken care of.

Guessing the needs

It's surprisingly easy to figure out what to say when you remember those seven words. You don't have to be a genius to guess that if your future spouse hears you want to postpone the wedding, she might:

- need not to be humiliated in front of friends and family.
- need to feel reassured that the postponement does not mean that the wedding's going to be canceled.
- need to know what it really means that you want to postpone the wedding (including whether it means there's something wrong with her).
- need to know what to expect.
- need to express her feelings and be accepted for having those feelings.
- need to know that this isn't part of a pattern of your saying you'll do something and then changing your mind.

I think guessing at least some of these needs is well within the capacity of most people. In fact, in my experience, if you guess even *one real need,* you'll have gone a long way toward preventing a huge mess. But why do the minimum? The best thing to do is to try to guess as many of the important needs as possible that the other person might have.

Meeting the needs

You already know how to do this. If someone comes to visit you and he's had a long drive, you figure that he probably needs to go to the bathroom and have something to drink and a bite to eat. So you directly offer all of those things. If you have an employee who seems unhappy on the job and might be getting ready to quit, you could just ask her what she needs, and if you're already guessing that she needs more money or more autonomy or more flexible hours, you offer what you can and give hope or at least an explanation about what you can't offer. Even if you can't completely meet every need, you can show a willingness to address her needs. That's what it means to say to someone, "I see you as a real person": you acknowledge that she has needs and you do what's reasonable to meet those needs.

Let's apply this to our I-want-to-postpone-the-wedding example.

Needing not to feel humiliated

If one of her needs is not to be humiliated, then you can acknowledge her need by saying, "You're probably afraid this will look bad to everyone," and then offering that the two of you could announce this as a joint decision. You could even say that you're willing to announce this as *her* decision, if she prefers. The point is that as part of telling her the truth of your feelings, you go to the heart of her needs and offer a solution.

Needing reassurance

Suppose you guess that she has a need to feel reassured that you're not indirectly canceling the wedding. You could address this need simply and directly by beginning your request for a postponement by saying, "I definitely want us to have a wedding, so I'm not backing out but . . . ," and then talking about your desire for a postponement. Then end by saying, "Is there anything I can do to make it clear how absolutely committed I am to our getting married? Do you want to set a new date immediately? Let me pay for the new deposit for the caterer." It's a very different experience to hear a difficult truth such as "I want to postpone the wedding" when your needs are met.

Needing to express feelings

Suppose you understand that your fiancée will be very upset in spite of any of your reassurances, but that she'll need to express her feelings and be accepted for having those feelings. If you want to postpone the wedding, she's got to be allowed to yell and cry, if that helps her. One way you can meet this need is to speak your truth and then do nothing to interfere with her expressing her feelings: not interrupting her, not judging her, not even commenting.

Needing to know what's really going on

Let's try one more. Suppose you feel that your talking about postponing the wedding is going to press all her paranoia buttons. You just know that she'll have an overwhelming desire to know what this bid for a postponement really means. Does it mean you're trying to back out of the relationship? Does it mean you find something wrong with her? Does it mean that you see yourself as some kind of entitled asshole who can do whatever he wants? Does it mean you want something from her and this postponement is an indirect threat to get it?

Again, the simplest way to meet this need might be to deal with it directly. Just say, "You probably wonder what this means. All it means is . . .

and I want you to know that it most definitely does not mean . . . Tell me what I can do to reassure you about what this postponement means." And then listen.

You can do it

The point is that you can do it. No matter what your difficult truth is, and no matter whom you're saying it to, you can do a good enough job of identifying the needs it will stimulate, and you can do a good enough job of satisfying those needs.

Let me tell you a little secret. You don't have to completely satisfy all the needs your truth stimulates. The *most* important thing is not to act as if those needs don't exist, and in particular don't act as if the other person's most important need doesn't exist or is stupid or is unworthy.

At an absolute minimum, acknowledge the fact that the other person has needs. Then try to meet some of those needs, particularly the most important ones.

The Secret of Uncovering Needs

How do you identify the other person's needs in the first place—if you can't guess or you don't already know—if you're completely clueless? You do it by *asking what the other person is afraid of.* Fears are the most reliable, direct indicators of needs. And the needs you should meet are the ones that calm these fears.

Suppose you and a friend are hanging out and it starts raining and your friend begins to act nervous and distracted. She obviously needs something. What? It depends on what she's afraid of. So you ask, if you don't know, "What are you worried about?" If she's afraid of getting wet on the walk home, you can offer to lend her your umbrella. If she's afraid of getting stuck in a traffic jam, then you can offer to let her stay with you until the rain stops. If she's afraid those traffic jams will make her late for an important appointment, then you can say you won't mind if she leaves early.

The point is that whenever you don't know what someone needs, asking yourself what they're probably afraid of is the best way to accurately guess what they need. It's easiest if you can ask the other person. But if that's not possible, you can ask yourself.

Breaking Out of Fear and Silence

"Tell the truth but meet the need" changes everything. It's been so hard for you to say certain things because you were afraid of how the other person would react. Your fear of his reaction trapped you in silence. But now you no longer have to focus on *your* fears. You can focus on what the other person needs. The other person would have reacted a certain way because of the needs your words created. If you can identify those needs (and you now know how easy that is) and if you can try to meet those needs (and you now know how easy that is too), then you can prevent the reactions that have made you afraid to speak in the first place.

Even the stupidest person in the world does a better job telling a difficult truth when he just tries to think of the other person's needs than does the smartest person in the world when he's just trying to think of the "right way" to say it. What to think about to successfully tell difficult truths is the other person's needs. And if you can't locate those needs, then exploring possible fears is the secret to discovering what those needs are. I'm talking about the specific *needs* your words create because of the *fears* your words create.

Needing to know our love was true

When I told my wife I was involved with another woman, I barely thought about her needs at all. But to the extent that I did think about her needs, I thought about her need for us to have a happy marriage. Well, that was a need of hers, but it wasn't the need my words created. To see what needs my words did create, you just have to think about how my words scared her.

The words I used to confess my secret made her afraid that our lives together had been empty. She'd thought we'd had something special, but now she was afraid that our love was a lie. She'd thought we'd meant something to each other. Now she was afraid she meant nothing to me, and therefore it was ridiculous for me to mean anything to her.

If her fear was that our love was a lie, her need was to know that our love was true. If her fear was that we meant nothing to each other, her need was to know that she really did mean everything to me, and therefore it made sense for me to mean everything to her. I had a truth to tell. But how would I meet her needs? If I was completely clueless, I could still say, "I'm sorry for what happened but I want to show you that I really love you. How can I show you that? And I want you to know that you mean everything to me. How can I show you *that?*" I could have just asked.

Doing something solid

The more concrete you can be in what you do to calm the other person's fear, the more likely you are to meet her needs. If telling your fiancée you want to postpone the wedding makes her afraid of humiliation, telling her you don't intend to humiliate her addresses one of her fears. But actually doing something or promising something specific that provides solid protection against humiliation is even better. It's like the example of your friend who's upset because it started to rain. If you understand that she's afraid of getting wet, it's helpful to say, "Let me lend you my umbrella."

Now you'll be able to understand one of the many mistakes I made in telling my secret to my wife. I actually tried to calm her fears at one point, but I failed to do something concrete enough. I said I really loved my wife, but when she asked me to promise not to go out for lunch with this other woman anymore, I dug in my heels. I was busy trying to convince my wife that nothing was going on. So like an idiot I figured that if nothing was going on, why shouldn't I keep going out to lunch with that woman from time to time?

There was my wife with her fears and the needs that grew out of her fears, and stupidly I was trying to prove a point. Promising not to go out for lunch anymore with that woman was the single most concrete thing I could have done then to allay my wife's fear that she didn't mean anything to me.

There's an important lesson here. When you think about telling your truth and meeting the other person's need and doing something to allay the fear that's fueling that need, it's more important to be concrete than clever. That's why when I talk about postponing the wedding and the fiancée's needing reassurance that you aren't going to break up with her, a concrete gesture such as paying the deposit on a new date for the wedding reception will be as important as any words you say.

Instant Magic

You see, there's something magical about trying to meet the other person's needs when you have a difficult truth to tell. The magical thing is that there are a hundred and one ways to do it right. A hundred and one people with their hearts in the right place could all look at the same situation and make good guesses about the needs a difficult truth will create and about how to meet those needs. They will probably all be right. They will certainly all do better than the person who's not thinking about this real person with real needs who's hearing his words. The health and healing you want will follow.

APPLYING THE PRINCIPLE TO THE SIX KINDS OF TRUTHS

Life can be so complicated and our hearts can be so mysterious that it can be tremendously reassuring—and, as you'll see, useful—to understand that all difficult truths fall into only six categories. To tell the truth effectively all you absolutely require is the basic principle *Tell the truth but meet the need*. Let's apply this to the six categories difficult truths fall into:

1. Confessing a secret.
2. Criticizing the other person.
3. Asking for something you are uncomfortable asking for.
4. Sharing charged, potentially explosive feelings.
5. Revealing sensitive personal information.
6. Bringing bad news.

Let's take these one at a time.

Confessing a Secret

You and another woman are partners in a graphics design business. Business is good, but that means the two of you are stretched to the limit. What your partner doesn't know is that you've been trying to have a baby and have gotten pregnant. The last time the two of you talked about this, she'd said, "Thank God neither of us is going to get pregnant." Imagine how she'll feel when you tell her that you're pregnant.

How can you possibly meet her need when you're confessing a secret like that? Then you start thinking about what she'll be afraid of: being swamped and the business's going under. So you could suggest that while you'll keep your share of the profits, you'll also pay for someone who can temporarily take your place. And you promise to be as available as possible yourself until you return to work. Instead of blowing up, your partner's happy for you.

In general, people go nuts when you confess a guilty secret to them because they feel betrayed. They feel they can't trust you or themselves anymore. They feel you're a person who does whatever she wants, who's hurt them now and will hurt them in the future.

What they need is a sense of balance, stability, and compensation. They need you to do something to demonstrate that they haven't lost the most important thing your betrayal threatens to take from them: you can still have a business, you can still have a relationship, you can still be friends. And they need you to see what your betrayal means by paying some substantial price that not only balances things between you but convinces them that you know what you've done.

Criticizing Someone

A sixty-five-year-old mother constantly criticizes her thirty-five-year-old daughter and the daughter's sick of it. She wants to give her mother some feedback. She wants to criticize her mother for criticizing her. But we all know how mothers are. She might say, "Fine, I won't ever say anything." Or she might say, "For all the times I bite my tongue, this is the thanks I get." Or she might say, "What will I talk about with you if I don't criticize you?" What the daughter wants is for the mother to simply hear the criticism and accept it and understand that her being so critical is a problem for her daughter.

But what need does the mother have that her daughter could meet?

One daughter figured that saying, "I hate it when you criticize me" would be heard as her saying, "I don't need you in my life anymore and you have nothing valuable to offer." And what mother wouldn't be terrified to hear that? So the daughter began and ended her bit of feedback with "I need you in my life and I know you have a lot to offer." The mother heard her daughter's truth and said, "Well, I suppose I do criticize you. I can try and change."

In general, criticisms scare people because they think, "What will happen if I change? What will happen if I can't change?" In other words, they're afraid of loss of the familiar, they're afraid of failure, they're afraid of abandonment. So in general their need is to be reassured that the familiar will continue, to be encouraged that they can change, and to know (if this is at all possible) that the worst that will happen if they can't change isn't so bad.

Asking for Something Difficult

You're an accountant for an ad agency. There's an attractive, hip copywriter you want to ask out. But you're afraid she'll think you're a geek. You're afraid that when you show her that you think of the two of you as date material, she'll just laugh or brush you off.

So what's her need in the face of the difficult truth that you're attracted to her? You're not sure, but you figure that she's got to be afraid of getting stuck on a long, drawn-out date with a guy she finds boring and obnoxious. So you decide to ask her out for a midweek lunch at an out-of-the-way restaurant where you probably wouldn't be seen together. That way she can check you out without getting stuck with you. She says yes!

In general, people get upset when you ask them for something because they feel trapped and powerless, afraid they'll lose if they say yes and lose if they say no. That's what makes a request difficult to hear. So in general their need is to feel free to decline but also to see that saying yes doesn't get them stuck in anything, and that it's not only easy to say yes but easy to follow through on what they've promised by saying yes. And when someone gives you something, he generally needs or wants something in return, and you have to show him how he'll get that.

Sharing Charged Feelings

Sometimes the truth we want to reveal is how we feel about something or someone, but we suspect that the other person will find it unwelcome or it'll shake up his sense that everything is okay. But you just can't keep those feelings to yourself. You're sick of not having any money, for example. You and your husband both work, and you're doing the best you can, but with two kids and a mortgage, even what you eat for dinner has to be carefully calculated. You're on the edge without a buck to spare.

You just want your husband to know how you feel. But you don't want him to feel guilty or depressed or annoyed with you.

What does he need so you can tell him your truth? You realize that he'll probably be afraid that you think he's not good enough, that you're sorry you married him. If, for example, your anniversary is coming up, you could arrange a private little ceremony between the two of you where you'll renew your vows and each speak from the heart. As part of saying you're happy you married him, you can be honest about how you feel about your problems, including the lack of money. Chances are he'll feel safe enough to be grateful for your honesty and intimacy.

In general, the kinds of feelings that are hard to say and hard to hear *scare* people because they make them think that either their world is going to turn upside down or that you think they're worthless. So in general the *need* is to reassure them in whatever way possible and appropriate that their world is going to keep spinning as before and that you do think well of them.

Revealing Sensitive Personal Information

When do you tell someone you're dating that you have diabetes? Not on the first date. Then on the second date you're really getting into each other, but things are still at a delicate stage. On the third date you're just starting to have feelings for each other and you don't want to screw that up. But if too many dates go by, it will appear as if you were holding back. But you've been down this road before. And you know that the diabetes disclosure can be a turnoff. How do you tell him?

What does the other person need? You decide that what the person is afraid of is being stuck with a sick partner and is too afraid of the unknown. So instead of minimizing your diabetes, this time you give as much definite information as possible, letting the other person know all the implications, both how likely it is that you'll be able to lead a full, healthy life, as well as the risks. And this time you discover that your revelation is accepted with no problem.

In general, when you disclose sensitive personal information, the other person is thrown because she doesn't know what this means for her. So in general her need is for you to spell out the difference the thing that you revealed will make to her and in her life: "You didn't know this about me before, and here's what's changed and here are all the things that will stay the same."

Bringing Bad News

You're working on a project at your job. As the days go by, it becomes clear to you that you're not going to have it done by the time your boss needs it. You could've told your boss sooner that the project would be late and given him more time to deal with your being late, but you kept hoping you'd be able to catch up. Now it's really late and you're sure he'll be pissed, and so you're really afraid to tell him. Well, the solution is to tell the truth but meet the need.

But what will he need? He needs the project to come in on time, which you can't give him. So what is he afraid of? Perhaps you realize that his big fear is getting in trouble with *his* boss. So when you tell him your bad news, you make it perfectly clear that you're willing to fall on the sword and take full blame for what happened. Your boss takes the bad news much better than you expected.

In general, when people hear bad news, they're subject to hopelessness and panic. Your reaction to hearing that a project you cared about has fallen through is only different in degree from hearing that a loved one is ill. So in general you address the other person's need by giving him a sense of hope, particularly about his worst fears, and clear directions for what will happen next.

Easy does it

That's how simple it can be. But each example is only one way to do it right. A different person telling the same truth to someone else might focus on a different need and address it in a different way. But what really makes an enormous difference is that you're trying to address the other person's needs in this moment of truth telling.

So there are two paths you can follow.

Here's the path of disaster: you blurt out the truth; the other person has fears; those fears create unmet needs; there's a huge mess.

Here's the path that combines honesty and harmony: you speak the truth in words designed to offer something concrete to allay the other person's fears; there are no unmet needs; both of you have the sense that telling the truth made things better.

Telling the truth while also addressing the other person's needs creates *closeness*—you can be close because it's safe to tell the truth. Paying attention to needs creates *trust*—you can trust each other because it's safe to tell the truth. Telling the truth in a way that deals with needs creates *hope* because you see that difficult truths can make things better.

Plus your truth gets heard.

A Look Ahead

Let's get more specific. The following seven chapters will give you detailed advice for how to tell the truth for each of the six categories.

4 Scripts for Responsible Truth Telling

You've come a long way. You now know that something is hard for you to say because you sense it will shake the other person's world. Her world is shaken because your truth suddenly creates a bunch of unmet needs. A truth is a bombshell when there's an explosion of unmet needs.

That's why difficult truths are such a threat to our relationships. Most relationships are in a delicate balance. A huge influx of unmet needs creates tremendous stress because of all the new resentment and anger and disappointment and frustration that go along with unmet needs.

Truth, good. Unmet needs, bad. That's the dilemma we all face. That's why the deepest, most fundamental secret about handling difficult truths is *tell the truth but meet the need*.

Things are easy for you to say when they don't create unmet needs. So everything you do to meet the other person's needs converts something that's hard to say into something that's easy for you to say. And how do you meet another person's needs if you don't have a clue as to what they are? Just ask yourself what the other person's afraid of, and do or say something to help him feel less afraid.

And how do you figure out what someone else might be afraid of? Go with what's most obvious. If you have to tell an employee that she's not going to get the promotion she was counting on, it's obvious that she'd be afraid that she's not going anywhere in the company, that there's something wrong with what she has to offer, perhaps that someone in the office is out to get her. And you address these obvious fears in the most direct way. You simply say, "I'm afraid you're not going to get the promotion, but I want you to know that you do have a future here. There's nothing wrong with your performance, except that you could show a little more initiative. This was a straightforward decision based on merit."

By addressing her fears, you've helped meet her needs. This reduces the likelihood of a painful scene and a resentful employee.

Telling the truth is an opportunity for two people to get close and help each other out. Telling the truth should be a moral act that emphasizes healing instead of damage. Then people are left with the feeling that it makes sense to tell the truth the next time.

WHAT KIND OF TRUTH IS IT?

The first thing you need to do is figure out which of the six categories your truth fits into. I know that the truth can be complicated and confusing. Telling someone something like "I want to postpone our wedding" can seem to fit into more than one category, or no category. But it's best to figure out the category if you can.

You can determine which category your truth fits into by thinking about which *response* would make you feel satisfied. The response that would make you feel satisfied is the response you should be looking for. And that's what determines the category your truth fits into.

Here are the guidelines:

1. If the response that would make you feel satisfied is the other person saying that he forgives you, then the truth you want to communicate is a guilty secret. In other words, you want to make a confession.
2. If the response that would make you feel satisfied is the other person saying that he'll try to change, then the truth you want to communicate is a criticism. In other words, you want to give feedback.

3. If the response that would make you feel satisfied is the other person saying either that she'll try to give you what you want or that while she can't give you what you want, it's okay that you asked, then the truth that you want to communicate is your need for something. In other words, you want to make a request.

4. If the response that would make you feel satisfied is the other person saying that she hears how you feel, then the truth you want to communicate is simply the truth of how you feel, and that's all.

5. If the response that would make you feel satisfied is the other person saying that she can let in this new information and accept you with it, then the truth you want to communicate is a sensitive personal disclosure.

6. If the response that would make you feel satisfied is the other person saying that he accepts what you're telling him and doesn't blame you for it, then the truth you want to communicate is bad news.

The Benefit of Deciding on a Category

I can show you the power and importance of deciding on a category by using the postponing-the-wedding example. Obviously that could fit into any of the six categories. But you've got to pick the most important category *for you* to make sure your experience of telling the truth works out the way you'd like.

For example, if you'd be happy with your fiancée simply saying something like, "Yes, I hear how you feel. I certainly understand. I've felt the same way myself from time to time. It's natural to feel that way," then why give her a heart attack by making it sound as though you want her to actually rearrange all her plans? The category your truth fits into is sharing feelings, and you can make sure you tell your truth so that your fiancée knows that she only has to hear your feelings.

If you'd be happy with your fiancée saying something like, "Well, I want you to pay for the lost deposit to the caterer, but I'll go along with your request," then why put her through the agony of making her think that you're doing this because there's something wrong with her? Your truth fits into the category of a request, not a criticism, and by keeping that clear you make things easier for both of you.

And if you do want her to change something specific that she does, such as being so negative and critical, why get her focused on the details of a wedding postponement? You'd be surprised how often people make hard-to-swallow requests for someone to do something when they just want the other person to change a little. They're really threatening the other person, but the attention gets focused on the threat, not the needed change, and that makes things far more explosive than they need to be.

You're entitled to want whatever you want. You're even entitled to be confused. But you're not entitled to speak to the other person while you're still so confused that you'll make the other person's head explode. The *clearer* you are about what you're trying to make happen, the easier it will be for your truth telling to go smoothly.

What Are You Going to Say?

You know what category your truth fits in and you know how you're hoping the other person will respond, but when you get to the point of speaking your truth, what will you actually say?

This is about speaking from your heart, so it's best for you to begin by writing down what you'd like to say in your own words. Imagine that the setting's perfect and you have the other person's full attention. Now when you open up your heart and speak your truth, what you have to say is . . .

_____

_____

_____

Now this is probably not what you're going to end up saying. But you have to make sure, as a first step, that it's actually what you want to say.

Here's a way to check. Imagine someone saying these words to you. If someone did say this to you, what would you guess is in his heart? Is it what's in your heart right now as you think of saying it?

Now think about how you'd respond if someone said this to you. Is the way you'd respond the way you'd like the other person to respond?

These are hard questions, but for most people they make a big difference. One woman, when she imagined herself speaking from the heart, wrote down the truth she wanted to say to her friend as "I always have to make everything happen in this friendship. I always call you and you never call me. I'm just a backup when you have nothing better going on."

This woman later told me that she'd been rehearsing these words over and over in her mind for a year. But when she saw them written down in black and white and thought about how her friend would respond when she heard them, she realized they would get into a big argument about who calls whom how often. In other words, they'd argue about whether the woman had a basis for feeling the way she does. That's exactly how this woman would have responded if she'd heard these words.

As she thought about what would actually happen as she told the truth, her truth itself changed. The truth was that she wanted her friend to call more often and initiate their getting together more often. That was her real truth. The other was just a complaint that masked the truth.

Thinking about your truth as something that someone hears instead of something that you say should help you change the words you use. So now write down a new version of the truth based on thinking about what you really want and how you'd like the other person to respond:

_____

_____

_____

Maybe you haven't changed a word. And that's fine. But most people have gotten just a step closer to finding the words that work.

The Six Basic Tools of Responsible Truth Telling

There are specific scripts to follow for each category of truth. They don't exist to put words in your mouth. On the contrary, our goal here is liberation: helping you do whatever is necessary to be free to tell the truth. The scripts provide the safeguards that liberate the truth.

But before I give you the scripts, let's look at the tools we'll be working with, because they're the same for all the scripts. These are the tools that all effective truth tellers work with. They are the reason the scripts work.

Tool 1: Attention

Believe it or not, when I told my wife the secret that almost ruined our lives, I didn't even have her attention. Our kids were still young, so there were countless distractions, and I began by talking about a movie, so she thought I was just indulging in movietalk. Then when I started talking about our relationship, she thought I was going to nag her, which pretty much guaranteed she wasn't paying attention, because who wants to be nagged?

The point is that you've got to create a moment. Getting the other person's attention means carving out a block of time in which you've made it clear to the other person that you have something important to say. Think of it like this. You'd never ask someone to marry you while the two of you were rushing to leave the house to go to work. You'd create a moment. Well, you do the same thing when you want to tell someone any important truth.

This might sound obvious, but it's something blurters need to hear. Remember, blurters are either afraid of confrontations or not sensitive enough to other people's reactions. Either way, the temptation is enormous to pop out with the truth at the worst possible moment, when the other person can neither take it in nor deal with it. But hit and run is just as bad when it comes to telling the truth as when you're driving your car.

Tool 2: Framing

A "frame" is a way of drawing a verbal circle around something you say that tells people the kind of thing it is and gives them an idea of how to respond. It's like the first tool, but more specific. It not only says pay attention, but it shows what to pay attention to. When people simply say, "I have some bad news for you," they're providing a crude frame.

But people usually don't frame their truths, and it makes the people they're telling nuts not to know what the frame is. If you happen to enjoy the sitcom *Seinfeld,* you'll notice in many episodes something like this: A man will say to a woman "I love you," but it will be said so casually that the woman has no idea whether this is a meaningful declaration or an offhand remark. They spend the rest of the episode sorting it out. That's what it means to talk without a frame, and it's a bad thing to do.

Each of the six categories is a specific frame. If you have something that's hard for you to say, no one will know what you're talking about unless he knows what category it fits in. That's why most of us feel uncomfortable when someone starts complaining. We ask ourselves what the hell he is doing. Is he just saying how he feels? Is he criticizing? Is he asking for something?

Every time I get a phone call from what turns out to be a telemarketer and that person begins by sincerely asking, "How are you today, sir?" I get confused because I don't know who this is or what she wants. It sounds as if we're having a friendly chat when it's really a sales pitch. The minute I realize what's going on, I get pissed.

It makes most people angry when they don't know what's going on. And if you're telling someone the truth about something and he doesn't know what it is that you're doing, he'll get mad from not having known the frame, and that anger will affect his response to your truth. So you always have to make it clear not only what your truth is but what kind of a truth it is. Only when the other person knows what category it fits into will he know how to respond.

Tool 3: Acknowledgment

If it weren't for the emotional power of acknowledging someone's feelings, we would never be able to help a person deal with a difficult truth we've told. By acknowledging what the other person shows you in return, you're saying, "I get it." It's like when the UPS guy brings a package and you sign for it, acknowledging delivery.

It might sound perfunctory, but in fact it's magic. One of the worst human nightmares is to be invisible. On the other hand, most people find there's real emotional nourishment for them in being seen for who and what they are. And that's because we feel a certain level of acceptance when we're seen. But when we reject something, we pretend it's invisible.

Acknowledgment is a major tool in meeting the other person's needs as a part of telling the truth. If you're telling someone you want to postpone your wedding, she might have an incredible need for you *not* to be postponing the wedding. You can't meet that need, of course. But by acknowledging her truth, acknowledging how hard it is to have a wedding date you were counting on pulled out from under you, you are seeing the other person, and that has a magical kind of effectiveness in helping her with her need.

This becomes all the more important when you realize the degree to which we try to minimize the impact of what we're saying in our hopes of making the truth less difficult to hear. When I told my wife about the "other" woman, instead of acknowledging how devastating my news was, I tried to make her feel like an idiot for making a big deal of it. As if that would convince her it was no big deal! What she needed was for me to see what my confession meant to her. If I'd acknowledged her feelings and the impact of my truth and stopped telling her what it should mean to her, there would have been a lot less pain and we wouldn't have come close to breaking up.

Tool 4: Compensation

Acknowledgment occurs through emotionally powerful and meaningful words. Compensation is something concrete that you do or offer to do that makes a practical difference in someone's life. Acknowledgment happens when you tell your employee that you understand how bad it feels to get fired and how scary it is to look for a new job. Compensation happens when you offer severance pay and real assistance in finding a new job.

One of the challenges for any of us who has a truth to tell is to find ways to offer compensation as a way of meeting the other person's needs. If a lawyer's reading these words, she might be alarmed because an offer of compensation could be construed as an admission of guilt. Indeed, it's in trying to deny our guilt that we withhold compensation.

But don't make things complicated. Your truth is difficult because it shakes up the other person's world. You can make your truth easier to take if you give the other person a little solid help putting his world back together.

Tool 5: Cooperation

This is the ideal feeling you want to create when you tell someone the truth: we're cooperating. You're not dumping a load of garbage on him and saying, you deal with it. You're saying, instead, that here's a problem the two of you have and you'll both be much better off if you work together to solve it. In my research what I saw over and over was that no matter how difficult a truth was, when there was a spirit of cooperation, people remembered the good feeling.

As you'll see when we go through the individual scripts, the best way to get this spirit of cooperation started is by being direct. You simply say that you want to work with the other person so that you can both get your needs met.

But you've got to watch out for the hundred and one ways cooperation gets eroded. The two of you can fight over what's real. The two of you can fight over who deserves to get what. Or over who should be required to do what. Even something as basic as telling someone how you feel can find the spirit of cooperation destroyed if the two of you fight over who deserves to feel what.

But the ball is in your court. You're the one with a truth you want to tell or need to tell. You know it's going to be hard for the other person to hear. If you're the one dropping the bombshell, you're the one who's got to clearly indicate a willingness to deal with the fallout.

Tool 6: Meaning and perspective

When my daughters were little and they'd fight, I'd get upset. Their fights seemed so full of angry passion. But I'd been an only child, and so I had no basis for comparison. My wife, who did have siblings growing up, helped me see what it meant and gave me some perspective: "You know that siblings fight. Well, this is what it looks like. The fact is that sisters who fight can grow up to have a warm, loving relationship."

I'd known *what* I was seeing. But once I got meaning and perspective, I knew *how* to take what I was seeing. We talked about framing earlier, which has to do with how to contextualize the truth. Meaning and perspective are about what to do with the truth after you've got it.

Let's say you tell your husband, "My mother's coming to visit for a long weekend." Your husband goes nuts. A whole weekend with his mother-in-law! But then you remind him that it's only one weekend out of a whole year and you show that by being nice to your mother, he's really being nice to you. You've given meaning to this news and you've given him perspective. A major part of the problem people have with hearing the truth is that they don't know what to do with it. And so you help the other person by telling him what it means or by giving him some perspective on it.

INTRODUCING THE SCRIPTS

As you read the scripts for telling the truth, watch for how all six tools are used. Think of the tools as the ingredients and the scripts as the recipes. When you start out, you're focusing on the recipe, and that's fine. As you become more sophisticated, you'll understand how important the ingredients are and see that as long as you rely on them, you can form your own recipes.

That's important. These scripts are suggestions, not commands. They're designed to give you ideas, not write your lines for you. They're supposed to help you see what's important, not tie your hands.

Now here's something amazing. No matter how different the things we have to say are, when people tell a difficult truth effectively, there are only four stages, and when you tell the truth in each of the six categories, you follow the same four stages:

- First, you *make an appointment* or arrange some uninterrupted time for what you have to say.
- Second, you *set up what you have to say,* so the other person understands what you're doing and is in a receptive frame of mind.
- Third, you *say your truth.*
- Fourth, you *make things come out right* by dealing with the aftermath and achieving some kind of resolution.

The first stage in the script is the same for all six categories of truth.

Making an Appointment

As I said earlier, you don't tell a difficult truth on the run. You don't tell it when either of you has no time to respond to it or hash it out. You don't tell it when either of you is preoccupied by anything else. You don't blurt it out impulsively in an emotional moment. The spontaneity that might seem so noble to the gods of truth will seem evil to the gods of relationships.

Most of us understand the importance of setting aside a time and place for an important truth. And we know not to criticize someone in front of others.

The words to use

First, what *not* to say. Don't say, "We need to talk." This has become a definite signal to the person hearing these words that she's about to go through a harrowing experience. Even words that are almost identical do not convey the dread sense that the ax is about to fall the way "We need to talk" does.

The best way to avoid the "We need to talk" jinx is to say words such as "There's something I'd like to talk to you about. Do you have time now, or when would be a better time?" The point is to use the word *like:* "I'd *like* to talk to you," not "We *need* to talk."

You could also say "I want to talk to you" or "I'd like us to get together," but always use the language of wanting or liking, not needing. That way you don't create a sense of dread.

Take the time

You've got to come up with some estimate on your own of how big a deal whatever you have to say is. Then when you ask for the appointment, you have to make sure to *say* how much time you'll need. If it's not a huge deal, then just making an appointment to talk is enough. But anything that would discombobulate you if you heard it will take at least a half an hour, and anything heavy-duty will take at least an hour.

Some examples:

Criticizing an aspect of an employee's overall performance, unless it's a minor detail, could take a half an hour. Telling an employee about how she needs to shape up if she's not going to be shipped out could easily take an hour.

Confessing to your current lover that you ran into your previous lover and chatted for a few minutes might take a half an hour. Confessing that you slept with your previous lover will take at least an hour, if not days and weeks.

Options

Sometimes you can get away without making an appointment. If the other person is someone you often go out for lunch with or meet with in the office, then you don't necessarily have to schedule a time. But even here you've got to be careful. You still have to say, "There's something I'd like to talk about. Is this a good time for you?"

You'd be shocked if you saw the disasters that come into my office, the terrible hurts that result because someone in effect schedules an operation when there is only time enough to open the patient up and no time to sew him back together.

For example, Carrie had been married and divorced by the time she was twenty-three, and for the last twenty years she'd been in a same-sex relationship. Three hours before her lover was going to leave for a long, important business trip, Carrie "mentioned" that she was thinking of possibly having sex with a man she thought she might be attracted to. Carrie and her lover might have worked this out under other circumstances, but I'm convinced that it was her bad timing alone that destroyed their relationship.

By making an appointment, you've already gotten the other person's attention and indicated your willingness to cooperate. But you need to take care of yourself here. Some people get antsy when you tell them you have something you want to say. They might insist on hearing it immediately even if they don't have time right then. You have to make sure that he really does have time and that in fact this is a good time. If not, hold firm to your scheduled appointment and keep your mouth shut for the time being.

Now you're ready to follow the scripts for each of the six categories of difficult truths.

5 "I Want to Tell You How I Feel"

You KNOW HOW IT'S BEEN when you've shared some of your feelings in the past with people and the very things you do to get your feelings heard end up making the other person feel threatened. There's a huge fight because the other person feels insulted or threatened with abandonment or scared about what you may do given the way you feel.

Here's a story that illustrates how things can go wrong. We'll use it to demonstrate our script for how to responsibly tell the truth about how you feel.

Michelle and Jennifer

They'd been best friends since boarding school, but after college their lives took very different paths. Michelle went to Wall Street and made a ton of money. Jennifer lived in the country, where she barely made a living as a reporter for a local paper. They remained best friends, but the friendship was based on their ignoring the extraordinary differences between their lifestyles.

As you can imagine, it was much harder for poor Jennifer to ignore the differences than rich Michelle. Finally, one day Jennifer opened up to

Michelle and revealed all of her long-held feelings of resentment and jealousy. Like most of us, Jennifer naively thought that sharing the truth would keep their relationship healthy. But Michelle felt attacked. The way Jennifer told her truth made it impossible for Michelle to feel safe or comfortable with her. Within six months their friendship had ended.

When we share our feelings with someone, we're basically trying to do what Jennifer was trying to do: let in some air, bring down some barriers, feel less pent up inside, feel the relationship is more honest. But too often the other person feels attacked and the whole thing is a disaster. Here's what you can do to prevent this from happening.

THE SCRIPT FOR SHARING FEELINGS

Make an Appointment

First, you make an appointment, as I've described.

Set Things Up

Before you say how you feel, make sure the other person understands what you're about to do and why. This is, of course, the step that blurters always leave out. But the result of leaving it out is that the other person feels confused and dumped on, and that means your truth can't get through and you've made it much harder to heal the relationship.

Think of yourself as a storyteller. Jennifer is about to tell Michelle that she's resented her. Before those words leave her mouth, she has to set the scene. In her case she could say something like, "You know, you're my best and oldest friend, and when we're old ladies, I hope we'll still be best friends." (Here she's offering meaning and perspective on the feelings she's about to reveal. She's putting them in context and saying how she hopes the whole thing turns out.)

Jennifer might go on to say, "We've always been open and honest with each other, but I have one feeling I've wanted to share with you for a long time, but I was afraid that I wouldn't say it right or that you'd take it the wrong way, and so I didn't say anything. What I want to do now is just get it out in the open and then I can let it go and we can move on. That's all we need to do about it. Okay? And after I tell you how I feel, I'll be here as long as you need for us to talk about it. I just want to get this out of the way so we can be closer than we've been before."

Tell the Truth

Then it's time for Jennifer to tell her truth. The mistake Jennifer made that cost her Michelle's friendship grew out of her feeling guilty for the way she felt. She decided there was something wrong with her for feeling resentful of Michelle. Most of the time when we have a feeling that's hard for us to put into words, we feel guilty for feeling the way we do or we're angry with the other person for making us feel that way. That's how we end up making the mistake Jennifer made: we attempt to justify how we feel. But our justifications make the other person feel attacked.

When people talk about the value of "making 'I' statements," they're really talking about the importance of not making the other person feel attacked in a vain attempt to justify your feelings.

Jennifer's saying "It's always been hard for me to deal with your success" is just about Jennifer. But it's precisely because Jennifer didn't feel justified for feeling the way she did that she added on a discussion about the huge gap in income and success between her and Michelle. Adding that on might have made her resentment more understandable to a third party, but it made Michelle feel attacked, particularly when Jennifer added little details about things Michelle had said and done that deepened Jennifer's feelings of resentment.

Your truth falls into the category of "saying your feelings" because all you want in response is the other person to say, "I hear how you feel." If you were criticizing the other person or wanting him to do something for you, your truth would fall into a different category.

Don't justify your feelings

And because all you want is for the other person to hear your feelings, you have to do something paradoxical: you have to make it seem as though there's *less,* not more, reason for you to feel the way you do. The more you downplay your justifications, the less the other person feels attacked and the less the other person will talk about who did what to whom, who said what, who was right, who was wrong, and all the other painful and confusing details people always get into. These details get you and the other person madder and madder at each other, when all you wanted was to say how you felt.

So what Jennifer should have said was something like this: "I need you to hear how I feel. On some level it doesn't make any sense that I'd feel this way. You've always been fair, and if there are differences in our lifestyles, they're the result of choices we've both freely made. But even though I know there's no incredibly good reason for me to feel this way, I have to say I've felt jealous and resentful of all your money and success. There's nothing you have to do about it. I'm not asking you for anything. I don't even want this to make a difference between us. I just want to make myself feel better by getting this off my chest, and I'm hoping you can hear how I feel without having to do something about it."

The way Jennifer actually shared her feelings destroyed their friendship because it made Michelle feel she was being judged and found guilty for having done something wrong, all because of what Jennifer said to justify her feelings. If Jennifer had said her feelings the right way, minimizing her reasons for why she felt the way she did, Michelle would have felt safe in being her old self with Jennifer.

Basic principles

Of course, the details of your situation are probably vastly different from Jennifer's. But the basic principles are exactly the same. A parent disappointed in her child, a wife afraid of her husband, someone on the job annoyed with a coworker—if all these people want is to hear the other person say, "I know how you feel," then they have to do just what Jennifer should have done and, when they tell their truth, make sure to get these points across in their own words:

- I just want you to hear how I feel.
- You're not to blame.
- My feelings are probably all out of proportion to anything you've done or to any underlying reality.

- On some level it doesn't make any sense that I'd feel this way.
- Here's how I feel . . .
- There's nothing you have to do about my feelings and I'm not asking you for anything. I don't want this to make a difference between us. I'm just hoping you can hear how I feel without the need to do something about it.
- My goal is to feel better because I've gotten this off my chest and to have a better relationship with you because I've been honest.

That's the script for saying how you feel. Notice that I didn't put any of these points in quotes, because they're there simply as indicators of the kinds of things you need to say, not as word-for-word commands.

Let me deal with some questions people often bring up.

First of all, you're *not* minimizing how you feel. In fact, you can be as vivid and passionate as you like in describing your feelings. What you *are* minimizing is the degree to which the other person will feel attacked. You minimize his sense of blame by not talking about things that make *you* feel justified but make *him* feel it was all his fault. It's exactly because you minimize your *reasons* for feeling the way you do that the other person does not feel attacked.

Sometimes people wonder what they'll talk about if they don't go into all the reasons they feel the way they do, but when it comes to sharing feelings, less is more. The fewer words you use, the better able the other person will be to hear how you feel. It's hard to hear painful feelings. When I work with couples and one person has extremely painful feelings to share, the other person can usually not tolerate listening for more than about thirty seconds. It's just too intense, too overwhelming. But the basic principles of communication are all on your side. The fewer words you use, the more the pure note of your feelings will come through.

The two of you will have plenty to talk about when it comes to other feelings and other issues. The last thing you want to talk about is stuff that might destroy your relationship.

And sometimes people wonder if doing it this way won't seem odd to the other person. After all, we're so used to having to justify our feelings that it feels strange not to. So we assume it must feel weird to the other person. But the opposite is true. If someone asks you what time it is, it doesn't occur to you to wonder why he doesn't know. And you'd be annoyed if he launched into an explanation of why he'd left his watch at home.

Well, that's how the person you're talking to feels. We've talked about the importance of acknowledgment, so now think about what's going on for the other person. It's hard enough for him to deal with negative feelings. By leaving the justification out, you're acknowledging how difficult what he's going through is. He's also probably wanting to tell you, "Oh, you shouldn't feel that way." By leaving the justification out, you're acknowledging precisely what he's wanting to tell you.

Don't get drawn in

And what do you do if the other person asks you what he's done to make you feel the way you do, as if he were trying to draw you into a discussion of why you're justified in your feelings? If the other person sincerely wants to know what's made you feel the way you do, you can talk about what's real, but the rule is *downplay, downplay, downplay*. Jennifer, for example, could have said, "Well, you always have a nicer, newer car than I do. But so what? You're entitled, and that shouldn't make me feel as silly and jealous as I do."

Notice how by saying it this way you make it infinitely harder for the other person to say, "So are you saying I rub your nose in the fact of my nicer, newer car?" Instead, what you're doing is making it hard for the other person to say anything *except* that he hears how you feel.

Make It All Come Out Right

Finally comes the fourth and last stage in the script. Here's where you do what you can to make it all come out right. On one level this is easy. You don't really have to do or say anything as long as the other person says she hears how you feel.

If Michelle had said, "Okay, the differences between us have been hard for you, but you're not blaming me and you're saying I don't have to do anything about it, so I guess that's it," then Jennifer would have been done. All she'd have had to do is reach over, pat Michelle on the hand, and say she was glad she had gotten that off her chest.

But as you must realize, it's usually a lot harder than this. When we hear someone share a feeling that's difficult for us to hear, we all do things that muddy the waters. So to make things come out right you need the part of the script that gives you responses to things other people say.

Dealing with silence

Although it doesn't happen often, you have to be prepared for the other person to say nothing. This means you have to *say* that you're open to hearing the other person's feelings. In doing so, you're using the tool of compensation: in exchange for having had your say, you offer to listen to the other's feelings. But since those feelings are in response to your own, you've got to have the discipline to do what you're hoping she does, and that's to simply say, "I hear how you feel." If you don't do that, then because you have feelings about her feelings, she'll have feelings about your feelings, and the two of you will be on a runaway escalator to disaster.

Dealing with self-blame

You have to be careful that the person to whom you're telling the truth doesn't blame herself. If she does, don't get lured into a discussion of what she actually did or didn't do, or what actually had an impact on this or that. Instead, just keep repeating that it's not the other person's fault and that you're not blaming her. But don't get drawn into details.

So if Michelle had said something like, "It's all my fault that you've resented me. I think I unconsciously did things to flaunt my money because when we were teenagers, I was jealous of you because you were so beautiful," instead of arguing about this, all Jennifer should say is, "Maybe that happened, but nothing you did made me feel the way I do. You were fine."

Beware of Mr. Fix-it

You have to beware of the other person's attempt to "solve" your problem. Michelle, for example, might have started talking about helping Jennifer out with money or being overly careful not to ever suggest that they go out to an expensive restaurant. You might say, well, what's wrong with this? Nothing, if Jennifer had come to Michelle with a request for help.

But all Jennifer's doing is saying how she feels, and if she starts getting into solutions with Michelle, although she'd started out just saying her feelings, that's when Michelle might start feeling manipulated. The next thing you know, Michelle could be arguing about why Jennifer shouldn't feel the way she does, and they're back in the soup.

If you're clear in your mind that all you want is for the other person to hear how you feel, don't accept the offer even to talk about solutions. There's nothing to solve.

Spiraling feelings

The most likely thing that will happen, and what you must prevent from getting out of hand, is that your feelings will stir up a whole bunch of feelings in the other person or will cause her to bring up other issues. Jennifer resented Michelle, but maybe there's stuff Michelle resented Jennifer for, and this is when Michelle will bring it up. "You want to talk about unfairness," Michelle might say, "well, what about . . . ?"

Another possibility is that instead of matching you resentment for resentment or disappointment for disappointment, the other person will try to broaden the discussion: "If you resent me, then maybe you hate me." Or, "If you resent me, then maybe you resent a lot of other people." Or, "If you resent me, then maybe you're also very depressed."

You have to watch out here. On the one hand, you really do want to have a free and open discussion about what you brought up. So, for example, Michelle would certainly be entitled to bring up all these issues when Jennifer told her how she felt. But if you're wise, you'll be careful to prevent things from spiraling into total confusion. That is a prescription for disaster if you're dealing with feelings that you were afraid to talk about in the first place.

Remember that all you wanted to accomplish was for the other person to hear how you feel. If what you wanted was a wide-open discussion about how both of you feel about a whole range of things, then that's a *request* and it falls into a whole different category.

So it's absolutely crucial that you keep things within bounds, if for no other reason than if you talk about important feelings you're not prepared to talk about, you'll end up blurting out things that you'll regret. They will only be the truth of the moment, not a truth you'll want to stand behind, but they will do damage nonetheless.

Here's what you do. If, like Jennifer, you talk about something you've resented the other person for and he starts talking about how he's resented you, then you acknowledge his feelings and tell him you're willing to talk about his feelings. But first your goal is simply to make sure he's heard your feelings, and then the two of you can move on.

Things in boxes

I know that there's a part of us that doesn't like having things put into boxes. And I understand that this might make you feel constrained. You'd like to flow as free as the wind.

I agree. To use one of the tools I've mentioned, I acknowledge the way you feel. I've spent many years feeling that way myself. But let me tell you a story about the value of boxes.

When my inexperienced cat had her first litter of kittens, she wandered all over our large house dropping blind, helpless kittens in one room after another. It was "nature," but it was a mess. One kitten got lost and we later found it dead. Another kitten was barely found in time. And poor Tippy, the mother, had the look in her eyes of a small, first-time traveler lost in a huge airport the day before Thanksgiving. Giving birth is hard enough without running around in search of a safe enclosure.

By the next litter she had learned her lesson. When she was pregnant, she sat in an open drawer every day until we got the point and cleaned it out and put newspaper in it. Then when she was in labor, she stayed put in the open drawer until all her babies were born.

There's a certain comfort and sanity in keeping everything in its box, whether you're delivering a kitten or a truth from your heart. So, yes, we'd all like to run free, but we put things in their boxes to create safety and sanity. When we make a mess telling the truth, that momentary feeling of freedom fades fast, and what we're left with is a relationship that's undermined and a greater reluctance to tell the truth again in the future.

This may be more important when it comes to feelings than any other category of truth. We therapists like to say that "a feeling is just a feeling." But ordinary people in real life experience feelings as actions, things that are done to them. In short, we feel assaulted by other people's feelings. Putting challenging feelings in a box prevents the other person from feeling assaulted and lets the feeling come through.

Creating hope

Ultimately, sharing feelings is about creating hope. We feel hopeful when we can speak from our hearts. By following this script as I've outlined, you give yourself the hope that you can say your feelings again, and you give the other person hope that your relationship is a place where she can say her feelings too.

I think it's good to end by referring to this hope. You could simply say something like, "I'm really glad I got to tell you how I feel. And I appreciate your hearing me out."

Summing Up

- First say, "I'd like to talk to you about something," and work out a convenient time.
- Next say what you're going to do and why you're going to do it: you're going to share a feeling but there's nothing the other person needs to do about it.
- Make it clear that the other person isn't to blame for this and that your feelings are probably out of proportion to anything the other person's done.
- Say how you feel simply and with the focus on yourself. Don't talk about anything the other person's done that might justify your feeling.
- Again, make it clear that there's nothing the other person has to do about what you're saying. Say that you're just hoping that the other person can hear how you feel.
- Hang around to answer any questions but don't get carried off into a discussion of other issues you're not prepared to talk about. If they need to be talked about, you can do that at another time.

Following this script, or any script, might feel unfamiliar, but you will soon be able to do it without thinking.

6 "I'd Like to Tell You What's Wrong with You"

SOMETIMES WE WANT TO GO FURTHER than just saying how we feel. We want to criticize someone or give him negative feedback or express disapproval. We want to tell someone who's important to us that she's doing something wrong and that we'd like her to do it differently.

What we're hoping is that this criticism will ultimately benefit everyone. But you know why criticizing someone is so hard and why we're so reluctant to do it: people hear what we think of as "helpful feedback" as a put-down or an attack, and they respond by getting upset or angry or defensive.

Here's a story that illustrates how things can go wrong. We'll use it to demonstrate our script for how to responsibly tell the truth when the truth is a criticism.

Linda and Robert

They were sister and brother. Their parents had been schoolteachers and they grew up in a close, middle-class family. When Linda first got married, Robert spent lots of time at her house. Then their paths diverged. Robert went on to teach in college, while Linda, whose husband, Henry, was a bar owner with underworld ties, gave up her nursing career to stay home with her three children.

As the years went by, Robert grew to hate the atmosphere in Linda's home, which he felt was coarse and crude. Finally one day Robert let Linda have it with both barrels, attacking every bit of the life Linda had made with her husband. Deep inside, Robert was hoping that this criticism would somehow wake Linda up and make her change. But Linda only felt terribly hurt by Robert's feedback, and it felt like a matter of emotional survival for her to tell her brother she never wanted to see him again.

THE SCRIPT FOR CRITICIZING SOMEONE

Make an Appointment

If you have a criticism that's a big enough deal for you to be nervous about saying it, make sure that the other person has enough time set aside to hear you without being distracted and for you both to have time to deal with whatever fallout there is.

Set Things Up

Think about what you're about to do for a moment. On some level, you're about to say, "You suck." You're about to say, "I'm entitled to sit in judgment of you." Of course, sometimes in special relationships feedback is expected. Bosses, for example, tell employees how to do their jobs better. Coaches criticize their athletes nonstop. Wives and husbands criticize each other too, but outside of that short list of special relationships, most of us have the experience that criticism makes trouble. That's why we're nervous when we want to give feedback or when we're on the receiving end of it.

So when you set up giving feedback, you've got to make sure three things come through: hope, benefit, and the fact that your relationship has a future.

Hope

Before you even say what needs to be changed, you've got to have hope and offer hope that the other person can change in the direction your criticism indicates. The tragedy is that so often in our attempt to make the other person realize how bad he is, we paint a picture that destroys hope.

For example, the sales manager, concerned that his salesman doesn't fight hard enough to close a sale, paints a portrait of the man as someone weak and unfocused. This convinces the salesman that he can't do the very thing the sales manager is asking him to do.

But you don't criticize someone to convince him of how badly he's been doing something. You do it to get him to change. And nothing spurs change like hope.

How do you convey hope? You just need a brushstroke. For example, the sales manager could simply say, as he's setting things up, "You know, you're one of the more likable people on my staff." That creates hope because while likable people sometimes have trouble twisting someone's arm, likable people also have an easier time getting others to say yes.

Benefit

As you set things up, make sure you hold up before the other person what he'll get as a result of taking in your feedback and changing. Of course, in some contexts the benefit is obvious. The same sales manager who destroys hope might be very successful at communicating the money his salesman can make if he does it right, and the unemployment he'll face if he doesn't.

But in our more personal relationships—friends, family, lovers—we often completely leave out any mention that there will be any benefit at all from heeding our criticism. The wife who says to her husband, "You never listen to me," and constantly criticizes him for not listening never mentions what benefit he'll get from listening.

You've got to make clear some benefit from heeding your criticism if you want to motivate a person to change, if you want him even to hear your criticism. And threats don't work, unless you're a sales manager. Let me make this simple. Telling someone you love "I won't hate you" if he changes is *not* a benefit. Telling him he'll be living with a happy person who will be willing to do things for him if he changes *is* a benefit.

A future

And you have to emphasize that your relationship not only has a past but a future as well. You don't simply want to give your friend feedback about how much time she spends complaining and how annoying her complaining is. The point is that you're hoping to stay friends with her for a long time and that your whole future together will be affected by whether she can take in your feedback.

People are vastly more motivated to take feedback well when they feel they have a future with the person who's giving it to them.

Even people who are married often inadvertently convey something like this: "I want you to know how awful this thing is that I'm criticizing you for. It's so awful that it makes me wonder if we have a future together." But by questioning the possibility of a future, people who do this make it all too easy for the other person to say something like, "Well, if we don't have a future together, why should I change?"

When giving feedback, you have to explicitly say that you have some criticism to offer the other person but that you wouldn't say it unless you believed he could change. And you have to make clear what the other person will get from changing. And you have to make it clear that the two of you have a future together.

And when I say you have to "explicitly say" this, I mean it. Let's go back to Linda and Robert.

To set things up right, Robert should have said, "The reason I wanted us to talk is that I'd like you to do me a favor. I'd like you to listen to some feedback I have. There's nothing wrong with you. I'm just talking about a change that, as your brother, I think you need to make. Look, I wouldn't give you this feedback if it weren't important and if I didn't think you could change. If you think my feedback is fair and you do change a little, then what you'll get is a brother who feels a lot freer to visit you and spend time with you and your family. We're going to be brother and sister for the rest of our lives, and I think it'll make us a lot closer if you can let in my feedback."

In this way you create a receptive frame of mind, which is the only frame of mind that lets in criticism.

Tell the Truth

Remember what you're after. You want the other person to change. It's not that you want him to do a specific thing. The change you're after is broader, more general.

Robert wanted his sister to live in a less "coarse and crude" way. All that meant was that he wanted her to take his feedback to heart and be more like the person their parents had been and had raised her to be. There was no one thing Linda could do to accomplish this. Robert just wanted solid evidence of change. And that's all any of us want when we give feedback. If we wanted anything as specific as a loan of money or help painting an apartment, we'd be making a request.

And that's what you highlight when you speak your truth—your desire for and hope for a certain kind of change. So you could say something like what Robert should have said to Linda:

> So I'd like to ask you to change something. It's just one thing. Otherwise you're fine as far as I'm concerned. But this one thing really bothers me and I'm hoping you can hear my feedback because it's important to me. I'm not asking you to agree with me, but I'd like to be able to come and visit you more often, and from my point of view the way you live with your husband makes me uncomfortable. Tell me how to say this. Do you want me to be blunt or should I sugarcoat it?

In almost every case I've seen, when people are presented with this choice—shall I be blunt or shall I sugarcoat it?—people respond by saying something like, "Well, just come right out with it. You don't have to tiptoe around with me." Of course you're not going to be blunt. But you've gotten your green light, and this is an important part of the script.

And now you have permission to say in direct words something like:

> Look, from my point of view, the way you live is coarse and crude. I'm talking about the drinking and the yelling and the cursing. Please, I know this is not who you are. But this is what I see and it's important to me that you change. Please don't be insulted. If you don't agree with what I'm saying or it doesn't make any sense to you, we'll talk about it.

You want to maximize the likelihood of change and minimize the likelihood that the other person will get insulted or start acting defensive. You see, you're not the other person's boss. Criticizing him or her is hard for you precisely because on some level this is not something you're supposed to do. Even people in a marriage who bruise each other with criticism all the time feel that they should be accepting each other for who they are and that there's something wrong with setting yourself up to pass judgment.

Watch out for your anger

When you criticize someone who's important to you, it isn't your fear of the other person's bad reaction to your criticism that creates a mess but your anger at him for needing the criticism in the first place.

Criticism is one of those classic things that we keep bottled up inside. So, propelled by your anger and in an attempt to drive your point home, the criticism comes across as a harsh judgment. And the result is that it's your own vehemence, not the change you'd like to see, that becomes the subject of the fight you have afterward.

That's why people who criticize someone end up so often apologizing. Now you see why my script was so apologetic in the first place. The apology is what you need to get the criticism heard so that when you talk about it, the whole conversation isn't about the other person's criticizing you for being so critical.

And you won't be viewed as overly critical if your apologies are up front. Don't worry about your criticisms not getting through if you cushion them. The cushioning is what *enables* them to get through!

Let my words be heard

People sometimes question this approach, arguing, "But if I don't shout, he won't hear." What they're suggesting is that people are impervious to criticism unless you're vehement about it.

Here's the right way to think about this. People are impervious to vehemence unless you're someone's boss and they're dependent on you for their very livelihood.

What people do respond to is knowing that you care. What makes people cooperate is not your vehemence but your ability to convey that your feedback is important to you. You're not just criticizing the other person to hear yourself talk or to complain or to be on a power trip or to put the other person down. You're criticizing because the change you want is deeply meaningful to you. And you convey this by saying that the change is important to you and by saying *why* it's important to you.

Robert criticized his sister because he wanted to be close to her and comfortable with her again. Her fully realizing that she is really important to him is what lets his feedback get through.

It's all in the follow-through

What usually happens when you do a bad job giving feedback is that the experience is so painful that you don't want to go near it again afterward. So what you made a big deal about on Saturday you don't talk about on Monday or Thursday or the following Saturday. In your attempt to avoid more pain, you communicate the worst possible thing: that you never really cared about what you were criticizing in the first place.

Otherwise, the other person thinks, you wouldn't have let drop the very thing you were so vehement about.

So you have to reverse this pattern. That means you start out *not* being vehement but then you repeat your feedback at every appropriate moment.

For example, every time he saw his sister being what he called "coarse and crude," Robert could gently have said, "You see, Sis, that's what I was talking about. That's exactly the kind of thing I was saying really bothers me." And when he saw Linda giving any evidence of having changed, even slightly, he could have said, "Oh, that's great, that's my old Linda. I knew you could do it."

This consistency, this staying on message, can't really be part of the moment of telling. But you have to reassure yourself that you will be there later for your own criticism, that you won't let yourself down when it comes to sticking to your guns. That way you'll know that you have another shot at saying the truth if you don't blow it now. And your knowing this will help you be less vehement and will increase the chance of your feedback getting through the first time.

Basic rules

What is the essence of this stage where you actually say your criticism? Three things.

One, be absolutely clear about the change you want. Suppose the other person really wants to let in your feedback. How would she know what to do? Suppose the other person really does let in your feedback. How would you know? The way you'd know that the other person took your criticism to heart is by seeing her exhibit the change you want, and that is something you have to make absolutely clear. Robert would have to be absolutely sure that Linda understood what he meant by not being "coarse and crude."

Two, let the other person know how important this is to you. Make her see why you care. Help her understand why it makes a difference if she does things one way as opposed to another way.

And three, cushion your criticism. People defend themselves against attacks, but they let in information. *Information* about what bothers you or about what you need will get through.

Make It All Come Out Right

Now it's time for the last stage, making it all come out right. The first thing you have to do is say that you hope the other person doesn't feel attacked or insulted.

Next you have to make it clear that you weren't judging the other person. Some people find it effective to say, "Look, I'm not any kind of expert on how to be a human being [or whatever area it is you're dealing with]. All I'm talking about is what works for me."

Now you have to listen to what the other person says. You might not have to ask anything to elicit a response. People often aren't shy about speaking up when they've been criticized. Here are some standard things the other person might say to you and ways you might respond.

"You have no right to say that to me." The best response is "I'm sorry if I made it sound as if I'm judging you. I'm just talking about what I need to feel better."

"There's no way I can correct what you're criticizing me for. It's just the way I am." The best response is "I like you the way you are. I'm not trying to change who you are. I'll be happy if you change this behavior I'm uncomfortable with a little bit, like ten percent. Look, just try. I know who you are; I wouldn't have said this if I didn't think you could change."

"I don't know what you're talking about. I don't even do what you're criticizing me for." The best response is "Look, I'm not saying it's intentional, but let me give you an example of what I'm talking about." (If you can't give a specific example, you have no business giving feedback in the first place.) "Maybe you don't remember doing that, but I do. But look. I don't want to get into an argument with you about who did what. Maybe you didn't do what I'm criticizing you for. But I think you did. Let me do this: next time I see it, I'll point it out to you. You may not realize you're doing it or it may mean something completely different to you, but at least we'll see what we're talking about."

Don't label

It's even better to prevent the other person from saying she doesn't know what you're talking about. The best way to do this, if you have to give feedback, is to criticize someone only for observable, specific things he does, not for a general state of affairs or a psychological state of mind.

For example, one guy had a close business associate who never seemed to answer his questions. When he couldn't take it anymore he criticized him for "being evasive." This almost destroyed their working relationship because the guy being criticized never for a minute intended to be evasive, hated evasiveness himself, and was deeply insulted. They were able to start repairing their relationship when the first guy apologized for the "being evasive" criticism and said, "Look, all I'm saying is that sometimes when I ask you a question, you don't answer. You probably think you've answered, but you haven't."

I'm really talking about labeling. People *hate* being labeled. If you talk about what the other person *does* instead of *who he is,* you get away from labeling and people can more easily let in your criticism.

Move toward change

Once you get beyond these predictable responses, if they occur, you have to ask the other person something like "You've heard how I feel—are you willing to change a little?"

The other person will probably talk about what his behavior has meant to him or what he thought he was trying to accomplish by doing the thing you were criticizing him for. For example, Linda said to Robert, "Well, what you call 'coarse and crude' is the way my husband likes to live. What do you want me to do? Divorce him?"

It might sound as if the other person's giving you a hard time about your feedback, but he's really helping you by saying he needs a substitute for the old behavior you were criticizing. For example, the person you criticized for complaining needs a way to express her feelings and needs that's not complaining. And Linda needed to be given a clue for how she could change in a way that wouldn't start an ongoing battle with her husband; otherwise Robert's criticism was completely useless. And the parent you feel is still too controlling needs to feel she has a role to play in your life if she stops bossing you around.

If you want your criticism to register, you have to help the other person get over these obstacles.

Notice how it all comes back to "Tell the truth but meet the need." The other person doesn't need to be doing the thing you were criticizing, but he does need *something.* And if you work with him to find out what that is, his need will be met and he'll be free to change. His objections just point to his needs.

Summing Up

Here are the essential ingredients in the script for giving feedback:

- First say, "I'd like to talk to you about something," and work out a convenient time.
- Next say what you're going to do and why you're going to do it: say that you have some criticism to offer but you wouldn't say it unless you believed the other person could change. Make clear what he will get from changing and that the two of you have a future together.
- When you actually give your feedback, be absolutely clear about the change you want. Let the other person know how important this is to you; help her understand why it makes a difference if she does things one way or another way. And cushion your criticism; remember that straightforward information about what bothers you or about what you need will get through in ways that vehemence won't.
- Finally, when it comes to making it all come out right, you have to say that you hope the other person doesn't feel attacked or insulted. Make it clear that you weren't judging the other person. Listen to what the other person says and acknowledge whatever emotional difficulties he has hearing your feedback. Focus your own efforts on helping the other person change.

Remember at the beginning you felt torn. You'd wanted to tell the truth to someone important to you, and that truth was criticism. But you were torn between telling the truth and preserving harmony. This script will help you achieve both of your goals.

7   "There's Something I'd Like to Ask You For"

W<small>HAT MAKES THIS CATEGORY DIFFERENT</small> from criticisms is that you're asking for something specific, solid. You might criticize your boss because she's never nice to you. What you're hoping is that in a general sort of way she'll be nicer. A request, on the other hand, is for something like a raise. It is, quite simply, a what, not a how.

If criticisms cause problems because they make the other person feel one down, asking for something can be difficult because it makes *you* feel one down and puts the other person in an awkward position as well.

Of course you'd like the other person to agree to your request, but the key thing you're hoping for is that if he can't give you what you want, you'll at least feel there's still a sense of respect and comfort between you. The door will still be open to your asking for other things in the future.

But you know how it's been in the past. Your request makes trouble. The other person seems to think less of you for needing what you do. And you feel in a bind. If you make a big deal about what you need, the other person will be afraid of you for being so needy and will move away from you. Or she'll start resenting you. On the other hand, if you minimize what you need, either you won't get what you want or the other person will feel manipulated. So you're not just afraid that the other will say no—you're afraid your request will damage her opinion of you and put a strain on your relationship.

Here's a story that illustrates how things can go wrong.

Mike and Jim

Mike owned a small printing business. Bills were mounting, sales were down, and he was in danger of going belly-up. He was way past the point where any bank would help. But his brother Jim had some money. The problem was that Mike and Jim had had a strained relationship since childhood and had never been close as adults although each had made the occasional, halfhearted attempt to reach out to the other. So it was out of the blue that Mike called asking for a loan of $10,000.

Mike tried to make it sound as though the amount was no big deal and he'd easily be able to pay it back within a few weeks. Jim felt both insulted and suspicious because Mike was obviously hiding the precariousness of his situation and was so obviously taking Jim for granted, particularly when they hadn't been close. Jim had $10,000, but he couldn't afford to throw a sum like that away. He apologetically said no, even though he resented Mike for the position he put him in. Years have passed and they haven't spoken since.

First Decide This

The first thing you have to do is make a decision. You want something but it's hard for you to ask for it. Well, you have to decide which is more important: Is the most important thing getting what you want, at almost any cost? Or is it preserving the good feeling in your relationship? In other words, do you want to win or do you want to feel good?

I'm not going to show you how to win when winning comes at the price of your relationship. But if the relationship is most important, the people who are important to you will give you what you ask for more often than not if you follow this script.

This is a book about strengthening your relationships, even when your truth is a real challenge to them. You can trust the spirit of cooperation that exists in most relationships to create the possibility that you can get what you need if it is at all within normal bounds. The tragedy this book is designed to prevent is a relationship that's destroyed because of a request that might have been handled much better.

So our goal, obviously, is to help you get both, the thing you're asking for and a healthy relationship with the person you're asking. But if you have to choose, you must decide to keep the relationship.

THE SCRIPT FOR ASKING FOR SOMETHING

Make an Appointment

The first stage, as always, is making an appointment. In this case, I've found it works best to explicitly say something like "I need to ask you for a favor. When would be a good time for us to talk?" The reason you're signaling in advance that you're going to ask for something is that otherwise the person might feel he's been "had" when he discovers that your "talk" has turned into your asking for something. Also, he'll try to anticipate what you're going to ask for, and in most cases your request will be less of a big deal than his worst fears.

Set Things Up

It's important to understand that whenever we ask someone for something, the way Mike asked Jim for a loan, we're really asking for a bunch of other things as well.

On the simplest level, we're asking for permission to ask—to know that we have the right to ask for this thing, or for anything, even if we can't get the thing we're asking for. It's one thing to be turned down when you ask for a raise. It's another thing to be told that you had no right to ask for a raise.

And we're asking for our request to be listened to and taken seriously, not dismissed out of hand. We're also asking not to be humiliated because we've asked for something or because we've asked for this particular thing. In effect when we ask for something, we're saying, "I'd like you to give me what I'm asking for, but if you can't, I want to come away feeling that it's okay that I asked." Before you actually say what you want, you have to set things up so the experience of asking feels okay afterward.

When Mike, in his attempt to get the $10,000 loan from his brother, tried to make it seem as though $10,000 was no big deal, he was making a big mistake. If $10,000 is a big deal to someone (and it is to most people), then saying to him it's no big deal makes him say, yes, it is a big deal. And once you've gotten the other person saying it is a big deal, he's already gone most of the way toward saying you don't have a right to ask for it.

That's why by his minimizing the size of his request, Mike was actually putting Jim in the position of having to say something like, "How can you say it's nothing? Ten thousand bucks is a big deal, and I can't believe you don't understand that." And those words made Mike feel it wasn't okay that he'd asked.

So when you set things up, you can't minimize the ways the other person will analyze your request. But don't make a huge error by going in the opposite direction. Most people like to think of themselves as generous and as having a lot of resources, not as being stingy and depleted. So if you go so far as to make a too-huge case about how what you're asking for is an unbelievably big deal, then the other person could respond by saying, "What kind of a stingy, selfish person do you think I am?"

So you have to steer between not making the other person feel taken for granted and not making the other person feel insulted.

The words to use

When it comes to setting things up, here's how you do this. What Mike should have said was something like, "I need to ask you for something that's important to me. Is that okay?" The other person will probably say yes, but it's crucial that you get that yes. By asking if it's okay to ask for something, you're making the other person feel empowered, not disempowered.

If the answer is yes, then you can go on, "But this is something that's hard for me to ask for. It's not you that's making me hesitate, because I'm sure you'd do this if you could, but it's the thing I'm asking for itself that's a big deal. So I just want you to know that our relationship as brothers [you can state what your relationship with the other person happens to be—

patient/doctor, husband/wife, friends, colleagues, and so on] is the most important thing to me. I hope you'll say yes, but I'd rather you'd say no than jeopardize our relationship. And if there's anything I can do to reassure you about my request, I hope you'll tell me."

I know that this is a fairly long speech, but your request is a big deal to you and you're nervous about it. Setting things up this way gets both the other person and you in the right frame of mind not to experience your request as a kind of combat situation. And the more you practice asking for things that are hard for you by setting things up in the right way, the more hitting the right notes will come automatically in the future. The essential thing is to create a nonthreatening atmosphere while at the same time being careful to avoid setting the other person up to feel that you're not acknowledging the impact of what you're asking for.

Tell the Truth

Here's how to make your request. Don't say, the way Mike did, "I really need ten thousand dollars to tide me over during the next period in my business." There are two things wrong with this. There's an arm-twisting quality to it that the other person will resent, and your reason for asking isn't completely believable. People are more likely to give you what you want when they trust your reason, but when people feel pressured they simply resist.

What you should say is something like, "We can do this however it works best for you, and I'm willing to do whatever you need to feel you can give it to me. But I need ten thousand dollars for my business. I'd like this to be a one hundred percent business-like loan, but you'd know I was kidding you if I made it seem as though I didn't need this really, really badly, which means I'm in trouble, which means there's the possibility I won't be able to pay you back, at least not for a very long time. I know I'm asking for a lot. Whatever's hard for you about this—let's talk about it."

The essentials

What's essential here is that you show your willingness to cooperate, you say clearly what it is you're asking for, you acknowledge whatever problems or suspicions the other person might have, and you indicate some kind of process in which the two of you can work things out.

And no matter how entitled you feel deep down to make your request, if it's something that's hard for you to ask for, then you must indicate clearly and specifically how you'll repay the other person or what he'll get in exchange. Asking for a loan and offering to sign a precisely structured promissory note with a meaningful interest rate is what Mike should have done but didn't. He didn't do it because, like most of us, he already felt bad enough making a request like that; offering to sign a note would have felt humiliating. But he might have gotten the money, and being shot down by his brother felt even worse.

No pressure

In one area you have to walk a fine line. You have to let the other person know *why* this request is important to you, because that helps him see what it means and it makes him feel you're treating him with respect. But you can't make it seem as though you're bullying or pressuring or guilt-manipulating the other person into saying yes. In the short run that might seem to increase the chance of your getting what you want. But in the long run that tactic destroys relationships. It's important to emphasize why the request is important and at the same time underemphasize the dire consequences that will follow if you don't get what you want.

In other words, Mike should have spent more time talking about how he'd use the $10,000 and how that $10,000 would help him than talking about how his life would be ruined if he didn't get it. I call this the Seem Cooperative Not Desperate Tactic. It's not obvious to most people.

Most of us play the desperation card either when we're asking for small favors—"Can you lend me twenty bucks till tomorrow? I've got to grab a cab but I haven't any cash"—or when we're asking for something from someone who's in a special position to grant or not grant certain kinds of requests—"Doctor, you've got to see me right away because I'm in terrible pain." But these requests are *within* the bounds of your relationship with these people. The things that are hard for you to ask for are hard precisely because they're pushing against the boundaries of your relationship, and that's where and why desperation will backfire.

Make It All Come Out Right

When it comes to making things all come out right after you make your request, there are three possibilities.

Sometimes *the other person says yes right away*. But if your request was a big enough deal for you to be uncomfortable about making it, then you should be just a tiny bit uncomfortable about having it met so readily. In other words, if the other person says yes, ask him if he's sure, and ask him if he needs anything from you in return.

Sometimes *the other person hits you with questions or objections*. If that happens, have the right attitude. Have the attitude that everything that's not a no is a maybe, and even a lot of nos are maybes. So any question or objection, no matter how challenging, means a possible yes. Think of them as signs that the other person is looking for a way to say yes but doesn't know how to get past his own objection. This is important, because if you start getting discouraged, you'll start acting bummed out or pissed off and that might guarantee getting turned down.

You have to deal with the questions or objections with a helpful spirit.

Dealing with delegitimization

The first thing Jim said to Mike was "We've never been close. Now you're asking me for all this money."

When he heard this, Mike said, "But I'm your brother." You can probably guess the mistake Mike made: he failed to acknowledge Jim's reality. Mike should have said something like, "I know we haven't been close. I'm sorry for that. I'd like us to get close in the future, particularly since we're getting older. And I hope that happens whether you lend me the money or not. I can understand why our not being close makes it harder for you to lend me the money. All I can say is that when I found myself in a tight bind and I thought about getting help, you were the only person who came to mind."

Even if you never ask to borrow money from your brother, any request can meet with the same kind of reaction. It's what I call *delegitimization*: the other person's saying that for some reason your request ain't legit. Your girlfriend says, who are you to ask me to stop smoking? Your assistant says, but that's not in my job description. Your husband says, you've asked me that before and I've said no and now I'm tired of your asking me.

Delegitimization is the "You shouldn't ask" response. And whenever the other person deals with your request by saying you shouldn't ask, then the only correct response is to fully acknowledge the anomaly. Yes, you say, I can see why you feel I shouldn't ask, but I'd like you to consider what I'm asking anyway. And if there's a gap in your relationship somewhere, acknowledge your responsibility for it and offer to do your share to bridge the gap.

Dealing with impossible-izing

There's another kind of question or objection people raise. It's not "you shouldn't" but rather "I can't." This is what I call *impossible-izing,* and it's what salesmen deal with all day long.

Jim had this response when he started talking about how $10,000 was a lot of money for him: he was basically saying that he couldn't afford to lend it. But people "impossible-ize" in many different ways as they bring up obstacles as a reason for why "I can't." They can't perform oral sex with a lover because it's "gross." They can't help you move because they've "been hassled" all week. They can't okay your proposal because what you're proposing has never been okayed before.

Here's how to deal with impossible-izing. Anytime someone you're asking for something gives you a reason why he can't do it, your response should be something like, "But I can help you with that." No objection is a slammed door—we haven't dealt with nos yet. Instead, objections should be seen as eliciting cooperative problem-solving from you. What Mike should've said to Jim was something like, "Look, if you really don't have the money, I understand. But if you're afraid I won't pay you back, I'll be happy to sign a promissory note or do anything else to make you feel confident you'll get your money back."

By seeing the other person's objections—whether they're delegitimizing or impossible-izing—as opportunities for problem-solving, you're really accomplishing two things. First of all, if you can solve his problems, you can get what you're asking for. I know (although I learned this too late) that Jim actually had the money to lend Mike. He could have kissed $10,000 good-bye without a lot of pain, although it was still a significant sum of money to him. By quieting his fears and showing him what he had to gain, Mike could have made Jim feel a lot more comfortable about lending him the money.

But, second, there's a gain to your relationship with the other person if you show your willingness to solve problems with him. Whether or not you get what you're asking for, people feel good about each other when they cooperate. Both people feel, "This is someone I have a future with." So unless your goal is to win at all costs, you can't lose when you try to cooperate with the other person.

In the face of no

But sometimes when you ask for something, *the other person simply says no.* The first thing you have to do is make sure that what you think is a no isn't really just a worry. To determine this, you have to ask. You can say something like "If you really can't do it, then I can accept that. But it would really help me if I understood why you're saying no."

When you hear the other person's response to this, it's often immediately clear that the other person is concerned about something that you can solve, and when you do, the other person can go from saying no to saying yes. When I was in high school, there was a tradition of staying out till dawn after the senior prom. When I suggested we do this to my girlfriend, she said no, this was impossible because her mother said no, and that was a no that was a no. I immediately understood that my girlfriend didn't want to get in trouble with her mother; but staying out all night wasn't a problem. So we worked out a solution. I brought her home in time to satisfy her mother. She and her mother went to bed. And then I came to pick my girlfriend up and we stayed out until dawn.

Maybe that was the beginning of my career as a therapist because therapy is like dating in some sense: it's a process of converting nos into yeses.

But if you intuit that the other person's no is for real, then you immediately have to focus on preserving the relationship, particularly since you've already decided that the relationship is more important than getting the specific thing you're asking for. You've got to say this explicitly: "Look, if you can't, you can't. The important thing is our relationship. And I don't want you to feel that your saying no jeopardizes it."

Finishing up

There's one more thing you have to do to make sure things come out right after you make your request. You have to make sure that the other person doesn't have any unfinished business. Perhaps he feels you now owe him something. Perhaps he has questions for you. But you have to go after this directly by asking if he's okay with what he's agreed to and if he needs anything from you in return.

In case making a request still seems daunting, just remember that the script is only a more detailed version of "Tell the truth but meet the need." Your truth is that you want something. Not speaking that truth is getting in the way of your feeling that you can be open with the other person. But every word of the script is filled with acknowledgments that the other person has needs and that you're willing to meet them.

We'd all like it to be that the things we're asking for are no big deal. If your request is a little deal, it's easy to grant. But when this seems, to the other person, to be minimizing the big-dealness of our request, it comes across as if we were minimizing the needs the other person has about our request, even if the biggest need the other person has is simply to get an acknowledgment for the way your request feels like a big deal to him.

Just remember, if what goes up must come down, what you play down must be played up by the other person. If you're the one to play up the difficulties—in a problem-solving kind of way—the other person will play them down.

Special Tips

To help you ask for things more often and get more of what you're asking for, here are six tips I know people have found useful:

1. *Caring.* Don't bother asking for stuff you don't really care about. You have only so much energy and the other person has only so much to give. This

is a problem for some people. If you feel deprived or if you constantly feel you must be testing the waters of the other person's generosity, you might be asking for things all day from coworkers and friends and your spouse, so that when it comes to asking for something that you really need, the other person's just tapped out. People ignore the boy who cried wolf and they will ignore your requests unless you limit them to things you really care about.

2. *Size.* Think carefully about how big a thing it is you're asking for. If it's really important to you, okay, but the bigger it is, the harder it'll be for the other person to give it to you.

For example, suppose you want to ask a close friend to spend a weekend helping you move. You feel that a really good friend should want to do this for you. Maybe so. But if you begin to think about her needs, you might see clearly that she's under so much emotional and physical stress at work that most of her weekends are a time to collapse.

Of course she could just say no. But if for some reason she also feels obligated to you, then a request that big in the face of needs that are just as big could really damage your relationship.

3. *One thing at a time.* Ask for only one thing at a time. Never ask for something and then just as the person is giving it to you, slip in a request for something else. You'll just generate resentment and mistrust.

You'd be surprised how often people do this, though. As a clinician, nothing is more shocking to me than the degree to which the average person goes around feeling deprived. So when we ask someone for something, we're all too typically carrying around a laundry list of other things we'd also like to have. Once he says yes to our first request, in our relief we start going down our list of other requests. Paradoxically, this usually works at first. But what from your point of view is opening up a floodgate of goodies, is the opening up of a Pandora's box from the other person's point of view. If you have a bunch of things you want to ask for, in other words, let the other person know this in advance.

Lots of times people say no to a request because they feel if they say yes, you'll never stop asking for things. You have to make sure the other person knows this isn't true. Maybe it was true in the past, but no more.

4. *Focus.* If it's hard for you to ask for *this thing* from *this person,* that usually

means that you have a number of emotional issues connected to your request. For example, you might be resentful about all the things the other person's asked you for. You might be angry about all the things you've asked him for that he hasn't given you. You might feel deprived because of all the things you haven't gotten from other people in your past.

Remember, asking for something is in a different category from saying how you feel, and even though we keep smooshing our categories together, it works much better to keep them separate. If you want something, focus on that and on helping meet the other person's needs connected to giving you that. Bringing in any other issue, such as your feelings, means losing the focus and makes it likely not only that you won't get what you want, but that you'll put a strain on your relationship.

5. *Reality.* Discussions about what happened in the past or what's really happening now are rarely productive and usually leave everyone feeling angry and frustrated. So particularly when you're asking for something that's hard to ask for, if someone says, well, you did this or I did that, don't pick up that conversational ball if you don't want to end up in a big mess.

It would be nice if we agreed about what's real, of course, but when we don't agree, the problem is that there's no way of coming to an agreement. Our personal lives are not like a barroom discussion about who had the highest batting average in 1947, where you can go to a reference book and look it up. If you say that I never paid you back the twenty bucks I borrowed from you five years ago and I say I did, there's no way we can determine the truth. We'll just get madder and madder at each other.

So if you're asking someone for something and a discussion about who did what and said what starts up, either agree to disagree or concede that the other person's *probably* right. Focus only on what you want now.

6. *Optimism.* And be optimistic. If you have a negative attitude, the other person will probably pick up on that, resent it, and be less likely to give you what you want. But if you act hopeful, others will be more likely to meet your requests. We all like to feel that we live in a world of abun-

dance, where there's a lot to get and we have a lot to give. Project that attitude and people will be more likely to feel good about doing what you ask for.

Summing Up

Here are the essential ingredients in the script for making a request:

- First say, "I'd like to ask you for something," and work out a convenient time to talk about it.
- Ask if it's all right if you ask for something.
- Indicate that your relationship is more important to you than your getting what you're asking for.
- Show your willingness to cooperate with the other person in helping him get his needs met, say clearly what it is you're asking for, acknowledge whatever problem or suspicion the other person might have, and indicate some kind of process in which the two of you can work things out.

Before you ask someone for something, put yourself in his shoes. That it's hard for you to ask for this thing probably means that it's something the other person will have some trouble saying yes to as well as some trouble saying no to.

Everything we've talked about has to do with giving the other person options. When people have options, they feel rich, instead of feeling trapped and powerless. With options, the other person will win if he says yes and win if he says no.

8 "I Want to Tell You a Secret"

I<small>F ASKING FOR SOMETHING MAKES YOU FEEL ONE DOWN</small>, it can be even harder to confess a guilty secret. You're not a bad person, but you did something you feel bad about that affects another person, and now you want to confess. What you're looking for is the other person to say he forgives you, or at least to say what it will take to forgive you.

What we're hoping is that confessing our secret will relieve us of guilt and fear. We're also hoping that bringing the secret out into the open will clear things up in that relationship, perhaps enabling us to solve some problem we've not known how to solve. Plus we know that confessing our guilty secret is the right thing to do. And let's face it, we want to confess before the other person finds out.

But we've all had experience going back to when we were kids of how when you tell someone about something bad you've done, his first reaction is shock and deep suspicion because you hadn't told him sooner. You're not a saint for your honesty, you're a sinner because of the bad thing you're being honest about. And because we all instinctively expect this reaction, we end up with some unhealthy combination of hiding part of the truth and distorting the other part. We act like liars even when we're being honest, which only causes more suspicion and anger.

We can't change the truth, but we can change the way we tell the truth, and that will make all the difference.

Of course, I've talked about how badly I told my own secret, but to present a script for how to do it right, let's use the experience of Dave and Matt.

Dave and Matt

They were partners in an ad agency. Dave was the inside guy, taking care of money and management. His secret was that over the past years he'd lost a lot of their money in bad investments. All Dave could think about was getting Matt's forgiveness so he could put things right and they could go on together. But Dave was so eager for Matt to forgive him that he told a half-assed, sugarcoated version of what had happened—a too-easy-to-forgive version that aroused Matt's suspicions. Matt checked into things and found Dave was still holding a lot back. In fact Dave had lost much more money than he'd confessed to losing and had lost it in riskier ventures than he'd admitted.

This destroyed Matt's trust and their partnership. It turned a potentially forgivable mistake into an unforgivable act of deception.

It would be wonderful if none of us ever had anything to confess in the first place. But even without evil intent we do bad things. And so a lot of us end up carrying around a guilty secret we know we need to tell. Here's what you can do about it.

The Script for Confessing Guilty Secrets

Make an Appointment

You set up a time by saying, "There's something I'd like to talk to you about, but I don't want to do it unless we have some uninterrupted time. When would be good for you?" If your confession is important enough for you to be nervous about, then it's important enough for the other person to have enough time to deal with it. People who've heard a guilty secret have told me over and over how they wished there'd been more time to ask questions and say how they felt. By saying that you need time for what you want to talk about, you're meeting the other person's need from the very beginning.

Set Things Up

When it comes to setting things up, there's something you have to do when you confess a guilty secret that you don't have to do with the other categories: you have to write a brief letter in which you spell out exactly what it is you did, how you feel about having done it (hopefully very sorry), and that you're willing to make amends. The letter should be short, but it has to include all of this.

The letter method

Long experience has shown me that this letter method is a powerful tool for turning something as potentially damaging as revealing a guilty secret into a healthful experience for your relationship. Just think about your frame of mind: you feel guilty but you're eager for forgiveness. You're so eager for forgiveness, in fact, that it's almost impossible to resist the temptation to try to convince the other person that what you did was no big deal.

A confession is all about trust and sincerity. You're trying to rebuild trust even as you're breaking it down, and trying to convince the other person that you're sincere even while you're providing evidence of how you haven't been sincere. But I know what happens to us when we have to confess something. Just as Dave and I both did, you try to pretty up the picture of what happened. There's simply less bad stuff to confess that way.

When it comes to confessing a guilty secret, the more important your relationship with the other person, the more likely he or she is to dig and probe. The stuff you left out will be found out. The stuff you downplayed will get played up. And then the trust you weakened will be shattered.

By writing things out, you're creating a fixed text where what you're confessing is, as it were, carved in stone. If I'd done that with my wife, for example, writing down exactly what I did and when I did it with the other woman, we would never have gone through the nightmare where the more she probed, the more I revealed, and the more I revealed, the more she probed, until having pulled out of myself every last drop of truth, I discovered almost all of her trust in me had evaporated.

Speak now or forever hold your peace

When you reread what you've written, ask yourself if that's the whole story, your final version, what you're committing yourself to reveal beyond any possibility of change or revision, a truth that cannot be proved false and that you won't later confess was not completely true. If you're confessing an affair and you write that you slept with the other person four times but she never meant anything to you, it should never come out that you slept with the other person five times and no letter should ever appear in which you wrote "I love you" to that woman. Neither you nor any future development should ever contradict what you say in that letter.

I'm *not* saying that you absolutely must confess the truth, the whole truth, and nothing but the truth in this letter. The "To Tell or Not to Tell?" chapter makes it clear what issues come into play when you're deciding where to draw the line.

For example, if some part of your story is hurtful and its coming out will be of no benefit, and the person you're confessing to could not possibly learn of this, then that's a reason to leave this out. *But* if that part of the story ever does come out, there will be much more damage than if you'd confessed it in the first place. The letter is a way of reminding you that this is a time to speak or forever hold your peace.

Unshakable details

Details are all-important when you're making a confession. I vaguely confessed to my wife that I'd gone out for lunch "a number of times" with that other woman and that we'd never talked about, for example, my marriage. Of course my wife said, "Well, how many times did you go out for lunch with her?"

It seemed that every time we talked about it I added another lunch date to my record that I'd "forgotten" the previous time. And I "remembered" something we'd talked about that I'd previously claimed we'd never talked about, such as what was going on in my marriage.

If your story changes, you seem like a liar at the very moment you're telling the truth. Instead of writing out your confession as the ultimate, final, unchangeable truth, you make the whole experience sheer torture as you lead the two of you into a world where there's no end of pressure and suspicion because every time pressure is applied it yields a drop of new truth, which creates more suspicion and results in more pressure.

Creating something solid

Writing a letter accomplishes something else. Not only does it prevent the truth from wobbling, but your having a physical letter that you've taken the time to create conveys a sense of solidity and responsibility that has an amazing power by itself to prevent much of the craziness that occurs when someone hears you reveal a guilty secret. That letter is your way of saying that you take the whole thing very seriously, rather than making the mistake most of us make, which is to try to minimize the seriousness of what we're confessing.

By putting your story in letter form, everything you want to make happen is on a piece of paper, so if your feelings start pulling you in wild directions, you can go back to basics. The letter will prevent you from saying things you'll wish you hadn't said.

How to write the letter

Just as cakes come in many flavors but without certain things it's just not a cake, when you show up for the appointment you've made with the other person, you should have a letter in your pocket in which you've said

- what your relationship with the other person means to you (this provides meaning and perspective and gives hope).
- what you've done.
- how sorry you are for having done it and that you're asking for forgive-

ness (this acknowledges what it's like for the other person to hear what you have to say).
• what you intend to do about it (this offers compensation).

By writing the letter, you're almost done setting things up. You just tell the other person that you have a secret to share, that you'll be there for him and for all his feelings and needs and questions, and that what you're hoping to accomplish is, first of all, getting the other person to forgive you and, second, creating more of whatever it is you'd like there to be in your relationship.

Of course, this last varies from person to person. Dave just wanted Matt to trust him again. I wanted my wife and me to stop growing apart. Whatever you want, this is the time to say it directly, before you actually make your confession.

Tell the Truth

Now it's time to tell the truth. It's best to give the other person some options. You could say something like "As I've said, I have something to tell you. But don't worry—this is something I know we'll survive. [This reassurance is important.] How do you want me to handle this? I've written it out—do you want to read it? Or do you want me to read it to you?" Occasionally the other person will agitatedly say, "Well, just tell me." The best you can do in this case is hold the letter open in front of you and, glancing at it, paraphrase it as closely as possible.

But you might be nervous. You might not want the other person to have a choice. If it feels to you that the only way you can get through this is for the other person to read your letter, then just add, "I've written it out, because I'd really like you to read it."

I've had the privilege of seeing many of these documents in my work. I've seen professional communicators from poets to judges to actors do a terrible job. I've seen poorly educated people or people who never use language professionally, from gardeners to computer programmers to teenagers, do a beautiful job. I now know that anyone can do a good job, but we're all at risk of doing a bad job.

Basic principles

What's long been the missing part of the puzzle in the experience of telling guilty secrets is knowledge of what it's like for the other person to hear the secret. People who have a confession to make, in spite of their fear of the other person, are almost completely self-absorbed. Even if you're a sensitive person and feel very connected to the person you're confessing to, it's easy to lose sight of her as you think about telling. But people who've been on the receiving end, by the hundreds, have taught me these principles:

- When it comes to saying what happened or what you did, use the simplest, most direct language.
- Don't explain or defend yourself in any way when you're telling your secret.
- Just give the facts. Make sure you include *all* the important details, but don't go on and on with irrelevant information.
- As we've discussed, make your letter complete and accurate, beyond the need for later revision.
- Say you're sorry and mean it. Don't worry that you'll make yourself seem even guiltier because you apologize passionately. The biggest thing that will increase your guiltiness is your seeming lack of remorse.
- Do give some kind of explanation by putting what you did in context. It's incredibly difficult to explain without seeming defensive, but you must try. The key is identifying a motive or circumstance that led you to do what you did but does not seem to diminish your guilt.

My telling my wife that I got close to the other woman because in our marriage we were drifting apart was bad because it sounded as though I was blaming my wife for my actions. Instead, saying I did it because I was irresponsible and thoughtless and too unskilled to be able to bridge the gap between us would have been good because it would have maintained my guilt while still making sense of my actions.

- Don't make it seem as though you couldn't help doing what you did. It's tempting because it seems to relieve you of responsibility. But you're trying to increase trust. And the other person will trust you more if you understand that you could have done otherwise.

- Acknowledge the impact the thing you're confessing has on the other person. Allow yourself to feel her pain. Again, we're reluctant to do this because we're afraid that talking about how much the thing we did hurts the other person will somehow remind her of how hurt she is and make forgiveness harder. The opposite is true. Imagine every possible way your deed might have hurt the other person, practically and emotionally, write it down, show you understand it, and apologize for it in your letter.

- Don't seem as though you're an expert on how painful it is to hear what you're confessing. Fully acknowledge the other person's pain, but be sure she understands that you know her pain is even greater than you can imagine. This is a good time to say that you're available to hear how your deed affected her.

- Explain what you want from all this. Make it explicit that you want the other person to forgive you. Say that you know how hard it will be, that you're willing to do what's necessary to earn the other person's forgiveness. Ask what you can do to be forgiven.

- Don't forget that there may be other things you want from this confession besides forgiveness, and make sure that you talk about them. For example, one thing Dave wanted was a realignment of responsibilities between him and Matt. Say whatever it is you'd like that's important to you, even if it's selfish, as long as it will go toward making your relationship work better.

- Ask what you can do to earn the other person's forgiveness. Make it clear that you're willing to do whatever's reasonable to attain this.

- Don't make it sound as though sincere remorse and your desire for forgiveness are enough by themselves to earn the other person's forgiveness. No matter how bad you feel, the fact that you're making a confession means that in real terms the other person was hurt worse, so *merely* feeling bad is not enough.

Sample letters

Here are some samples of actual letters written by people in the same kind of circumstances you might be in.

Let's go right to a biggie: confessing an affair. Basically, this was a guy in his thirties, married with two young kids, who made frequent extended visits to his firm's home office, where, it turns out, he also made extended visits to a coworker's home.

A bad letter

I'm writing to tell you that for the last almost two years now I've been sleeping with a woman I see whenever I go back to Dallas. I'm going to break off my relationship with her the next time I go back. I never meant to hurt you and I hope this doesn't hurt you too badly. I hope you will not make too big a deal out of this because frankly it's really nothing anyone should make a big deal about. I suppose I cared about this woman but I certainly never loved her, and I suppose you could say that our relationship was basically about sex. At least it was for me; she might have seen it differently. Anyway, it's basically over. I know what I did was wrong, but you really can't completely blame me. I mean, you were sort of pushing me away in bed and refusing to do stuff in bed, like we talked about. If you shut a guy off like that you've got to expect he'll be tempted to go elsewhere. I'm just saying what I did was wrong but I did have a reason. Anyway, I'm sorry and I just hope we can forget about it.

There are many problems with this letter, but I want to focus on what I believe is an important source of these problems. The guy who wrote it made the mistake of "performing honesty." What I mean is—and I know this for a fact—this guy thought that if you're going to tell the truth by confessing a guilty secret, you have to act like a "blunt truth teller" and behave as if you are resisting any attempt to sugarcoat things. The attitude of people who feel they have to "perform honesty" is that if you're not brutally honest, you're not honest at all. "Let me be brutal, so you'll know I'm being honest."

But as you know, this is a book about making relationships and honesty work well together, and that means telling the truth in a way that both saves the relationship and leaves people with a desire to be honest again.

But it's strange: even as this guy was "performing honesty" he seemed evasive, as if unwilling to give up full claim to the facts he owned. It's as if he were saying, "I can confess, but you can't make me tell you everything." That's where you get the evasive-sounding sentences: "I suppose you could say that our relationship was basically about sex. At least it was for me; she might have seen it differently." In reality, his relationship with this woman was definitely about much more than sex, and he was lying when he said she "might" have seen it differently. He knew she did, as he knew he did.

When it comes to achieving the healing that you want from a confession, seeming evasive is just as bad as being evasive.

A good letter

Let me show you a letter by someone who did a good job when she confessed her affair. If you remember the principles for how to do this right, you'll see that she mostly kept to them:

> I have a confession to make. I did something I'm very sorry for. I did it of my own free will, but I'd give anything now to take back what I did. I'm telling you about this because I'm hoping that by my confessing what I did we can find a way to strengthen our relationship and put it on a more honest and loving footing.
>
> I'm sorry I have to confess this to you. But what I did was have an affair with a guy at work. Do you remember back to that period last winter and spring when they needed me at the hospital so much and I was always working late? Well, many of those times I was with

this guy and we had sex together. I don't remember exactly how many times, but a dozen would be close enough.

Ever since, I've been wondering if I had "feelings" for this guy. It certainly felt like it at the time. I can't deny that this was a passionate affair. During that whole period I thought about being with him a lot, but I never wanted to marry him or end our marriage.

I really don't have an excuse for what I did. I think now that on some level it was just an exercise in selfishness and self-indulgence. I wanted it because it felt good. I even think I wanted it because I wanted to see if I could get away with it. I had a funny feeling the whole time, both guilty and yet very powerful.

I ended it last April because I knew I had to or it would destroy our marriage. I'm confessing it to you because we've been sniping at each other for a couple of years now, and if we don't patch things up, I'm afraid for us. Part of me even thought I was stupid to confess because how would that help things, but I just know our relationship has got to be a place where we can be honest with each other. Besides, you know people from the hospital and there's just a slight possibility that you might find out about this, and I wanted to confess it first.

What I haven't told you yet is how sorry I am for what I've done. Back when I was actually having the affair, at first, I can't really say I was all that sorry. But as time went on, I guess I sort of realized what I was actually doing, and I was just hit with feeling incredibly sorry and guilty, which is why I ended things. I guess once it dawned on me that I was really doing this terrible thing, I just couldn't let go of feeling incredibly bad. And I've been feeling that way since.

I don't know how to show you how sorry I am. What can I do? I mean, you tell me if there's something I can do *to make it up to you, whatever it is, because that's what I want to do. I guess I draw the line at your hitting me. But anything else. I mean it. I'll do a penance like in the Bible. I'll do whatever you want me to do so you can say we've balanced the books.*

I can't bear the thought of your reading all these words. I know it's got to be a lot easier for me to feel all sorry and guilty than for you to read about what I've done. I can imagine you're shocked and hurt and devastated and ready to kill me and unbelievably confused and all kinds of other emotions. I just hope you don't feel humiliated—you know, like the guy whose wife had cheated on him, even though that's what happened—because whatever else terrible it was that I did, it wasn't a judgment on you or who you are or what you have to offer. Maybe it was a comment on our marriage, but really it was only a judgment on how incredibly stupid and selfish I realize I was capable of being.

I guess I want to end by giving you my solemn word that this will never happen again as long as we're married. I don't know if you can believe that now, but I hope you'll come to know it's true in the future.

I love you and I'm very sorry for what I've done, and I hope this doesn't hurt too much and I hope you'll find a way to forgive me eventually.

This is a wonderful letter. This woman wasn't performing honesty, she was simply struggling to be honest and to repair her relationship at the same time. A good letter doesn't have to be perfect. This woman left out two things. She didn't say that she's available now to listen to her husband tell her how he feels. And she didn't go into enough detail.

But there's one kind of detail you shouldn't go into. I advise people who are making a sexual confession like this to tell the whole truth as far as how many meetings there were and what feelings were involved but don't go into explicit sexual details such as who did what to whom and in what position. These details create an indelible image that makes forgiveness much harder. If you're in this situation, you're confessing to having had an affair, so if the other person pushes, you can say, "Look, we had sex, that's exactly what I'm confessing. But I'm not going to go into graphic detail. That's not going to add anything to the truth I'm confessing to you."

The essential point of this letter is this woman's willingness to take the full measure of guilt and sorrow, without trying to shift any of the blame or minimize the damage. She gave some context, showed that she was willing to do what was necessary to wipe the slate clean, and gave some real hope for the future. There's no reason why you can't do the same thing. If necessary, use that letter and paraphrase it sentence by sentence, inserting your own words and feelings.

Remember Dave and Matt? Dave had invested a lot of his and his partner Matt's money and lost it. When he confessed to Matt, he did so in such an arrogant, trust-eroding way that an otherwise highly productive business relationship was destroyed. Of course Dave could have done a much better job. He didn't get the chance, but a guy named Kevin did have a chance and he made good use of it.

Kevin's situation was a little different. He was a doctor, a partner in a group cosmetic-surgery practice. The good news was that he didn't lose any money. The bad news was that he *stole* some. He repaid it before anyone realized it was missing, but it was theft nonetheless. Kevin had been going through an expensive divorce. He needed cash desperately and he panicked. He was going to let the whole thing go without saying anything to anyone since the books were balanced again, but he had this horrible nagging fear that a sharp accountant examining the books would immediately understand what had happened. Better to bite the bullet and confess than be found out.

For someone in a business, where money is a real issue, Kevin did a fine job with his letter.

Another good letter

In our profession trust and credibility are all-important. As a group practice, our ability to depend upon each other is all-important too. So it is frankly with a great deal of trepidation that I make this confession. I hope you will be able to forgive me, but I'll understand it if you can't. I just hope that after you've read these words, we have the opportunity to talk and "process" whatever problems you have so if there's a chance we can work things out, we don't lose that chance.

To get to the heart of the matter, there's no other way to put it than to say that I stole money from you. I've since repaid all of it, but I stole it nonetheless. I know you all know about my divorce from hell, but you don't know how scared and desperate I was back then. Kate was going after everything she could, and I simply had no liquid assets. I'm not excusing what I did, but I guess I do hope that if you know the context, it'll be a little easier for us to rebuild trust.

I basically wrote myself a check for $57,000 as if that money would be used for buying equipment for the practice. Nine months later when my situation was clearer, I was able to get a loan for that amount and I paid it back to you guys. But I did steal from you, and maybe just as bad as possibly destroying your trust in me, I withheld my trust from you by not telling you about my situation and asking for help.

If you want me to withdraw from the group, I'll understand and I will do so at the time you deem most convenient. But I hope you won't ask me to withdraw. Let's face it, the issue is this guy stole once, why wouldn't he steal again? And if he stole, why wouldn't he cut corners some other way?

I frankly don't know how to respond to this. All I can say on my behalf is that I've never done anything like it before, and given how bad I feel about it, I can't imagine doing anything like it in the future. That's why I think we need to talk about this. Maybe there are some questions

> *you can ask me that you'll find helpful in determining*
> *whether or not my crime was a onetime thing or not. Let*
> *me just say that I will do whatever is necessary to earn*
> *back your trust and that I deeply hope that it's still possi-*
> *ble to do so. Please forgive me for stealing from you in the*
> *first place.*

Again, the essential elements are all there. Kevin didn't hide anything. He didn't pull any punches. He didn't minimize what he did or the impact it might have had. He didn't try to excuse himself, although he did offer an explanation. He made it clear how sorry he was. And he said what he wanted for the future.

There's a funny twist on this story. Four of the other five doctors in the practice, after they got over their anger and confusion, were strongly in favor of Kevin's staying with them. One doctor wanted Kevin out and wouldn't budge. Kevin stayed and a year later the doctor who wanted Kevin out was gone himself.

But of course writing a letter like this and giving it to the person to whom you want to confess your secret is only part of the process of actually telling the truth. Let's talk about what will happen with the letter. You're sitting with someone. You've either handed him the letter so he can read it for himself or you've read it to him. Then what?

Now for the most important part of the process.

Make It All Come Out Right

After they read a confession letter people have a lot of feelings and a lot of questions. "How could you . . . ?" "Why didn't you . . . ?" "What were you thinking when you . . . ?" "Didn't you realize that . . . ?"

Most often feelings and questions are all smooshed together, so that a lot of feelings come out in the form of questions and vice versa. Here's the key to avoid falling into terrible traps at this stage. You will be asked questions that will tempt you to minimize what happened or to evade responsibility for it. Therefore what you have to do is respond to any question by continuing to drive home the point that you are responsible, that what you did was terrible, and that you're incredibly sorry.

So when the other person says, "How could you [do whatever it is you did]?" don't be misled into thinking that the other person is interested in some kind of explanation. This is *not* the time to talk about how you were lonely or in deep debt or were feeling you couldn't talk to the other person. Instead this is the time to say that you're sorry for what you did and that you shouldn't have done it. If there are *facts* that are important in explaining what you did, they should be in your letter. No matter how upset the other person is, no matter how hard he pushes you, you should never, never, never say something that significantly adds to or changes what you've said in the letter.

But after you've talked about how bad you feel about this terrible thing you did, you're not finished. You have to talk about two other areas.

First, *what does it mean that you did it?* I'm specifically referring to what the other person can expect from you in the future, *not* your excuse for what you did in the past. If you cheated on your spouse, the two of you are going to have to deal with what you did. But soon enough your spouse is going to want to know if she can expect you to cheat on her again in the future. And, let's face it, you're not in a great position to prove otherwise.

Here's how you handle this, and you should handle it during the session when you're confessing your secret.

One thing you should do (assuming that it's true for you) is *say* that you'll never do it again. That might sound obvious, but some of us hate like hell to eat crow, and the whole business of making a confession is hard enough, so saying "I'll never do it again" makes you feel like a child. But you need to say it anyway.

Another thing you should do is ask the other person what *he* needs to start feeling confident that you'll never do it again. He probably won't know the answer to this, or else he'll say there's nothing you can do or that only time will tell. But at least you've started a conversation about rebuilding trust. You can't rebuild it overnight, but you've got to show you can talk about it.

Let me say what the game really is here. You have to indicate that you're willing to do whatever it takes to rebuild trust back to the point where this relationship is viable again. The other person doesn't know what she needs, but she needs to put you to some kind of test or set some kind of task in front of you.

The explosive ingredient here is humiliation. Generally, when we can't trust someone, we treat him like a child. So often when there's a need to rebuild trust, you're asked to do something humiliating. When I confessed my involvement with another woman, to rebuild trust my wife asked me not to have lunch with her anymore. Like an idiot, I reacted to the humiliation of this. How could she tell me whom to have lunch with? But I should have understood that doing something that feels humiliating is almost always a part of doing what's necessary to rebuild trust.

Let me put it this way. If you're not willing to eat a little bit of crow, then you really don't care about that relationship. If you think the other person is deliberately trying to humiliate you, then you shouldn't care about that relationship. Otherwise, accept that you'll have to do something beyond merely uttering words to rebuild trust. You probably won't like what you have to do, but the other person didn't like whatever it was you were confessing.

We've just touched on the second area you have to talk about. It's *what you need to do to rebalance things*. Anytime someone does something that's a big enough deal for them to worry about confessing it, there's a terrible imbalance in that relationship. If you borrowed someone's golf clubs for an afternoon and ruined his expensive putter, there's an imbalance there and most people understand that you right the balance by buying the person a new putter. If you broke it, you pay for it. Imbalance, balance.

The problem with most of the things we have to confess is that the damage is abstract. When Dave lost a lot of his and Matt's money in bad investments, he couldn't afford to pay for the financial damage, but there was also damage to Matt's sense that he could rely on Dave, and how do you pay for that?

You have to acknowledge that questions of this sort are legitimate and deserve a sincere attempt to find an answer. Neither you nor the other person has to know the answer. But you have to say that you are willing to do whatever's necessary to rebalance things. That's what your relationship is going to be about in the near future: finding your way back to a new balance where instead of making it seem as though the other person's a jerk for holding a grudge, you make it clear that you'd be a jerk if you didn't do something to fix things.

Summing Up

Here are the essential ingredients in the script for confessing a guilty secret:

- Make it clear that you have something serious you want to talk to the other person about and that you'll need a good chunk of time. Make an appointment to get that time.
- Prepare a letter in which you say what your relationship with the other person means to you, what you've done, how sorry you are for having done it, what you intend to do about it. The essential point is that you take on yourself the full measure of responsibility, without trying to shift any of the blame or to minimize the damage.
- Then when the two of you get together, you tell the other person that you have a secret to share, that you'll be there for him and for all his feelings and needs and questions, and that what you're hoping to accomplish is, first of all, to get him to forgive you and, second, to create more of whatever it is you'd like there to be in your relationship.
- Finally, stay with the other person for as long as it takes for you to answer fully, honestly, and patiently all his questions and to deal with all his responses.

Confessing a secret is a moment of incredible opportunity. Guilty secrets can destroy relationships because of the way people deal with them. So your confessing your secret is your chance to save this relationship. If you're effective in the way you confess it, you will save the relationship.

9   "I've Never Told You This Before"

SOMETIMES WHAT WE FIND DIFFICULT TO SAY is a simple fact about ourselves. We haven't done anything wrong, but we know the other person will be upset anyway.

Whenever we tell someone personal information about ourselves, we want him to know something that we feel is important for him to hear or we want to feel closer to him or we want to create more honesty in the relationship. In case you're in doubt, if the response that would make you feel satisfied is the other person's saying that *she can now let in this new information and still accept you,* then what you want to do is reveal sensitive personal information.

What we're hoping is that indeed honesty is the best policy. But when you've done this in the past, it's often caused the other person to change how she feels about you for the worse. She's shocked or disturbed. She starts wondering what else you haven't told her. She starts wondering how what you've told her might harm her. And so you start wondering if honesty is in fact the best policy.

Kim and Jason

Kim came of age in the sixties and had been at the forefront of liberal/feminist activities. She always hated the things people kept from each other in her family when she was growing up. By the midnineties, though, Kim had something personal to hide from her liberal husband, Jason: she'd turned conservative. Finally she decided she had to tell him. But as she told Jason, she sounded defensive. Her revelation came across much more belligerently than she'd planned. What he heard was not an attempt to create openness but a declaration of attitudinal warfare that eventually poisoned their relationship.

THE SCRIPT FOR REVEALING PERSONAL INFORMATION

Let's begin by talking about the obstacle you have to overcome here. People who are in ongoing, not-completely-impersonal relationships expect that others will tell them important things about themselves. If you're in college and become good friends with someone, you'd be hurt if he kept from you that he is gay. If you're in your thirties and dating a woman, you'd be upset if she kept from you that she is divorced.

The problem is that the things we'd want to hear about are not things we always feel safe telling. That's why it's instinctive to wait before you spill the beans about something that's a big deal. And that's where the obstacle comes in. Instead of making your revelation right away, you waited, which means that you're setting it up for the other person to get mad because you didn't tell him sooner. But the fact that you hesitated about making your revelation at all means that there's the possibility that the other person will get upset because of what you're telling him. In other words, the obstacle we face is that after we finish saying, "There's something I have to tell you about me . . . ," the other person will say, "Oh, that's gross. Why didn't you tell me sooner?"

So your task is to get the other person to accept whatever it is you're revealing without making a big deal about your not having revealed it sooner.

Make an Appointment

As usual, you begin by making sure you have time that won't be interrupted. I've found that it's not quite as important here to actually make an appointment, since this is precisely the kind of truth people expect others to make spontaneously, but you have to make sure you have a little pocket of time so that the other person won't feel you've left her high and dry. It's not leaving time for questions that makes other people feel dumped on.

Set Things Up

Once you get together, you have to make sure you set things up right. You must deal with the you-should-have-told-me-sooner issue. The best thing is to say that explicitly: "I have something to tell you about myself. I know I should've told you sooner, and I wish I had. I'm not going to make any excuses about waiting for the right time. I was just afraid that what I have to say would be a problem for you, and I'd hate for anything to hurt our relationship." Just admit you were wrong for not having told sooner, and don't make any excuses for yourself. Most of all, don't blame the other person—"You always get upset when I tell you things"—even if it's true.

Next you say what you want. You could say something like, "My deepest wish is that this won't change anything between us. I just want you to accept this fact about me for what it is. But I'm still me."

Notice how important it is with this kind of difficult truth, as with all the others, to know what you want to get out of the experience. I think of it like this. If telling the truth were a newspaper story, what you want to get out of telling it is the headline. So if you're going to tell something personal about yourself, you've got to have a clear idea of how you specifically want the other person to respond. Then say directly what that response is that you're looking for. For example, you might want your revelation to make no difference between you. You might want your revelation to make one specific difference. You have to make it clear.

Tell the Truth

By now the other person's completely on pins and needles, and it's time to throw open the curtain and tell your truth. The mistake most people make (and this is the mistake Kim made) is to reveal this truth about themselves with the attitude "This is no big deal, and you're a jerk if you think it's a big deal." In other words, don't try to manage the other person's response instead of acknowledging it. You've clearly indicated the response you want when you set things up, but for now you have to focus on acknowledging the response the other person does have. As you'll see, it's precisely by acknowledging his real response that you make it possible for him to come around to having the response you're looking for.

Simply convey that you understand if the other person thinks it's a big deal, and that just the way you want to be accepted for what you're revealing, you accept the other person for initially having trouble accepting what you have to say.

Then you have to make sure you delineate just what your revelation means and doesn't mean, as if you were saying, "Look, if you want to make a big deal, let me point out what you should be making a big deal about."

Here's how Kim did it wrong, and I was in the room when she said it: "Look, there's no way to sugarcoat this, but we haven't talked about politics in a long time, and you should know I've changed. I'm tired of helping people who don't want to help themselves, I'm tired of paying taxes, and I'm just basically realizing that I'm a conservative. I don't think that should shock you or anything; I mean, I think there's something wrong with you if you don't turn conservative as you grow up. We're not children anymore."

Doing it right

What Kim should have said was, "You know how we were all militant and liberal and everything when we were younger? Well, we haven't talked about this stuff in a long time, but the fact is that I've become more conservative recently. I know lots of people are conservative, but that's not the woman you married, and so I realize that there's this huge issue now and that maybe you wouldn't have been with me if you knew I was conservative. I know some people think that it sounds stupid, but back in the sixties

I would never have gone out with a guy who was a Nixon supporter, and now I'm saying that in some ways I'm like the people we hated back then. So I totally understand if this is a really big deal for you. But I guess on the positive side I don't feel judgmental about it, like you're stupid if you don't agree with me, and in some areas like abortion I guess I'm more what you'd call libertarian, which means I'm pro-choice, which is the liberal position. I feel it's perfectly fine for us to agree to disagree about some things."

When we reveal something about ourselves, we're afraid of being rejected. In the first version, the one Kim actually used, Kim did what most of us do: she rejected Jason in advance because of the possibility that he might reject her. This might be instinctive but it's wrong. In the second version, the one she should have used, she overtly *accepted* him for feeling like rejecting her and therefore made it more likely that he would have accepted her.

People who have a successful experience coming out as gay to a family member or friend usually understand this. But some gay people don't. They put themselves at tremendous risk of destroying their relationship with the other person by essentially saying, "I'm gay, and if that's a problem for you, then I'd rather we weren't connected anymore."

But when the relationship is just as important as being honest, people who are successful at revealing that they're gay make it clear that they accept the other person for having trouble coming to terms with who they are.

Make It All Come Out Right

It's the hanging in there to work through the other person's reaction that's the essence of making things all come out right. People usually have a lot of questions. But even if they're stupid questions, answering them is the most important part of putting the relationship on a solid footing again. After all, a relationship isn't a place where everything is exactly what we'd like it to be; it's a place where we feel comfortable talking about things.

So as Jason contemplated this new abyss between himself and a suddenly alien Kim, the very questions that might make it sound as though he was rejecting her because she said she was conservative were really part of his having a relationship with her. It's only with someone whom you're close to that you can talk about whether, for example, his political beliefs mean he's selfish or not. When Jason asked Kim if this meant that she was growing selfish, she should have answered his question honestly and not seen it as his picking a fight.

Someone coming out to her parents might very well have to deal with their asking her, for example, what they did to "make her turn lesbian." That she rejects the very idea that something made her "turn lesbian" doesn't mean that the question isn't a serious attempt to build a bridge of understanding across an abyss. "I don't see it that way myself, let me tell you how I see it" is the way to begin responding to this. Even if you *feel* the other person's challenging you, respond as if it were a sincere request for clarification.

Don't look for rejection

It's difficult not to experience what other people say as a form of rejection when your fear of their rejecting you is what kept you quiet in the first place. Don't read rejection into the other person's response, even if she *says* she's rejecting some part of what you've revealed. The best way to see it is that it's hard to take in something new.

A woman I know told a man she was starting to get serious about that she was a diabetic who had to give herself an injection every day. She felt rejected when he said that sounded gross to him and he'd never want to see her doing it. But she was smart enough to respond by saying, "I know this is hard for you to get used to, but maybe in time you will." Eventually he did come to find it as easy to watch her giving herself an injection as anything else she did. And yet she could have blown up his difficulty into a complete act of rejection that would have destroyed their future relationship.

The magic phrase

Here's a wonderful phrase to use in responding to almost any question: "Look, what this means for you is . . . ," then go right to the practical implications of whatever it is you're revealing to the other person.

For example, Kim should have been able to say to Jason, "I believe in some things that you don't believe in that have to do with political decisions made in Washington that we have no connections with whatsoever. So what? I'm not going to start making love differently or start cooking my special lasagna in a suddenly conservative way."

This phrase works like magic in all situations where you have to reveal something to someone. For example, if you tell your parents you're gay, they need to hear you say something like, "Look, what this means for you is that pretty much nothing's going to change. I'll still be your daughter. You can still be proud of me. I'm not going to ask you to go on any gay pride marches. I'm still going to be leading a pretty middle-class lifestyle. I still hope to have children. The only thing that might be a real challenge for you is that I'm going to ask you to accept my life partner the way you would accept a son-in-law. And as far as what you tell other people, that's completely up to you."

Just be real and practical. Whenever you make some big, dramatic personal disclosure, all the other person wants to know is what difference it will make for him: the ways in which this new reality will make a big difference and the ways in which it won't make any difference. Just assume that any trouble the other person has accepting you is really about coming to grips with what it will mean for him personally.

Parts of what you have to reveal might be bad news. Kim had to tell Jason she couldn't join him anymore if he got active in liberal causes. Some gay men and women have to tell their parents that they probably won't have grandchildren. A medical condition you're revealing to a lover might mean you're at risk of dying at an earlier age.

When you tell the other person what your revelation means to him, you have to mention the bad stuff too if it's real and important. But he'll want to know the truth, and that means knowing the bad stuff. By revealing something you've kept hidden, you've disoriented the other person. The most important need to meet isn't for everything to be wonderful but for everything to be clear again. And if you bring up the bad parts of your revelation, you'll demonstrate that you care about making things clear again.

Don't overemphasize or underemphasize the bad parts. It's best to mention them somewhere in the middle, so that the other person hears good stuff first and something reassuring at the end.

Summing Up

- After you find a time that's free of distraction, say that you're going to reveal something about yourself, but before you say what that is, apologize for not having told the other person sooner and make it clear that you hope this won't hurt your relationship, that if anything it will make it better.

- Then reveal whatever it is you want to in a simple, direct way. Make it clear that you can understand that the other person might think that this is a big deal. Say that all you want is to be accepted for what you're revealing, and that in the same spirit you can accept the other person if she initially has trouble dealing with what you have to say.

- Make it clear that you're going to be there to answer all the other person's questions. Whenever possible, help the other person by saying just what this new truth about you actually means for the other person in personal, practical terms.

10 "I'm Afraid I Have Some Bad News for You"

With bad news, you haven't done anything that you have to feel guilty about. And you're not revealing a personal fact about yourself. What makes bad news difficult is that you know it will make other people unhappy, and beyond that, they'll blame you for bringing it and blame you for causing it.

What you're looking for is a way to convey bad news that will minimize recriminations and keep the focus on what the two of you can do to make things better. In other words, you want to be there for the other person, but you don't want to get involved in a messy, overintense, exhausting scene, and you don't want to end up getting blamed for anything.

We all understand that bad news is a bitter pill. But we've too often seen how bringing bad news creates shock waves of disappointment and distrust that destroy whatever healing power the truth might have. To avoid these shock waves we often do something similar to what John did. We tell it at the wrong time or try to slip it past the other person or try to minimize its impact. And that just results in the other person's feeling neglected and minimized.

John and his colleagues

You know how it is. When things are going smoothly, you don't like to bring up bad news because you don't want to make waves. But when there are problems, you don't want to bring them up because you don't want to make things worse. In fact, people are far more likely to blurt out their bad news when things are stressful than when everything's flowing smoothly.

John is an example of this. The way he brought his colleagues a piece of bad news damaged his career. He'd known for some time that for a variety of technical reasons the software application he'd been developing probably wasn't going to work out, but he said nothing about it. Then during the stress following the merger of John's company with another company, he suddenly announced his bad news.

His colleagues, old and new, were furious. The people who would've been sympathetic if John had spilled the beans early on were furious, less for the failure of the project than for his failure to trust them enough to tell them about it. Within a year John had been cut loose by the company with lousy references.

THE SCRIPT FOR REVEALING BAD NEWS

The old script for telling bad news goes something like this. Suppose you have to fire someone. In the bad script you'd say, "You've not been giving us what we need recently. Look, there's no good way to say this, so I'll just come right out with it. The fact is we're going to have to let you go. I'm sure you'll find a new job right away."

This approach is fine as long as your bad news is something with which the other person will have an easy time dealing: something like his dry cleaning not being ready when he expected.

But the bad news you're reluctant to give is usually the kind that the other person will have a hard time dealing with, and this approach is not right. Instead, the script to follow is based on these principles:

One, hope is good, blame is bad.

Two, action is good, analyzing history is bad.

Three, acknowledging pain is good, wallowing in pain is bad.

But before you give the other person the bad news, you should make sure that you're the right person to do it. You are the right person if you're the person responsible for the bad news—for example, you're the one who's made a decision to fire an employee—and if you're the person in the appropriate position to pass on the bad news. If you've got to be told that you have a serious disease, the right person to tell you is either the doctor who's made the diagnosis or your family doctor, but not a nurse, not an elevator operator, and probably not a family member, who wouldn't be in a position to answer your questions.

If you realize that you're not the right person to deliver the bad news, then your job is to find the right person and make sure he's the one who does it.

Here's what to do if you are the right person.

Make an Appointment

For some reason people put off telling bad news as long as possible, but once they've decided to tell it, they act as if they can't wait a minute to do so. But you should always provide a setting for telling your bad news, even if the news can't wait.

One guy had accidentally run over and killed a neighbor's cat. But he was smart enough not to tell his neighbor about this the minute the neighbor answered the door. Instead, he said, "May I come in?" and then led the way into the living room and sat down. Only after his neighbor followed him and sat down as well did he say what had happened.

Obviously you have to blurt out your news if it's a true emergency where seconds count. (However, even if it's a true emergency, the words you use make a difference. The mistake is to do nothing but describe the disaster. The right way to do it is to focus on what needs to happen. In particular, whenever and wherever possible and appropriate, *tell* the other person what he needs to do in specific, direct words.) But emergencies are rare. In almost every case you can make time to create a favorable setting for telling your bad news.

Set Things Up

Preliminaries are perhaps more important with giving bad news than with other categories. Context is everything. One owner of a small survey-research boutique was stupid enough to call a relatively new employee into his office at nine-thirty on a Monday morning to fire her. Unfortunately, once he got her into his office to give her the bad news, he couldn't get her out. She held him an emotional hostage the entire day to listen to her begging and crying.

So as you set it up, you have to think about what context would be reasonable and appropriate for both of you. If you're telling your fiancée you want to postpone your wedding, for example, you have a great many questions to answer and decisions to make. So doing it first thing on a Saturday morning would give your fiancée the time she needs to deal with your bad news.

If you have an employee whom you've decided not to give an important project to, even though he's been looking forward to it, then going to his office on, say, a Thursday a half hour before it's time to go home gives you enough time to answer some questions, makes it possible for you to leave, gives him time to go home to the bosom of his family, and gives him a whole Friday on the job to run around talking to people about the whole thing without taking a week to do it and yet without being stranded over the weekend with no information.

In other words, ask yourself how you want this to play out and, as a decent human being, how you should let it play out. To be respectful of the other person, he must be given the opportunity to ask questions and get emotional support. To be respectful to yourself, don't create expectations you don't want to deliver on.

Tell the Truth

When the truth is bad news, most people report that hearing it straight out but in a sympathetic, supportive manner is best. So if my doctor called me in to tell me that the lump they found had to be removed, I'd want her to say something like, "I'm sorry, but although the pathologist and I agree that it's probably not malignant, your lump needs to be removed. You're generally in good health and the operation should take you out of danger, but you are going to have to have this operation."

What's important is what this is *not,* as much as what it is. What it's not is a confusing tease. It's hard enough to get bad news, but don't make me crazy in the process. If I'm going to have an operation, don't tell me how wonderful it is. Don't tell me how close I came to not getting this diagnosis. And don't twist the knife. If I've got to be sick, don't blame my bad eating habits just to make it seem as though I deliberately got myself into this situation.

If the bad news is that you want to postpone your wedding, say that you are looking forward to getting married, but you absolutely need a postponement for whatever good reasons you need it. And those reasons should be valid enough that your fiancée doesn't feel she can talk you into not postponing it and yet not so devastating that she feels dumped on in addition to getting her wedding postponed.

Bad news shouldn't be made grimmer than it has to be. It's adding insult to injury to pile on reasons for your bad news as if to completely squash the possibility of any hope whatsoever, much less to give the impression that the news itself is still negotiable. In an attempt to avoid hearing the employee beg for his job, some bosses attack their employees so viciously that their morale is destroyed for any future job. Don't say anything that will make the bad news sound worse than it is.

Get the bad news out of the way sooner rather than later

What about John with his bad news that his computer project was screwed up? John's biggest problem was timing. He made the mistake many of us make: we hope we can fix things before the bad news gets out. We're like the embezzler who tries to pay back the money before it's found missing. The problem is that we end up being alone with our problems, we have no help, the problems rarely do get fixed, and then we're seen as making things worse by making the problem bigger.

When he'd held back the news for too long, John's truth was no longer primarily bad news at all. The truth he had to tell was that he had a guilty secret. Again, the right category is crucial. John needed forgiveness, not acceptance.

The point of this is that you've got to know what kind of truth your truth is or at least know what kind of response you want to get from telling it. If you have bad news to tell someone, tell him earlier so that the focus is on the news itself, which means that the focus is on what to do about it, rather than telling him later so that in effect you're confessing your guilt, which puts the focus on you.

Make It All Come Out Right

Once they've taken in the bad news, people need answers to three questions if you're going to make it all come out right. First, where is there hope? Second, what can I do? Third, what does it mean? You have to answer these questions for the other person even if he doesn't ask them.

Show how hope is realistic

You have to treat hope carefully. You cannot give hope by making it seem as though your bad news were negotiable. People often fall into the trap of giving reasons for firing someone, for example, that make it sound as though the person still has a shot if he fights for his job. Don't say anything that will give the other person reason to struggle to achieve something that can't happen.

If you want to bring your husband the bad news (for him) that you don't want to have any more children, fine, but don't give him the impression that you're still open to persuasion. This is a more important point than you may think. It's painful enough to be told your project is a no-go, but to be seduced into continuing to pitch it when it has no chance is merely cruel.

But while there may be no hope about this specific piece of bad news, *there should be hope about everything else.* This project was shot down, but others will get through. You don't want to have any more children, but you have wonderful children already and maybe one day you'll have grandchildren. You've got to postpone the wedding, but you look forward to going ahead with it at a later date.

The idea is that there may be no hope *here,* but there's plenty of hope *there.*

Show the person what to do

Now you have to help the other person figure out what to do next. Bad news means that a path someone was counting on has been taken away. He was moving and had momentum. Now he can no longer move in the same direction, and yet he still has the same momentum. In a way, when you give someone bad news, the most important thing that happens psychologically is that you're suddenly damming up energy that has already been channeled, and it needs to be rechanneled.

Besides, what people know least is what to do next. It's odd. If you fire someone, he knows he's got to look for a job. But he doesn't know what he has to do first thing next Monday.

So you have to make sure that you give the other person the best, most explicit guidance you can about the next steps he needs to take. This is important in reestablishing the other person's sense of momentum. "Yes, the wedding's postponed, but we have plenty of other things to keep us busy besides making wedding plans. And I think what you should do right now is call your mother, and I'll get on the phone with you, and we'll tell her together and figure out what to do and what to say to people because she's been in charge of all the arrangements."

John would have been in a much better position if he'd done just a little bit of homework and thought about the next steps everyone would have to take when they learned his project was a goner. That way he could have said, in effect, "The project's dead, but here's what we have to do right now," and then the focus would have been on what to do next, not on blame and history.

Make it clear what it all means

Finally, you have to help the other person understand what your bad news means in the scheme of things and give him a little perspective. In other words, you have to help the other person see just how bad the bad news is (maybe it's not as bad as it seems on the surface) and how bad it will make things in the future (maybe it won't make the future all that bad at all).

The trick is to make the other person feel better without minimizing whatever the bad news is about. No news is so terrible that you can't give perspective while at the same time acknowledging what the other person's going through. As Rabbi Kushner points out in *When Bad Things Happen to Good People,* even if you have to report that a loved one has died, while you're saying how sorry you are, you can say what a good person he was and how he didn't deserve to die. You can say, "I know this is hell for you but other people have gone through it and survived and you will too."

If you tell your fiancée the bad news that you want to postpone the wedding, don't forget to say that lots of happily married people postponed their weddings and, putting things into even more perspective, point out that it's better to do it right than to rush and feel bad about it afterward.

The key to giving perspective is for you to do what I call *finding the health*. Somehow, somewhere, there's some healthy process connected to your bad news. Even people who found themselves in concentration camps found the "health" in their situation by focusing on staying alive to bear witness to what had happened.

On a much more mundane level, people who work in fields where they must experience constant rejection, such as actors or salespeople, understand that being rejected is a normal part of their lives, that in fact it's a sign of health because it's a sign that you're in the game.

Summing Up

- Don't delay reporting your bad news, but do your best to provide at least some setting where the other person can take in the bad news in a dignified way and the two of you can process it responsibly and you can answer questions and offer support.
- The best way to tell is to give the bad news straight out but in a sympathetic, supportive manner. Don't say the bad news so that it seems negotiable if it isn't. Be clear.
- It's important to acknowledge the other person's feelings and respond to her questions. But whether she asks them or not, you've got to provide answers for these questions: Where is there hope? What do I do next? What does it mean?

Don't make the mistake of thinking that bad news is something extra-ordinary or catastrophic. Many of the truths that hurt us because we don't say them or say them badly are small, everyday, ordinary bits of bad news. But let me put bad news itself in context.

First, bad news is news. That means it's information. And information is the lifeblood of effective living. If you're my lover or boss or friend, for example, the bits of bad news I withhold from you deprive you of the ability to function at your best. And if I tell you the bad news so that you overreact or misunderstand, then I've distorted the information you need.

Second, bad news is an opportunity for people to connect. When you tell me your bad news, even if it's the trivial bad news that comes up in people's lives every day, there's an opportunity for me to commiserate and offer support and for us to get closer. We feel more connected to each other just because I know your bad news. And if you tell me your bad news effec-tively, in a way that takes my needs into account, I feel respected and sup-ported in turn.

PART III

PERSONAL
ISSUES

11 Getting Your Own Needs Met

• PLANNING FOR SATISFACTION

"TELL THE TRUTH BUT MEET THE NEED" capsulizes in seven words everything that will make you effective in saying something that's hard to say to someone who's important to you. The scripts I've given you for the six kinds of truths will help you know what to say and how to say it in order to meet the other person's needs.

But what about *your* needs? You have specific needs in your life, and you have particular needs that come up with this truth you want to tell. How do you tell the truth but meet *your* needs?

I'll show you how, but you have to do the work up front; you can't wait until after the truth you were agonizing over pops out of your mouth. I'll show you what is important to think about, and I'll show you how to think about it to get answers that are helpful for you. But you have to get your answers before you tell, and that means doing a bit of planning.

Planning's no big deal. We plan all the time. Let's say that tomorrow you're going to leave work to catch a 5:45 P.M. business flight to London. That means you have to plan. You have to pack the night before and know what to pack. You have to wrap up work at the office, and you have to know what to deal with to be ready for your trip. You have to leave for the airport on time, and you have to know how long it'll take you to get to the airport during a Friday rush hour.

You know you only have two alternatives: plan properly or invite disaster.

Why would you do any differently when it comes to telling a truth that could conceivably change someone's life, perhaps your own?

Secret Wisdom

You've seen how badly things turn out when people rely on blunt spontaneity to make truth telling work. You realize that spontaneity isn't a sign of commitment to the truth, it's a sign of irresponsibility, just as leaving for the airport at any old time is a sign you don't care if you miss your flight. You realize that telling the truth is a craft, and every honest craftsman is dedicated, above all, to how his efforts turn out.

This chapter contains the secret wisdom of the master truth tellers. Wisdom isn't knowing the answers; it's knowing the questions to ask. The secret wisdom here is captured by the four questions these master truth tellers have learned to ask themselves before they speak:

1. *What is the real truth you have to tell?* There's often a profound difference between the words you have in your head that you've been agonizing over and the truth you have in your heart. For example, you might be wondering how to tell your fiancée you want to postpone the wedding, but if you look into your heart, it may be that you really want to cancel the wedding. Or it may be that you want to tell your fiancée that she seems nice now, but you're afraid she's really cold and manipulative and you'd like to find out which it is.

2. *What do you really want to get out of telling?* People speak, things happen. When you speak, some things are going to happen. Do you want them to? Is there something else you want? For example, when you tell your fiancée you want to postpone the wedding, are you just letting her know how you feel or do you hope she'll break up with you? Having something happen that you don't want makes a lie out of your truth.

3. *What emotional baggage or issues are involved in this truth that will likely get in the way of how you tell it?* For example, are you so angry about your fiancée's controlling personality that it's going to affect how you tell her you want to postpone the wedding?

4. *What's most important in the whole picture, including you and the other person and your relationship and everything else?* The most important thing is what should have the biggest impact on what you say and how you say it. For example, as you think about postponing your wedding, is the most important thing that you avoid making a terrible mistake, even if that means risking not marrying a good person? Or is the most important thing not losing your fiancée, even if that means not postponing the wedding? Or is the most important thing your rich father-in-law-to-be, who happens to be your boss? Or is the most important thing that you have a long history of getting cold feet but you usually go through with things, so why make a mess now talking about not doing something you'll probably end up doing?

If you do not at least consider these questions and give yourself a chance to rethink the truth you want to tell, so that hopefully you end up telling the truth you *really* want to tell, then you're simply not a responsible truth teller.

Janice's story

Here's a story that illustrates how important it is to ask yourself these four questions before you speak.

"I'm not interested in sex anymore. I don't have any sexual feelings for you. I don't have any sexual feelings, period." These words were on the tip of the tongue of Janice, a forty-nine-year-old woman going through menopause. The problem was that, like so many other women, Janice felt scared and vulnerable at the thought of telling her husband this and having to deal with his . . . what? Anger? Disgust? Depression? She knew that her truth was going to cause a painful scene at some point, maybe right away, maybe later when she least wanted it. Perhaps they'd have this scene as they were going to bed and he'd say things to her that would keep her up all night and many other nights as well.

But at the same time Janice was a strong, confident, successful woman with a keen sense that she was entitled to her feelings, entitled to go through menopause however her body meant her to go through it, entitled to tell her husband, Greg, whatever was on her mind.

Janice ended up doing what my research and clinical experience show is what most people do with a bombshell like this. Instead of stopping and thinking about her own needs, Janice simply worried about how she'd tell Greg. Over and over in her mind she played out the same scene where she'd say, "I'm not interested in sex anymore. I don't have any sexual feelings for you. I don't have any sexual feelings, period." And in her mind Greg would have whatever horrible response she most dreaded at that moment.

Setting the stage for disaster

In a perverse way, this worry made Janice pissed off at Greg. What right did he have, she thought, to make it so hard for her to be who she was and to say what she wanted? In other words, before she'd even said one word, Janice resented Greg for making her feel it was hard to speak. As you've probably guessed, this was an accident waiting to happen. Fearful of speaking and yet resentful for being afraid, Janice was primed to blurt out her truth at the worst possible moment and in the worst possible way.

It was Saturday morning in bed, and true to his schedule, Greg turned toward Janice and started kissing her. Then he started kissing her body, the way he always did. But Janice lay there completely unresponsive. Finally, Greg asked, "What's wrong?"

"You always do the same thing," Janice said, her feelings bursting out. "It's always the same boring lovemaking. What do you want from me? Is this supposed to turn me on? No wonder I'm not interested in sex anymore. I don't have any sexual feelings for you. I don't have any sexual feelings at all. What do you think you're doing with me?"

That was the truth she ended up saying! Greg was overwhelmed. He couldn't figure out what he'd just heard. It was something about his being a lousy lover, he thought. And there was something in there, he thought, about Janice's not wanting to have sex with him anymore. At the heart of everything he felt attacked, and the element of truth in the attack—he was a boring lover—made him feel hurt.

And he *was* being attacked. In her pain and confusion about losing her sexual desire, Janice wanted there to be a way to make it better, and the person who was supposed to arouse her was Greg. Her disappointment in Greg wasn't as deep as her feelings about her loss of sexual desire, but it was much easier to express, and so she went with it.

Making things worse

That's what we all do when we don't think about the truth we really want to tell before we tell it. That's what Janice did.

The result was that in his hurt at being attacked as a lover, all Greg could do was remember the ways Janice had been unfair in their twenty-year marriage. And he attacked her for being unfair. And it made Greg so mad to think about her unfairness, and he was so intent on driving his point home, that he made it sound as if she were a completely unreasonable person, someone impossible to deal with.

How would you sum up their fight to this point? It was as if Janice had said, "I have no desire for you," and Greg had said, "I have no desire to deal with you." In no time at all they were talking about a dead marriage and about the possibility of a divorce. They were both hurt. They were both disappointed. And they were both furious. This is exactly the mess that Janice had feared.

Think about how differently it might have turned out if Janice had thought about what you're learning to think about.

Asking the Right Questions

First, what was the real truth Janice had to tell? Was it actually true that she wasn't interested in sex anymore? That's what she was thinking of telling Greg, but was it the actual truth? Or was the real truth that she was simply *afraid* that she was not interested in sex anymore? Facts are facts, but you owe it to yourself and to everyone who's important to you to identify the real truth before you speak.

Next, what did Janice really want to get out of telling her truth? You saw what Janice did get, and you know it's not what she wanted. But Janice needed to do herself a favor and think in advance about what she wanted to get beyond "letting Greg know." Did she want him to work harder at turn-ing her on? Did she want him to go get his sexual needs satisfied somewhere else? Did she want him to talk her into going to the doctor?

Janice had real needs and her needs were a crucial part of the truth she had to tell. If her need for reassurance was primary, then what she really wanted wasn't for Greg "to know" about her loss of desire, but for Greg to tell her that she was desirable. This is a completely different truth.

Then, what emotional baggage or issues did Janice have around this truth that would likely get in the way of her telling it effectively? Suppose Janice's need was for Greg to be more loving and tender, not just in bed but everywhere in their lives together. But suppose this was an old story. Sup-pose that Janice had been going around for years furious with Greg because she kept asking him to be more playful and adventurous in bed and he kept not giving her what she wanted. Her fury would be real. But if it got in the way of the truth she had to tell and what she wanted to get out of telling the truth, then it would be a completely different issue and it would have to be dealt with separately. Unless she dealt with her issues, the truth would come out that "I no longer have desire and it's your fault." If she did deal with her issues, a very different truth would come out, that "I no longer have desire but it has nothing to do with you as a lover."

Most of the emotional baggage we have ends up being about blame or regret, and blame or regret will end up being the main topic after we tell the truth if we're not careful.

Finally, what should Janice have focused on? What was most important to her? Let me make a distinction. Janice's goal was what she wanted to get for herself. But what was most important for Janice was what she'd be most afraid of losing. Suppose Janice's goal had been for Greg not to put pressure on her sexually. Fine. But, at the same time, the most important thing for Janice might have been preserving warmth and closeness and intimacy be-tween her and Greg.

Your goal might be getting to the airport on time, but if not getting killed on the way is what's most important to you, there might be a point at which you'd have to sacrifice your goal, and Janice might have to sacrifice her goal to preserve what's most important to her.

Now you see what's at stake. What a difference it would've made for

Janice if she'd tried to answer four simple questions before she opened her mouth. Maybe she wouldn't have felt quite so spontaneous, but she could still have told the truth and she'd also have saved her relationship.

So let me help you answer these questions for yourself.

FINDING YOUR OWN ANSWERS

1. What Is the Real Truth You Have to Tell?

We all know that when you take the witness stand in a court of law, you swear to tell the truth, the whole truth, and nothing but the truth. That's really the key in identifying the real truth you have to tell if you want to get your needs met. Ask yourself these questions: What is the whole truth? Isn't the truth I've been thinking of telling only a part of the whole? What have I left out of the truth I've been thinking of telling?

There's always more to the truth

This is important no matter what the truth is, even if it's something as seemingly pure as the truth of a feeling. Suppose your boss has given you a project that takes up a large part of every day, and you absolutely hate working on that project. All you can think of is confronting your boss with the truth of your feelings and letting him know how much you hate it. You know he can't relieve you of this responsibility right now, but you'll feel like a cowardly weasel if you don't tell him how you feel.

But suppose you appreciate the new level of responsibility this project represents, even while hating the work. Suppose you hate the project but you like the people you're working with. Suppose you don't mind the project but you hate the people you're working with. Suppose you actually like the work but don't like the client or what he stands for.

I can't say what your real whole truth would be. But think of the mess you'd make if you were to leave it out. Would you want your boss to think that you don't want responsibility? Would you want your boss to think that you don't like the people you're working with? Would you want your boss to think that you don't like doing this kind of work?

It's about perspective

I'm just asking you to have perspective. When I told my wife that I was getting close to another woman, I simply didn't have any perspective. The "other woman" was a fact, but as I put it all in perspective, it was a fact that illustrated, along with many other illustrations, the distance and anger that was threatening our marriage.

I'm convinced that if I'd simply asked myself to think about the whole truth and how the "other woman" fit into it, then just my *attempt* to gain perspective would have meant that the truth I ended up telling my wife was far more healing as well as being far more real.

The fear we all wrestle with when we have something that's hard to say grows out of our real experience with other messy situations. I think you'd be amazed to discover how many of these messes arose because you never told your actual truth in the first place.

2. What Do You Really Want to Get Out of Telling?

If thinking about what you're going to do before you do it is the secret wisdom of the master truth tellers, then the secret of secrets is to "begin with your desired ending." If you just want to "be yourself," then you throw your words out and you let the chips fall where they may. But if you realize that the truth actually resides in how things play out over time, then where you want to get to as a result of speaking your truth will have to guide everything you do.

Arthur's story

Arthur, whose business was struggling, wanted to ask his widowed mother, Dorothy, to give him some money. When I asked him what he wanted to get as a result of making this request, he said, "I want to see if she'll give me the money."

This shows how fuzzy our thinking can be when we try to speak our truths. I asked Arthur, "Do you want to know how your mother behaves or do you want to get cold cash? Are you a psychologist or a guy who wants money?"

This distinction between learning something about the other person and getting something from the other person haunts virtually every important truth people reveal.

Is a test your need?

There is a distinction between your telling your truth as a test and your telling your truth to get something you want that you're willing to go after. So when Arthur said he wanted to see if his mother would give him the money, either he was interested in testing her (it never hurts to ask) or he was kidding himself about how badly he wanted the money and what he was willing to do to get it.

And if you're kidding yourself about something you want to have happen as a result of telling your truth, you're setting yourself up for disaster. Janice wanted comfort, understanding, love, hope, and affection from Greg as a result of telling him about the changes that had happened in her body. She even wanted him to continue initiating lovemaking. If she'd focused on what she wanted from Greg, everything would have been different.

Needing not to have a scene

To zero in on this idea of what you want to get from telling your truth, think about firing an employee. The truth is simply the words "You're fired." But anyone who's afraid of confrontations will understand that what you want to get is not just the opportunity to say those words, but for the fired employee not to make a huge nerve-racking scene, with crying and begging and shouting. You don't want to *see if* she'll take this bad news calmly. You want her to take it calmly.

It's not manipulation

Thinking about what you want to have happen makes some people uncomfortable. This, more than anything else, raises the specter of your being manipulative. The question, though, is what kind of person will you be if telling your truth turns into a disaster? Janice didn't want to be manipulative, but she ended up furious with her husband. I didn't want to be manipulative, but I ended up with my wife furious with me. Arthur didn't want to be manipulative, but when he blurted out his request by saying, "How would you feel about giving me some money for my business?" and his mother didn't give him the money (of which she had plenty), he was hurt and disappointed, and he withdrew from her, which gave her a real sense of loss.

When we don't acknowledge what we really want, we're not acknowledging what's really at stake.

You're not a bad person if you think about the outcome you want from telling your truth. You're a bad person only if you're willing to be completely ruthless to get what you want. You're a *fair* person if you recognize that you and the other person both have needs and that you can take the other person's needs into account without minimizing your own.

To help you focus on what you want to have happen, let's look briefly at each of the six different categories of truth one at a time.

Sharing Feelings

The question to decide right now is what is it that you want to get out of sharing your feelings. What does it even mean to talk about "getting something"? You share your feelings because you're honest, right? Sure you do. But there are two other realities to pay attention to.

Real consequences

First, words have consequences. There are consequences to saying "I love you" for the first time to someone you're dating. There are consequences to saying you feel sexually attracted to someone you work with. There are consequences to telling a friend you feel bored when you're with him.

A young woman went with her husband to a faculty dinner shortly after he'd gotten a job at a university. The people at the table were talking about the Holocaust, and she hated the way they were doing it. Finally she couldn't contain her feelings. "What's wrong with you people?" she said. "You sound so glib, so dry. Don't you care? Doesn't this mean anything to you?" They were shocked but polite. But there were consequences. Her husband's contract was not renewed for the following year. The couple were just not considered "collegial."

Desired consequences

The second reality to pay attention to is that there are consequences you want. You have goals. You want things to turn out a certain way. Surely the truth of your feelings has to acknowledge the truth of your goals.

Think about this. Imagine that you've told someone how you feel. What happens then, and how do you feel about what happens? How does he respond? Does his response bring you closer to or further from your goals?

Saying "I love you"

Let's take this for a trial run. You want to tell someone you love her. It's the way you feel. But what will happen after you say it? Are these the words she's been waiting for, and do they make it possible for her to say she loves you the way she's been longing to do? And do you want the closeness and the sense of moving to a new level of commitment that your words might bring about?

Suppose you know that the other person is afraid of commitment right now, afraid of having to deal with some guy who's in love with her. Your words will make her feel uncomfortable, she'll need to create distance, and you'll only be further away from your goal of getting closer to her. If that's the case, then you need to change what it is you're going to say.

Suppose you wanted to signal your desire to get closer and form a deeper commitment without scaring her off. We usually say affectionate things because we want to tighten the bonds. In a new relationship we want to get closer, and we're also afraid the other person will drift away if he doesn't understand how we feel. But we've already said that this woman doesn't want the bonds getting tightened. So what you really want to signal is that you're good for her. Because that will strengthen the bonds you want to strengthen.

So given what you're trying to make happen and the way you feel, don't say "I love you." Instead say "I really want to understand what you need at this point in your life, and I want to meet those needs." That way you're not the sticky I-love-you guy. Instead you're the ever-desirable I-understand-you guy.

Is this the truth of your feelings? When you take your feelings out of your heart and make them function in the real world, the truth is that you care. Either way you're showing it.

So if you want to share a feeling with someone that's hard for you to say, make sure the words you use will get the response you want.

Offering a Criticism

The first thing you need to do when you think about sitting someone down who's important to you and unburdening yourself of this criticism that's been so hard for you to speak is to *ask yourself what you want to get out of this.* What do you want the other person to do differently? Surely you're not interested in just complaining.

But when you realize that you're asking for change, that may modify the criticism you thought of offering. Let me give you some situations to think about.

When change isn't possible

Suppose the other person simply cannot change. For instance, your mother criticizes and you want to criticize her for criticizing you. Since you don't want to be a complainer, your criticism is some kind of request or demand that she change. But can she change? Obviously it's theoretically possible for her never to criticize you again, but is this a realistic possibility? Is being a mother, being your mother, the most important part of her identity, and does she define "being a mother" as "someone who criticizes"? Has she simply never shown the slightest indication that she can behave differently?

You can instantly see that for someone who can't change, a criticism will sound like a put-down. "I need you to stop telling me what's wrong with me all the time" will be heard as "You're an awful person whom I don't like." But that wasn't what you wanted to get out of telling. And *that* means you've got to rethink the very truth you wanted to tell in the first place.

For example, it might be that instead of criticizing her you just want to let her know how you feel: "I just want you to know that it's hard for me to hear you criticize me all the time. I know you're my mother and I know that's what you do, so I'm not asking you to change, but I feel it's only fair for you to know how I feel about it."

Or it might be that instead of asking her to change in general you'll wait until after each specific criticism she makes and then ask her what she wants you to do differently. That way you're at least converting her criticisms into specific requests.

Or it might be that you'll end up asking for some other change, not that she stop criticizing you. One woman, realizing that her mother would never change but also knowing how destructive her mother's criticisms were, asked her mother to change the day of their weekly phone call to Thursday. That way her weekends wouldn't be spoiled the way they were when the calls were made on Saturday, and her weeks wouldn't be spoiled the way they were when the calls were made on Sunday. With Friday to look forward to and good shows on television Thursday night, Thursday was unspoilable. But what a difference from criticizing her mother for criticizing her to asking her mother to have their calls be on Thursdays. It's the same truth! But now she's getting her needs met.

Who the other person is to you

Criticism is like water. It flows easily downhill but has a hard time flowing uphill. Criticizing your boss is different from criticizing your assistant.

Whatever your intentions, your boss might respond to your criticism as if you were trying to usurp her authority. It's not that she can't change. She just doesn't like your trying to change her. What do you do about this? Anytime you feel like criticizing someone who's above you in the hierarchy or to whom you owe a certain amount of official respect or obedience, you've got to add something to your truth in order that it be heard. You've got to talk about the goals the two of you share and how your boss's changing will better enable the two of you to meet those joint goals.

You're seeing your truth as part of a larger truth. Even if you want to criticize your boss for giving you too much work and not praising you for the work you've done, the change you're asking for has got to be placed in the context of your overall effectiveness on the job: "Since we both want me to be as effective as possible, it will really help me if you . . ." If you want to criticize your boss and you want something positive to come out of the experience, you've got to frame your criticism by using those words "since we both want . . ."

It's different with a subordinate. Now *you're* the boss, and bosses are supposed to make demands, within reason. But if you have a criticism and you want it to be heard and you want your subordinate to do things differently based on your criticism, then the truth you need to think about telling is one that focuses not on what he's doing wrong but on how he needs to do things in the future and on how he's capable of doing these things and what kind of future he'll have if he does those things.

I'm not talking about routine matters. I'm talking about when you have to severely criticize something that's important about your subordinate. If what you want to get is change, your criticism also has to offer help.

Not being misunderstood

When your truth is a criticism, you must think about how the other person will respond. Then ask yourself if you want that response, because the response your criticism elicits *is* the truth you've told, whether you like it or not. Let me explain. Early in my professional career I criticized a patient for always blurting out the truth, no matter what the truth was, no matter whom she was telling it to. Look at the trouble you keep getting yourself into, I said.

Well, Barbara got upset. What was I trying to do, she asked—prevent her from being herself?

The next thing I knew she was blurting out the truth with even greater abandon and she was more confrontational. I could see that it was a matter of psychological survival for her. If someone was working to get her to be less truthful, as she saw it, she'd have to work harder to be as truthful as she was before.

Of course I wasn't trying to get her to be less truthful or less authentic. But Barbara kept making a lot of trouble for herself, and I was trying to get her to see that she had a choice about whether to do so. Her response of becoming even more confrontational was what happened to my truth. It's what my feedback turned into. My attempt to get Barbara to change in one direction resulted in her changing in the opposite direction.

When I realized the actual response my criticism was getting, I realized that a truth that gets lost in translation is of little use to anybody.

The response I wanted from Barbara was something like "Yes, I see how I alienate people and destroy opportunities for myself by being so blunt. If the people I'm alienating are really important to me and the opportunities I destroy are things I really care about, then my emphasis on absolutely authentic truth telling is really turning my life into a lie. Honesty is an absolute value for me, but my friends and my opportunities are absolute values as well, and I've got to figure out how to weigh them all in the balance."

As I thought about getting this response from her, I realized that no criticism, no attempt to change her, would give me this response. This response could come only from her seeing how things work in the world, from her seeing how things worked in her life. That was the truth I had to tell Barbara: this is how things work, and I'd like you to understand this.

So instead of criticizing her for being so blunt, I asked Barbara to tell me about what had actually happened to her when she'd told people the truth in the insensitive way I knew she did. Except I didn't label it blunt and insensitive, of course. The more stories she told, the more she painted a picture for herself of a woman who was destroying all her relationships and opportunities. I'd stopped trying to criticize her. I'd stopped trying to get her to change. I was just trying to get her to see how things worked.

Whenever you think of telling a truth that's a criticism, you have to ask yourself what will happen to that truth when the other person responds to it. If you can see that your truth will come back in shreds, then unless you only want to make an empty heroic gesture, unless you don't care about the other person's response, then you have to make sure your truth survives the process of translation from your heart to the other person's heart.

Awkward Requests

Remember Arthur? He wants to ask his mother to lend him $25,000 for his business. But is that request—"I want you to lend me twenty-five thousand dollars"—really his whole truth and nothing but the truth? What is the whole truth from the point of view of what he wants to get out of telling?

Why ask for one thing when you really need to and want to ask for something else?

Let me help you with some of the possibilities.

"I want you to know what I want"

Sometimes we think we want to ask for X when all we really want is for the other person to know we want X. Suppose you'd been thinking of asking your boss for a promotion, and you'd been agonizing over how you were going to ask. I know one guy who tied himself in knots because he was afraid he'd seem like a wuss if he asked for a promotion too weakly, and yet he knew that there weren't really any promotions to be had. So why ask for a promotion at all? If it's not possible, why put yourself in the position of being turned down? Why not, in other words, acknowledge that the truth of your request is that you just want your boss to know that you want a promotion? This is easier to say and easier to hear. "I'm not asking for X, I'm just saying I want X. I don't want you to give me X, I just want you to acknowledge that I want X."

This possibility is important to consider anytime your truth is a request. Do you actually want to start the wheels in motion for getting your request or do you just want your request to be known as a fact?

"I want to see what you'll do"

Sometimes a request is really what I call a *see if*. The truth is that you do want to set the wheels in motion for getting your needs met, but the price you're willing to pay and the risk you're willing to take are minimal.

That might've been the case with Arthur. The truth of what he wanted might have been that he really wanted to *see if* his mother would give him $25,000, but he didn't actually want to struggle with her about it.

When you ask to see if you'll get something, part of the truth of your request is that it's okay if you don't get it, at least for now. You're saying to the other person that there is no cost to him for not giving it to you. Now, you may not want to say that explicitly, because it'll make it less likely that he'll give it to you, but you know it's true, and as you'll see, that makes all the difference when you think about how to ask.

Compare it to the alternative. Sometimes your request has a bottom line attached to it. In this case the truth is that something meaningful is at stake depending upon whether you get it or not.

The truth of a request is the truth of what's at stake if that request isn't granted. Suppose Arthur needs that $25,000 because that sum will make all the difference between his business's dying or surviving, and suppose that Arthur feels with some justification that his prosperous mother has never really been there for him. What's at stake here might be the fact that no $25,000 means no business and means no relationship with his mother. What does Arthur really want to get? He wants to save a business and a relationship. But he wants to save the business first because that's his future. So in a way what he wants to get is the business even if that means sacrificing the relationship.

It's absolutely crucial when you think about what you're asking for to get clear about how badly you want it and what you're willing to do to get it. You're at a moment of extreme danger here. Things can go horribly wrong in two completely different ways. If your request is little more than a "see if," then if you ask for it too assertively, you risk making the other person feel unnecessarily bullied. If your request is absolutely crucial to you, then if you don't ask for it strongly and effectively enough, you risk terrible disappointment that could unnecessarily threaten your relationship with the other person.

You just have to be clear whether you really want what you're asking for or you just want to see if you can get it.

When you don't want what you think you want

Sometimes you don't really want what you're asking for at all. Gail and Leo had one of those iffy, rocky relationships, but Gail hoped it would work out. She wanted something from Leo that was so hard for her to ask for that she brought the two of them into couples therapy. She wanted to ask Leo to say he loved her. That request felt too difficult to ask for on her own. It took time for the two of them to feel safe enough with each other and with the therapist for Gail's request to come out. But when it did, there was a mess.

Leo had trouble giving Gail what she wanted. He didn't like the idea of saying the words "I love you" on demand. He didn't even like the idea of putting his feelings into words. He'd say things like, "You should know how I feel without my saying anything."

Round and round they went. By the time I was called in as a consultant on this case, something clearly wasn't right. It turned out that Gail wasn't asking for what she really wanted. She said she wanted to hear the words "I love you" because that seemed like something concrete. But what she really wanted (but was desperately afraid she'd never be able to get from Leo) was the sense that "he wants me." What she meant by that was feeling that Leo liked being with her and wanted to be with her.

But Gail had been rejected by men before in her life. So it was hard for her to acknowledge the truth of what she really wanted to ask for. For Gail, asking someone to say "I love you" was a lot easier than asking someone to say "I want you." The problem was that by not being clear about what she wanted to ask for, she kept giving the impression of being unsatisfied when she got what she asked for.

What can you do about this? I know it's hard. But if you have a truth that you have trouble saying and your truth is a request, then make sure that the thing you're asking for isn't standing in place of the thing you really want. I know that the reason you're not asking for what you really want is probably that it's scarier to ask for it. But if the thing you ask for isn't what you really want, you'll be unhappy whether you get it or not.

Just ask yourself how you'd feel if you got what you think you want. Would it really make you happy or satisfied? More important, would it make you feel finished with your needs in this area? If it would not, then what's missing? What would make you feel finished? That's the truth of what you really want.

Guilty Secrets

Okay, you screwed up. You did something that hurt someone else. For example, you lied to your boss by saying that you'd checked on some facts that you'd never checked. Or you did things behind your roommate's back that caused her to break up with her boyfriend. Now you want to confess. But the issue is what you want to get out of telling your guilty secret. If you think about *why* you're telling it, will that change *what* you tell?

It might sound as though this question doesn't make any sense. If you had an affair, you had an affair. You're not a fiction writer, you're a reporter. You can't make up what happened, you can only report what happened. "I had an affair" is the truth, the whole truth, and nothing but the truth.

Or is it? When is an affair not an affair?

An affair or any other guilty secret may not be what it seems, depending on what you want to get out of confessing it. The facts are still the facts, of course, but the words you use might change incredibly depending upon your needs.

Think about your guilty secret and ask yourself which of these you want:

- You want the other person to forgive you.
- You want him to appreciate that you're not the kind of person who usually does what you're confessing.
- You want him to understand that you had reasons for doing what you did and to know what those reasons are.
- You want him to see that there are real problems in your relationship and that what you did is somehow connected to these problems.
- You want him to maintain his respect or other positive feelings toward you in spite of what you did.

An affair is an event that's part of a larger whole the way Hiroshima is an event that's part of World War II. And what this larger whole is for you depends on which of the items on this list you want.

For example, if you want the other person to see that there are real problems in your relationship that you want to solve, then those problems and the solutions you'd like are the larger fact, and your affair is the result of or an expression of those problems. When you think of sitting the other person down and saying, "There's something I have to tell you," the truth you have to tell is one of a relationship with problems that somehow involved an affair.

To take another example, if you want to confess to your boss that you never did the background check on important facts in a proposal your firm sent out, it may be that what you really want is for him to appreciate that you're not the kind of person who usually does this kind of thing. You're not an irresponsible, not-checking-on-things kind of person. So the larger fact of which your lie is merely a part is that you do check on things, just not this one time. The truth you have to tell is about your care*ful*ness in which an incident of serious care*less*ness is embedded.

In other words, you want your boss to trust you in spite of an incident that would arouse mistrust. And so the other facts that would make his trust warranted are a central part of your truth.

The bottom line is that what you want to have happen points to a larger story of which the crime you're confessing plays a role but is not by itself the whole story.

So when you have to confess a guilty secret, tell the whole story based on what you want to get out of telling and give the other person a chance to see how your secret fits into the scheme of things.

Lead with your ending. What I should have done with my wife is to have begun by saying, "Look, I think we're drifting apart and I want us to be loving and close again. I want to tell you about something I did that I feel bad about, and I hope you'll find a way to forgive me. But I'm telling you now because, most important, I want to make things better between us again."

Whatever your guilty secret, you can lead by talking about what you hope will come from your confession.

Personal Disclosures

When I asked people why they revealed something personal about them-selves, here are the most common reasons they gave:

- Because the other person would find out anyway, so I might as well tell him sooner rather than later.
- Because it would hurt him not to know.
- Because I felt like a liar by not telling.
- Because I felt there was this huge barrier between us that wouldn't come down unless I told.

A fact is a fact even if it's a truth about who you are or what you've done. But the whole truth of what you have to say has got to include your reasons for saying it as well as the meaning for your relationship of your saying it. If you reveal a fact about yourself, there will be a mess if you haven't changed what it is you're telling to highlight your reasons and its meaning.

Gay men and women who've come out to their parents, for example, have a lot of experience with this. The disasters kept being those cases where the gay man or woman simply said in effect, "There's no good way of saying this, so I'll just come right out with it. I'm gay. And you'll just have to deal with it." Yes, they told the truth, but that truth was a lie because they left out what it meant and the reasons for telling.

But the experience of coming out was often a success, even with parents who seemed most unlikely to welcome their son or daughter for being gay. What helped make it a success was when the bald statement "I'm gay" was thoroughly embedded in a statement of the reasons for telling, such as, "I want us to be a close, loving family again and I don't think we'll ever be close and I don't think our love will ever be real unless you know the truth about me." Then the disclosure was also embedded in a statement of what it meant, such as, "I want you to think of yourselves as good parents. There's nothing wrong with me or with you. What this is all about is our accepting ourselves and each other even if the things we're accepting aren't necessarily the things we would've chosen."

In this latter case, the person has changed what he's disclosing. It's no longer a revelation of a personal fact. It's a revelation of a vision about love and family. If you have some fact that you need to tell someone, then you must make your reasons for telling and the meaning of the fact as real to the other person as the fact itself.

Bad News

This is where you and I most feel that our hands are tied. Regardless of what we'd like to have happen, the news we have to tell is what it is. How could it be different, no matter what outcome we'd like, no matter what outcome we're dreading?

You've already read a chapter on how to convey bad news in a way that meets the other person's needs; that will help you get through an awful experience. But when people have bad news to tell, they often have other needs besides.

One doctor who consulted with me had to tell a patient not only that she needed an operation on her spine but that there was a significant risk with the operation of her ending up in a wheelchair. Now, here's what the doctor wanted to get out of telling this to his patient: he wanted to get her to agree to have the operation. He knew that, in spite of the risks, it was her only alternative to a life of pain. The pain was bearable now, but it would get worse without the operation.

There's only one solution when you're in this doctor's position of having to give someone bad news but then also having to get something for yourself. You have to divide your task into two parts. You want to convey bad news. And you want to make a request. You treat your request just the way you would anything that's hard to ask for. But you embed your bad news in the request. Begin by saying you have a request. Say what your request is. Then give your bad news. Then explain why it's so important for the other person to do what you're asking.

To illustrate (in an abbreviated way), the doctor could have said, "Ms. Jones, I'm going to ask you to have an operation that I'm convinced is vital to your health and happiness. If you were my mother, in the same situation, I'd tell you I think you should have this operation. You need an operation on your spine to get rid of your pain. And I'm afraid that there's some risk involved with this operation. Eighty percent of the time it's a big success, but twenty percent of the time nerves get cut, which leaves people stuck in a wheelchair for the rest of their lives. I know this is hard to hear and I wish I could give you better odds. But I'd like to ask you to accept these odds and get the operation because it's your best chance to be pain free."

In this case, the doctor's needs were unselfish professional needs: to do the best job of helping his patient. But even if your needs are much more personal and less noble, they're still real, and you too can embed your bad news in a request that will satisfy your needs.

3. What Emotional Baggage or Issues Will Get in the Way of How You Tell This Truth?

You don't have a choice. If there's something you've found hard to say to someone who's important to you, then you have emotional baggage about that truth or about that person. Let's say you have an assistant at work. He's okay, but he's started showing up just a little late in the morning and taking just a little too long for lunch. At first it doesn't feel like a big enough problem for you even to mention without seeming petty, without destroying your image as someone who's interested in the big picture, without its making it just a little harder for you to leave early on Friday yourself even though your assistant still has work to clear up.

So you don't say anything. But the longer you stay silent, the more annoyed you get. To make matters worse, you've started to notice a devil-may-care attitude in him that might be bearable in a hardworking assistant, but is as annoying as hell in someone who keeps being late.

As you sit there wondering how to say something to your assistant, you may not realize how much baggage you've been carrying around until you say something and you sound so angry about his being a little late that you end up having to apologize for flying off the handle, at which point he thinks you've withdrawn your feedback about his showing up late.

You've made a mess without even accomplishing anything. And that's because you were carrying around rage that was out of proportion to the truth you had to tell. "You've got to show up before nine from now on" is a clear instruction. "You've got to show up before nine from now on or I'll kill you" is, to say the least, distracting.

How to be an emotional-baggage inspector

Before you think about how to say something that's hard for you to say, you've got to inspect your emotional baggage. But how do you do that without going into psychoanalysis? And what do you do after you've inspected it? Let me make things simple.

Here's the best, most simple way to inspect your emotional baggage: *assume anger.* That's the whole story.

Whatever complicated feelings you have, and whatever complicated sources for these feelings there might be, the most useful way to think about the emotions that will interfere with your telling your truth is to assume that they're about anger. Assume you're angry about the truth you have to tell—his coming in late has made a lot of problems for you. And assume that you're angry with the other person for making the experience of telling hard for you—his attitude puts you in the wrong for making an issue of his coming in late.

I'm not saying you don't have other feelings. I am saying that short of psychoanalysis, anger is the most productive feeling to focus on to prevent your emotional baggage from getting in the way of your telling the truth.

Alexis's story

Suppose you learn a secret that spells bad news for someone you like. Alexis, a therapist I supervise, brought a messy situation to me. Justine, a patient with whom she had a good working relationship, had seen Alexis's husband in a hotel lobby with another woman. It looked as though they were having an affair. Justine had thought about not saying anything about this, but it gnawed at her. And she had the feeling that if the situation were reversed, she'd want to know.

The anger below the surface

But the way she told this bad news was actually fueled by anger that destroyed her relationship with her therapist. You might wonder how she could possibly be angry with Alexis when her therapist was the innocent victim here. But my point is that there's often anger when there's something that's hard to say, and I'll show you where it comes from in this case.

For one thing, Justine was engaged to be married and was terrified that her marriage wouldn't work. Alexis had been trying to assure her that marriages can and do work all the time, and that in spite of misleading statistics, most marriages are happy. Seeing Alexis's husband in the hotel lobby made it seem as though Alexis was either naive or was deliberately misleading Justine. Either way she was furious with Alexis for essentially defrauding her. For another thing, Justine resented the time and money that therapy took and now she was having to use up more time and money to talk about what was basically her therapist's problem.

But Justine wasn't aware of her anger. And that meant that she didn't realize the way her anger changed the "truth" she had to tell.

The truth behind the anger

What I later found out was that the scene Justine witnessed in the lobby was far more ambiguous than the scene Justine had reported to Alexis. This was a Cambridge hotel that was the site of innumerable meetings and conferences. Alexis's husband had laughed at something the woman said, but there was no sign of anything romantic going on. In fact what Justine saw was perfectly consistent with Alexis's husband and the woman he was with being complete strangers who happened to fall into a conversation while attending a meeting at the hotel.

If Justine had been more aware of what her anger was leading her to do, she might've said nothing, because in some sense she couldn't be sure she'd seen anything worth reporting. Or she might've simply mentioned to Alexis that she'd seen her husband in that hotel lobby. Or that she'd seen him talking to a woman in that hotel lobby. It was Justine's anger that led her to take the crucial step of saying that it looked as though they were having an affair and shading the details so they'd sound more incriminating.

The moral of this story is that the truth is shaped by feelings that have little to do with what that specific truth actually is. In other words, you'd better be prepared for the likelihood that subtracting your anger from your truth will change your truth. In Justine's case, subtracting her anger from her truth made the truth less incriminating, less hurtful. Subtracting your anger from your truth might change it so that you're more genuinely sorry. Or you're more willing to negotiate. Or you're more interested in solutions than in blame. Or your statement is more balanced.

Do this. Think about the truth you have to tell. Assume anger. Then ask yourself what you would say if you weren't angry. Say that instead.

You don't have to ignore your anger. You might very well want to tell the other person how angry you are. That's the truth of your feelings. But that's a separate truth, to be told at a separate time, from this other truth you've just saved from being contaminated by your anger.

4. What's Most Important in the Whole Picture?

Let me be clear about what this question focuses on: the most important thing is what you're most afraid of losing. People get in trouble with this in two ways: either they are so focused on what they have to say that they forget to think about what is most important, or they simply have no hope of getting what's most important.

But you can *always* take care of what's most important. Hey, that's what "most important" means. Everything else comes second. And I mean *everything,* including the truth itself. It's just as we talked about in whether to tell or not. The truth is certainly a value. But in the world of human affairs it's the servant of the greater good. Doing what's best for everyone comes first. Truth is a soldier in morality's army, and if it must be sacrificed to serve morality, then so be it.

To zero in on what's most important to you that you might lose, ask yourself what's most *precious* to you. What is incredibly fragile and yet incredibly valuable to you in the little pocket of life where you would be telling this truth to this person? Life is precious. Love is precious. Hope or a sense of a future is precious.

Friendships are destroyed all the time because people get annoyed with each other or hurt each other while at the same time forgetting that what's most important is the precious bond of friendship itself, which can so easily be lost. The bond seemed so elastic they forgot how fragile it was.

Andre's story

Andre and Lowell had been friends and golfing buddies for about ten years. Recently Andre had started getting the sense that Lowell was a liar. It wasn't anything big, but it seemed to Andre as though Lowell was mentioning business deals that never came to anything but that made him sound important, as well as saying he knew semifamous people whom it didn't make sense for him to know. These lies didn't come up often, but they annoyed the hell out of Andre and he decided to confront Lowell with it.

"Look," Andre said, "I don't know if the stuff you're telling me is bullshit or not, but it sounds like bullshit and I wish you'd cut it out." It seemed to Andre like a frank, man-to-man way of dealing with the problem.

But Lowell was deeply insulted. "You're calling me a liar!" he said, and he broke off their friendship. Andre never found out, even though he asked around, whether Lowell had been lying.

Andre didn't ask himself what was most important. If he had, he would have realized that finding friends is hard for men, and he liked hanging out with Lowell. Lowell's "lies," if they were that, were only a big deal if Andre chose to make them a big deal. They were certainly not about anything that mattered between the two of them, like cheating at golf. Later Andre realized that if he'd thought for a minute about how precious friendship was, he'd have waited until the next time Lowell said one of his "lies" and then asked for some corroboration.

Other priorities

But asking yourself what's most important doesn't always mean focusing on your relationship. Sometimes the most important thing is some need or goal of yours. Andre had an associate at his small law firm who kept showing signs of being irresponsible. On one occasion or another she lost a client's material and forgot to forward an important message and filed a brief too late and left work before a job was finished. Andre kept giving her feedback, but he was polite about it because he didn't want to work with an associate who was pissed at him. But Andre forgot to ask himself what was most important, and in this case it was to have his law practice run efficiently. It was his professional survival that was precious, not his relationship with this replaceable associate.

Fortunately Andre realized this in time and switched from giving feedback to handing her some bad news: "If you don't shape up, you'll have to ship out." Andre was surprised that she did shape up. Only an ultimatum conveyed the truth: that Andre was deadly serious about what he needed.

It's a big deal

As you can see from the example of Andre and his associate, what's most important isn't necessarily what's most precious. It could simply be what the biggest deal in your life is right now. It's the dog that wags the tail, not the tail that wags the dog. For example, if you have a small business, keeping that business alive and thriving is the biggest deal in your life. Most other things serve the business, instead of the business serving other things. So if you have a difficult truth to tell someone, exactly what you say and how you say it has to be put in the context of what your business needs.

Sometimes what's most important is what is the highest priority in your life right now. This is more of a goal than an in-place structure. It's more something you're trying to accomplish than something you're trying to preserve. But it could be, for example, that while your career is the biggest deal in your life right now, you've gotten so incredibly stressed that you're practically on the verge of a breakdown, and so your highest priority is to reduce stress to a minimum. And that might mean that out of all the things that are hard for you to say, you say only the ones that will give you something that reduces stress, like asking for a vacation.

Let's go back to basics. You've already learned you can't just blurt out the truth, that there's a way to say it that takes care of people's needs instead of making a mess. And what we're seeing here is that when you think about people's needs, the most important need of yours is not to lose what's most important.

12 To Tell the Truth, Don't Make These Mistakes

A LOT OF LITTLE MISTAKES CAN STAND IN THE WAY of your telling your truth effectively. They're easy to make—and therefore all too common—but the good news is they're easy to avoid. And you'll be amazed at how successful you'll be in telling the truth if you can just avoid these simple mistakes.

Speaking Before You're Ready

Something pops into your head to say to somebody. You're suddenly burning to say it. You can't imagine not saying it. But this reminds us of what wise men and women have known since biblical times: only a foolish person speaks without thinking.

Spontaneity can be risky. It's one thing to spontaneously tell someone you care about "You're beautiful!" or "Let's go to New York for the weekend." But would anyone think it's wise to spontaneously say to someone you're married to "Let's get divorced" just because you're momentarily annoyed with him? The hotter, the bigger the truth and the more delicate your relationship with the other person, the more speaking your truth without thinking is like tossing a pitchfork into a steam room. Someone will inevitably get hurt.

But it's not enough to say don't speak before you're ready. What are you supposed to think about before you speak? What does it mean to get ready? You already have a general idea: you think about what everyone needs. And if you don't know what they need, you guess about what they're probably afraid of, and you figure that they need whatever would make them not feel afraid in this situation. Here's a simple checklist:

- Do you know what the other person's response will be?
- Do you want this response?

If you can't confidently check off both items on this list, then you are not ready to speak your truth, no matter how much you're burning to speak it. In fact, without being able to check off these two items, your truth isn't so much a truth at all as it is a shot in the dark, and by the time the two of you are finished, the truth you were trying to get through will be lost.

But when it comes to telling a difficult truth, I understand how strong the impulse is to blurt it out before you've thought it out. I remember what it was like when I got my first firecracker. I was seven. It scared me. I was afraid of the noise it made and I was afraid of getting hurt. But I couldn't wait to set it off.

That's how many of us feel about many of the difficult truths we have to tell. We're afraid to speak but we can't wait to speak. That's how we end up blurting out the very truth we were scared to say.

My grandmother would've said we get a bee in our bonnet. It's a pretty good description: there's this thing buzzing around in our head that we just have to let out. Even if your truth is the last thing in the world you feel like saying—like asking your brother for money or telling your wife she looks fat in pants—once you get it into your head, you've got to let it out. Even if that means doing the equivalent of lighting a firecracker in the schoolyard during recess, which is what I was stupid enough to do when I was seven.

And so even people who are huge confrontation-phobics, as I was, end up blurting out the most difficult truths.

How to avoid this mistake

The simplest thing for me to say is *just don't*. You don't need instructions on how to not go when you're sitting in your car at a red light. When the light's red, you just don't go. In the same way, any truth that's at all hard to deal with for you or for the other person means there's a red light. You simply never, never say it until you've thought about what your truth really is, what you want to get out of telling, what the other person needs and how he'll respond. The hotter your truth, the more sensitive your relationship with the other person, the more you have to make sure to work through all the issues we talk about in this book.

At the very least, make sure you can check off both items on the checklist:

• Do you know what the other person's response will be?
• Do you want this response?

Think of it as playing chess or bridge or any game that requires a minimum of intelligence. Remember the last time you played checkers with a seven-year-old? Remember how he'd move a piece without thinking about how you'd move your piece in response? You wouldn't dream of doing that yourself. Before you make any move, you always ask yourself what the other person will do in response to that move. I know that when I play chess, every time I make a move without thinking and get slapped down as a result, I feel like a silly child for not having been minimally thoughtful. But when you have a truth to tell to someone who matters to you, you can get slapped down far worse if you don't think about how he'll respond to particular words, and it's no game. If you pay a price, you pay a real price.

The demon spontaneity

It also helps to recognize that you and I have inside us an enemy of thoughtfulness. There's a part of us that hates the thought of having to think before we speak, of having to weigh words and gauge reactions. We want to feel free. We want to believe we're perfectly safe. We want to think we're at home, where we can do anything we want.

And this part of us thinks there's something evil about holding back the truth until we're ready to speak it. There might've been part of you, for example, that was uncomfortable when I used the chess analogy. There's something cold and calculating and inhuman about chess. Your relationships with the people you care about aren't chess games.

So we create this polarity inside ourselves. There's the "good" person, who is free with the truth. It's a kind of inner Forrest Gump, and it's hard to imagine him ever thinking before he spoke. Like a child. And we wish we could be like that. Then there's the "bad" person, who is an evil, Machiavellian manipulator who, because he thinks before he speaks, must be sowing selfish lies. And so we're in love with our spontaneity because it's a sign of our goodness and hope and freedom.

Being careful with the truth

What we forget is the way we get into endless difficulties when we speak without thinking. We don't realize that we're not limited to two choices: Forrest Gump or Iago. We have a third alternative, where we're fully committed to the truth while at the same time being fully committed to preventing the damage that's caused when the truth is spoken in a thoughtless way.

What I'm saying is that you need to see your waiting as something that's not merely good for you but good for everyone. You don't avoid this mistake merely because it's good medicine, but because it's one small step toward making the world a better place.

Thinking before you speak is very different from simply not speaking. We conflict-phobes will often go for a long time when we sit on some truth we're afraid to speak. But the fact that you sat on something for a long time that you were dying to say doesn't mean that for even one minute during those long months of silence you were actually thinking about the other person's needs and reactions. You were just not speaking.

The way to avoid this, if there's a truth you want to speak, is to decide to tell it and then use your decision to tell to motivate you to think about and work out a plan for exactly how you're going to tell. At a minimum, think about what category your truth fits into and then follow the script in the how-to-tell chapters.

The Mañana Syndrome

We've talked about how important it is not to speak your truth until you know what it is exactly and what category it fits into and what you want to get as a result of speaking it and how the other person will respond. But answering these questions isn't rocket science. If you just thought for a bit about them, you'd probably come up with good answers. Most people get into trouble because they haven't asked themselves these questions, not because they haven't been able to find answers.

But once you're ready, you're out of danger of blurting your truth. Now you face the opposite danger: delay. That's the mañana syndrome: dreading exposure or conflict so much that you keep putting off until tomorrow what you should do today.

If there's some truth you're needing to tell someone right now, read this book first, use the help I provide, then tell him as soon as you've seen what's best. Then for the rest of your life, always tell someone as soon as possible.

Why is the mañana syndrome such a mistake? Here's what people have told me who've been on the receiving end of it:

- "The fact that she waited so long to tell me just convinced me she had something to hide after she told. What else wasn't she telling me?"
- "Delaying seemed like a manipulative thing to do. I couldn't let in what he was telling me when I felt manipulated by him."
- "His delaying made me wonder what he thought of me. What kind of a person did he think I was that it would be a problem for me to hear what he had to say? It was the insult implied by the delay that was the hardest thing for me to hear."

It's important to understand how seductive the mañana syndrome is, and how much damage it can cause. If you and I are supposed to meet for lunch and I'm fifteen minutes late, it might be awfully tempting for you to say nothing about how annoyed you are. Maybe you're not that annoyed to begin with, because you figure what's fifteen minutes, and I'll probably never do it again. But let's say we start meeting for lunch regularly and I keep showing up late.

The longer you go without giving me feedback and letting me know how you feel, the angrier you'll get, the more I'll feel there's nothing wrong with my showing up late, and the bigger the blowup we're headed for. If you finally do say something, your annoyance will show through, and yet I'll wonder how you could really be so upset since you didn't say something sooner. To avoid that messy scene, you might just decide to say nothing and look for a way to get out of what would otherwise be pleasant or productive lunch dates.

Here's the basic principle. Silence means consent. It may not mean consent to you, but it always means consent to the other person. If you don't say anything about my being late for lunch every time, it means to me that it's okay with you that I'm late. Then if you start giving me a hard time about it, I'm either going to feel that you arbitrarily switched from not minding to minding (and then what kind of a nut are you?) or that you were pretending to consent (and then what kind of a sneaky person are you?).

The mañana syndrome is a mistake because the longer you delay saying what you have to say, the more it'll seem to the other that he can do whatever he wants regardless of the consequences. It's as if you were saying that you're not serious about the very thing you're finding so hard to say.

How to avoid making this mistake

I understand that we're all tempted to delay telling difficult truths. Fear and delay are inevitable twins in life, which is why people always put off going to the doctor or the dentist. But the way to avoid the mañana syndrome is to employ the "next time" principle: decide that the next time you and the other person meet or the next time this problem comes up or whatever "next time" is most relevant, you'll tell your hot truth.

Define in your own mind as clearly as possible what that next time is, then lock yourself into that definition so that when the time comes, you can't fall back into the mañana syndrome by dreaming of a better moment.

The Half-a-Loaf Solution

You make this mistake when you simply tell one big piece of your story and leave out or lie about another big piece. What you're hoping, of course, is that the other piece will never come out. And I suppose that if you're lucky enough that the other piece never does come out, then you got away with this mistake. The problem is that those of us with algolalophobia are so afraid of saying difficult things that we seriously deceive ourselves about how likely it is that the other piece will come out. We tell ourselves that it probably won't come out because we don't want it to come out.

Kirk's story

I think of Kirk, who still hadn't told his parents he was gay when he discovered he had AIDS. Because he dreaded confronting them with all this news he knew they'd find so difficult to hear, he convinced himself he could tell them he had AIDS without telling them he was gay. Of course, like most average Americans they connected AIDS with being gay and asked him if he was gay. Kirk denied it.

The majority of parents, even those with "traditional" values, end up accepting their adult sons and daughters when they discover they're gay or lesbian. Kirk's parents would most likely have done the same. But he subjected them to a long period when they had to think he was lying. Because they felt lied to, they felt rejected, and because they felt rejected, it made the lying even harder to handle. What it felt like to them was that they couldn't trust their son and that he didn't want them in his life. In fact, Kirk died alienated from his parents.

Kirk's story is dramatic, but where the half-a-loaf mistake comes up far more often is in something stupid that we algolalophobics do all the time. Instead of leaving out an important half of the story, which is definitely a mistake but at least makes some kind of cowardly sense, we leave out an utterly unimportant part of the story, which is just as big a mistake and makes no sense whatsoever. The classic instance of this is the guy who confesses to having had an affair and then lies by saying it only happened twice. Later when his wife finds out that he slept with the other woman four times instead of twice, he's completely blown his credibility.

How to avoid making this mistake

You must separate the decision of whether to tell from the question of how to tell when there's a hot truth. In a few specific circumstances it's better not to tell. But once it's clear that you should tell, you'll avoid this error if you know that telling your truth means telling your whole truth. Telling half your truth buys you a ton of trouble with little hope of gain.

The No-Big-Deal Approach

You make this mistake when you try to convince the other person that he shouldn't think of what you're saying as a big deal. You think you're softening the edge of whatever it is that's hard for you to say, but you're really twisting the knife. Here are some examples of what people do when they make this mistake:

- A man who'd dreamed of having a closer relationship with his sister wanted her to let his five-year-old stay with her for a couple of weeks while he went on vacation with his wife. Overlooking that this was a busy time for his sister, he said, "I don't see how you can object because he'll be no trouble whatsoever."
- A man told the woman he'd just gotten engaged to that he was adopted just as they were ending one of their evenings out. When she started asking questions, he shut her up by telling her it wasn't important, it made no difference to him, and she shouldn't be concerned about it.
- A sixty-year-old man's cardiologist told him he had coronary artery disease, but he wasn't a good candidate for heart bypass surgery. At first the man didn't tell his wife (the mistake of delaying), but when he did tell her, he said that he'd probably live, that if he died, she'd be better off without him, and that the whole thing was no big deal, so he didn't want to talk about it.

It's important to understand why the no-big-deal approach is such a big mistake. The fundamental rule of communication is that what you communicate to someone *isn't* what you intend to say or what you actually say; it *is* what the other person understands by what you've said.

Here's an analogy. What you eat in a restaurant isn't what the chef thinks he's cooking or what he had actually cooked the moment it left the pan; it's what you experience with your eyes and nose and tongue when the dish reaches your table. What good is a dish that leaves the pan hot but arrives at your table cold? What good is a dish that an aesthete chef thinks is exquisite but that the hardworking diner thinks is a paltry rip-off?

In the same way, what good is your saying it's no big deal if the other person hears that it is a big deal?

If you minimize, I gotta maximize

So that's the problem with the no-big-deal approach. You *intend* your words to convey the idea that whatever it is you're saying shouldn't be reacted to so strongly. But what *actually* happens is that the very words you use to minimize the impact of what you say magnify its impact in the mind of the other person.

Here's a simple illustration. Let's say you step on someone's foot. It hurts her and she says ouch. If you apologize profusely, as if you've done a terrible thing, then the other person has the impulse to say, "Oh, it's nothing, really." Because you make a big deal out of it, she's filled with the desire to tell you that it's no big deal.

But suppose, after the other person says ouch, you say, "What are you making such a big deal out of this for? I barely stepped on your toe." Now, because you try to tell her it was no big deal, she's filled with the desire to tell you what a big deal it really was. You've created in the other person's mind the impulse to magnify the very thing you're trying to get her to minimize. This mistake can have terrible consequences.

Tom and Mary

Theirs was one of those marriages where both people led separate lives and both felt distant. The difference was that Tom wanted to spend more time with Mary, but Mary was pushing to have even more time for herself. So Tom generally felt rejected and Mary felt harassed.

One summer started out typical for them. She lived at their beach house. He tried to be with her when his work permitted. Finally Tom had a free week. He showed up at the beach house and told Mary about the plans he had for what the two of them could do together. Mary didn't say anything, but she felt something. As she thought about it overnight, it became clear that she had something difficult for her to say to Tom. She wanted to tell him that she had activities planned with her friends and she didn't want to change her plans and she didn't want Tom to come along.

When she told him, she saw how hurt and upset he was. So in a mistaken attempt to minimize the damage, she said, "You really shouldn't feel so bad. It's no big deal. It's the way we live anyway." She acted just like the person who steps on your toe and when you say ouch tells you that you shouldn't be making such a big deal about it.

Of course, all this did was make Tom's reaction all the more intense. It's not only that he acted more hurt in an attempt to make her see the impact of what she'd said. But he actually felt more hurt because neglecting and minimizing his pain neglected and minimized *him*. He must be nothing to her, he thought, if hurting him was nothing to her, if she couldn't see his hurt.

Within a month Tom was having an affair with a woman in their social circle. Tom was rich and charming, and this woman had been attracted to him for a long time, but Tom had always put her off. Now after Mary tried to make him feel, from his point of view, that what she was doing was no big deal and therefore he was no big deal to her, a combination of anger and loneliness made Tom agree to sleep with this other woman.

There'd been problems before, but now someone had done something unforgivable.

How to avoid making this mistake

Put yourself in the other person's place. If someone steps on your toe, does it make the pain worse if he apologizes profusely? Of course not. Just the opposite.

Be aware of how tempted you'll be to minimize the impact of what you're saying. Just know that the more you minimize, the more the other person will maximize. If you're asking for something that's a big deal, say, "I realize this is a terrible imposition." If you're confessing to having done something that hurt the other person, say, "I know what I did was terrible and I know how much it hurt you." If you're giving someone negative feedback, say, "I can really understand it if you feel attacked or put down. It can be devastating to hear criticism like this." Whatever kind of tough truth you have to convey, if you say something like this, your words won't be drowned out by the other person's feeling that you don't understand the impact of your words.

The Fouling-the-Nest Error

There's a certain emotional geography in your relationships with everyone who's important to you. There are places that both of you recognize as safe and happy. There are places that make both of you feel uncomfortable, where the two of you feel awkward or don't get along. And there are neutral places. And a mistake many people make when they have something they know the other person will find hard to hear is to tell it to him in one of those safe and happy places.

The reason this is a mistake isn't that it screws up your saying whatever it is you have to say. It's a problem because it screws up the aftermath.

A simple dramatic example will make this clear. You're married and whatever problems there've been in your relationship, the bedroom has been a place for sex and romance and comfort and relaxation and safety. Now if you have to confess having had an affair, that's a bombshell with a lot of fallout. Don't you want to keep that fallout away from the bedroom as much as possible? If you do confess your guilty secret in the bedroom, you run the risk of contaminating an environment that you'll need to work for you if you're going to have a reconciliation.

You might be surprised to hear how powerful the forces of emotional geography are. But I've seen its effects over and over. Suppose you have a boss with whom you've developed a good working relationship and you usually hold meetings in her office. Then one day she has some pretty harsh criticisms of your work that are hard for you to hear. If she tells you this in her office, where you've spent so much good productive time together, it puts a defensive edge on how you feel about being in that office in the future. If she tells you at lunch, at a restaurant where the two of you rarely go, it's much easier to go back to her office and feel you're starting with a clean slate.

How to avoid making this mistake

If you have something difficult to say to someone, think about the emotional geography of your relationship before you say it. Think about the places that are good for both of you, whether "good" means happy, safe, productive, romantic, comfortable, fun, or whatever. Then rule those places out.

The simplest rule of thumb is to find a place that's emotionally neutral and that you're not going to need later to repair your relationship.

"I Thought You'd Want to Be the Last to Know"

Suppose you have something to say to person X that's hard for you to say. You make the last-to-know mistake when you tell other people what you want to tell X before you tell X.

Of course, you might get away with this mistake if X never finds out that you've talked to other people first. But tongues wag and it's hard for people to keep secrets, so there's an amazingly high probability that your person X will either learn your hot truth before you tell him or will find out afterward that he was the last to know.

Here's why this mistake is so destructive. When people hear something that's hard for them to hear, they feel violated. Peace of mind, personal integrity, even sense of self are assaulted when we hear bad news or someone asks us for something that's difficult and awkward for us to deal with.

This sense of violation was one of the most surprising findings as I talked to people who were on the receiving end of the kinds of hot truths you're needing to tell. But we never think of a sense of violation as one of the feelings the other person will go through. And so we keep making the mistake of talking to other people before we tell the person who deserves to hear what we have to say first.

Aaron and Lane

It's a surprisingly common story. A father builds up a successful business. He has two sons. They're both good boys. But one, Aaron in this case, is responsible and ambitious. The other, Lane, just wants to have fun. The father, torn among hope, love, and realism, sets things up so that after he dies, Aaron will have control of the business, Lane will have a part to play in it, and the family assets will be divided as equally as possible consistent with Aaron's maintaining control. It was a fair, savvy arrangement.

But ten years after the father's death Aaron wanted to change things. Lane was screwing up in his limited role in the business. And he seemed both miserable and uninterested in it. So Aaron wanted to work out a way, to put it bluntly, of paying Lane to walk away. Aaron certainly had the dough to do it, and Lane would certainly be happy to walk away. There was the possibility that everything could be fair and amicable.

But it's humiliating to be fired by your brother. That's what made it so difficult for Aaron as he tried to figure out how to tell Lane what he wanted. So Aaron made the mistake of talking to a whole bunch of people about his how-do-I-handle-Lane problem. He talked to a cousin. He talked to an old crony of their father's. He talked to the family lawyer. He talked to their tax man. He talked to a guy they both played tennis with. And more.

His intentions were the best. Like a young surgeon performing a difficult operation for the first time, Aaron wanted all the help he could get so he could carry out his mission as safely and effectively as possible. Then it all blew up in his face. In one weekend, three people called Lane and basically said, "You know, your brother's trying to do a really nice thing, but he's worried about how you're going to take it."

The blowup

Lane was humiliated at being fired by his brother, being fired in public, and being seen as someone who couldn't handle being fired. When Lane confronted Aaron with all this the following Monday, Aaron said, "Why are you so upset that those people know? Everyone knows. I knew this was for the best, but it was a delicate matter and I wanted to handle it properly."

This blew the deal and destroyed their relationship. What Lane should have, and probably would have, recognized as an arrangement that was both fair and in his own interest now seemed like a slick maneuver that would deprive him of his inheritance.

Lane was responding to the sense of violation we all feel when someone has a difficult truth to tell us and he tells others first behind our back.

It's important to recognize the different ways you can make this mistake. The most obvious way is doing what Aaron did: asking other people for advice on how to tell your truth. Another way is talking to other people and conducting trial runs, telling them your truth and getting their reactions before telling it to the person who needs to hear it. Probably the worst form of this mistake is telling other people in the hope that one of them will blab it and so relieve you of the responsibility of saying what's so hard for you to say.

How to avoid making this mistake

I'm not, repeat *not,* saying that you should never, ever consult with anyone if you have something difficult to say to person X in your life. I'm a firm believer in the value of wise advisers. The issue is how to use them while still avoiding the last-to-know error.

It's simple. If you must consult with somebody, find one person who's the wisest man or woman you know. Not more than one. Then make sure that you can absolutely trust him or her to maintain confidentiality. Most of all, make sure this person doesn't know the person you need to tell your truth to. Someone who knows neither of you is better than someone who knows both of you. A reasonably smart person who knows neither of you is better than the smartest person in the world who knows both of you.

The "Devil Made Me Do It" Strategy

You make this mistake when you tell someone something and at the same time deny your responsibility for it. If you criticize someone, for example, you try to make it sound as though everyone else is bothered by the same thing you're criticizing him for, so in a sense it's not your criticism but everyone's criticism. You act as though you don't even really want to make this criticism but everyone else sort of got together and made you their spokesman. In a sense, if it were up to you, you wouldn't have said anything, except that everyone else was so bothered.

Suppose you're dating Woman #1 and then without telling her you go on a date with Woman #2, then find yourself having to confess your guilty secret to Woman #1 before she discovers it. You make the devil-made-me-do-it mistake when you say that the real reason you dated Woman #2 was that Woman #1 gave you mixed signals about the level of your commitment or Woman #1 wasn't being nice to you.

But it doesn't play on Broadway. The other person's already upset because of what you're saying. Denying responsibility doesn't lessen the impact of your words. You still went on a date with another person. The facts behind your words are still the same. But now you have to add in that the person you're telling this to doesn't buy your excuse.

So now you've committed a double injury. You've revealed whatever you've had to reveal that the other person finds hard to hear. But you've also shown yourself for a bald-faced liar. You've shown yourself as someone so unconcerned and dismissive that you'll toss off a stupid excuse. Actually it's a triple injury. Not only have you treated the other person like a nothing, but you're saying she's an idiot because who else but an idiot would believe your stupid excuse.

Just think about this. You go to fire somebody at your job and you pretend that your boss made you do it. Now this person's been canned, lied to, treated like a nobody, and labeled an idiot. If you hadn't made this mistake, he'd still be canned, but he'd also have the sense of being treated with the maximum respect possible in this situation. He won't be happy, but he'll be far less unhappy than if you'd denied your responsibility.

How to avoid making this mistake

Accept that you're tempted. There's so much talk about "taking responsibility" these days that who among us would ever dare admit that we weren't taking responsibility? But algolalophobia means being scared of big emotional confrontations, and it's almost irresistible to want to hunker down and try to make the whole thing better by blaming someone else.

Once you know how tempted you are, recognize the most likely form this temptation takes in this psychological age we live in. It's the temptation to explain. You'll want to explain your motives: "to help you," "because I was angry," and so on. You'll want to explain the causes of whatever it is you have to say: "I was driven to it," "how could I resist," and so on.

To avoid blaming someone or something else, don't fall into the trap of offering an explanation that takes you off the hook, and don't do anything else that takes you off the hook. There will be plenty of time in weeks to come to go into explanations if they turn out to be necessary. But now is not the time.

Instead of blaming others, blame yourself. The more you pile the ashes of blame on your own head, the more the other person is likely to get to the point of saying, "Well, it's not your fault," and then point the finger of responsibility somewhere else than at you.

Whenever you have a truth that's hard for you to say, there's a problem somewhere. The person who's hearing that truth always feels a problem is being dumped in her lap (it's other people's reactions to having problems dumped in their laps that makes it hard for us algolalophobics to tell the truth in the first place). By blaming yourself you're taking some of the problems onto yourself. The other person feels relieved instead of feeling dumped on, and the whole experience ends up going more smoothly for you.

The "Bombshell? What Bombshell?" Switcheroo

You make this mistake when you tell a difficult truth, then take it back if the other person gets upset: "I'm sorry I said you were fat. You're not fat. I don't know what I was thinking. You're just right." Or "I'm sorry I said I was breaking up with you. I didn't really mean it. I was just upset. Things are fine between us."

Sometimes people even deny they've said what they said. One guy asked his boss for a raise, then when his boss blew up said the boss must have misunderstood, that he wasn't asking for a raise, only a performance review.

The principle is that when things are terrible, we deny reality. We can do it manipulatively in a deliberate attempt to save our butts, like the guy who denied he was asking for a raise. We can do it with full sincerity simply because we're horrified by the impact of our words, like the woman who denied she was breaking up with her boyfriend. But even though we may not like to think of ourselves as doing this, we do do it, just like the kid who wakes up feeling mildly ill, makes a big deal out of it to avoid having to go to school, then says he's fine when he learns that his parents are going to take him to the doctor to get a shot.

You need to know how common this is in its milder forms, because as upstanding adults we don't like to think of ourselves as taking things back. But it's common to feel bad when we see the fallout from saying things the wrong way. Then we do what we all see politicians do in virtually every campaign: try to control the spin when we see the real impact our words have. But it's important to recognize the subtler forms of this switcheroo mistake, which the following story illustrates.

Abby and Lenny

The session was specifically set up for Lenny to confess to Abby that he'd started drinking again. Lenny wanted to confess partly because he felt virtually crippled by guilt and partly because he knew he'd been seen drinking by people who knew Abby and so there was a risk that she'd find out anyway.

I wish I'd done a better job of coaching Lenny, but this happened long ago and I was still in my learning phase. Lenny made his confession with the kind of blunt, bluff honesty we hope will gain us credit for being upstanding people. And Abby freaked, as people so often do when you do a bad job of telling them you've lied to them and fallen back into a destructive pattern.

In response to her being upset, Lenny started sliding into the switcheroo mistake. Yes, he'd said he'd started drinking again, and he was sorry if he'd made it sound as though he'd really done some serious drinking, but it was really just a couple of beers and it was only to look good for business reasons. Yes, he could understand why Abby thought he had completely gone back on his promises, but he'd obviously created the wrong impression and in fact it was just one incident of a couple of beers.

If you'd been in the room with us, you'd have felt Lenny edging ever closer to saying, "Drinking? What drinking?"

You don't have to completely take back the difficult truth you've spoken to fall into this mistake. Even taking back a significant part of it or being seen as trying to take it back is enough to convict you of this error in the mind and heart of the other person.

But why *not* do this whenever possible? The thing is that few people are stupid and gullible. They know what you've said and they know you're taking it back. And to them your attempts to take it back are insulting. It's as if you'd stepped on someone's foot, and when he said ouch, you slapped him in the face.

How to avoid making this mistake

You've learned about deciding in advance exactly what you're going to say. It's easy to speak without thinking and to describe things in a loose way. But you avoid the mistake of taking back your words when you take the time to decide on your words in the first place. Then commit yourself to them. And being committed to them is easiest when you decide what they are in advance.

The "If I Apologize and You Won't Forgive Me, Then You're Bad" Maneuver

Okay, you've said something that's hard for you to say. And whatever it is, there is something there for you to apologize for: for what you did, for what you're asking for, for not having told sooner, whatever. And let's say you're smart enough to actually apologize, sincerely and profusely.

This mistake comes when you feel as though your apology should have smoothed all the rough seas ahead. Then if the other person is agitated instead of calm after your supposedly all-healing apology, they're in the wrong. "I told you I was sorry for cracking up your new car. I told you I'll pay for the deductible. So I don't understand why you're still upset. What more do you want from me? What's wrong with you that you can't let go of this now?"

Don't use this maneuver. I'm not saying you'd use it deliberately, but even if you just fall into it, it's a terrible mistake. It creates a huge backlog of unfinished business for you. Look, you've just said something that's hard for the other person to hear, and that's what the two of you need to talk about. If you cracked up his car and he's still upset after you've apologized and after you've offered to pay for the deductible, he's upset about something. You have to find out what it's about. You have to hear it and respond to it. It's not that you'll be able to make it all better, but at least you'll be able to acknowledge it and respond in some healing way.

Maybe the fact that his cracked-up new car will get repaired is beside the point. The point to him is that it'll never be a new car again. It'll never be perfect again. By saying he's in the wrong for getting upset after you've apologized means you haven't dealt with his specific sense of loss. And if you never deal with it, there will forever be a breach in your relationship.

How to avoid making this mistake

The reason certain things are hard for us to say to other people is that we know that our words will change their world. A sincere apology may be necessary, but their world is still changed. And they have to process that change. They might have to complain about it or mourn it or blame you for it or figure out what to do about it or any one of a dozen different things. You have to recognize that no apology by itself can do the work of helping other people deal with the change.

So you avoid making this mistake by understanding how far an apology will take you. It will let the other person know you're sorry. But then you have to know that there's still more work to be done. We've talked about the principle of compensation. "Tell the truth but meet the need" means that if there's a need for some concrete action to right the balance, you'll do it.

The Chinese Water-Torture Mistake

You make this mistake when you have something that's hard for you to say, but instead of getting it all out at one time, you leak or dribble out what you have to say a bit at a time.

If you have bad news to tell someone, for example, you might be so worried about how she'll react that you tell her only part of the bad news today and another part next week and another part a week later. If you have something that you want to ask for from the other person, for example, you ask for only part of what you want today, so it's not until weeks later that the other person realizes the full magnitude of your request.

Obviously, what it means not to make the mistake of employing Chinese water torture is to say whatever you have to say in one complete unit at one time. When five minutes or an hour are up and you're finished saying whatever it is you have to say, you really are finished and there's nothing more.

The big news about the Chinese water-torture mistake of leaking your story in bits and pieces is the enormous, horrible discrepancy between what you're hoping to accomplish and the pain and injury you're actually inflicting.

Daniel and Sarah

Breaking up is hard to do. It's hard whatever your relationship with someone: romantic, professional, casual. Part of what makes breaking up with someone so hard is that it involves most of the six situations where we find ourselves with something difficult to say. You're bringing bad news. You're being critical. You're asking for something. You're saying how you feel. You're even confessing the guilty secret of having harbored hidden thoughts of wanting to break up. And we all know how painful it is to be dumped.

That's why Sarah did what so many people do when they want to break up with someone. She didn't tell Daniel the whole story at once. She didn't tell him that she wanted to break their engagement. She didn't tell him she wanted to break up because he didn't make much money and probably never would, plus she was seeing a guy at work for lunch whom she was starting to feel romantic about. And she didn't tell Daniel that she couldn't be friends with someone she'd broken up with.

Here's what Sarah did instead. One Saturday morning while they were still lying in bed, she told Daniel that he should know that she wasn't as happy in the relationship as he might have thought. As you can imagine, this led to a weekend-long talkfest about what she needed and what Daniel was doing wrong. This conversation scared Daniel, but it also led him to conclude that Sarah was getting rid of problems so they could face their wedding on a solid footing.

A couple of weeks later Sarah came home from work late one Tuesday night, and when Daniel complained about her not letting him know she'd be late, Sarah said she was starting to feel she needed more time on her own, that he was suffocating her.

"I'm starting to feel you don't like me," Daniel said. They spent weeks talking about this, and while Sarah's words denied it, the message she conveyed to Daniel was that it must be true.

Then Sarah said, "Look, we're obviously both miserable here. Something must be wrong. We should go into therapy before we go any further." Again, from Daniel's point of view, there was that agonizing mixture of hope (therapy would fix things) with rejection and desertion (they'd been talking about a wedding and now Sarah was talking about therapy).

After a month of therapy, during which, from Daniel's point of view, they'd just begun bringing out their issues, Sarah suddenly brought up the idea that they "should" have a trial separation.

Sarah's hope during this whole period was that Daniel would catch her drift, literally, in the sense that he'd see her drifting away. What she didn't understand was how utterly connected people are with their own needs and how these needs make it difficult to take in new information. Daniel's need was to hold on to Sarah. So instead of catching her drift, each torturing drop of new information gave him new hope, along with making him sad and scared.

Making things hard by trying to make it easy

Those of us who find it difficult to say difficult things keep putting ourselves in Sarah's position. We make the mistake of thinking that if we leak out our stories one easy-to-swallow piece at a time, the other person will be able to accept without giving us a hard time what he would reject with a big messy fight if we told him all at once. But whenever we make the mistake of using Chinese water torture, the people who are on the receiving end respond the way Daniel did.

They don't believe you. When you get to the point of saying that you want to break up, they believe, as Daniel did, in the hope they've found in each bit and piece of the message you've tortured them with. Daniel wouldn't let Sarah break up with him. He fought with her when she tried to move out. He stalked her when she moved to her new apartment. When he heard about Gavin, the man in her office she'd been dating, Daniel went to where he knew they had lunch and confronted him there.

It's easy to label Daniel a nut, a control freak, just another guy who couldn't let go. But Sarah's part in this was to confuse the hell out of him. From his point of view, Daniel wasn't a guy who couldn't let go; he was a guy who felt he had reason to believe what he heard, not what Sarah ended up saying. And what Daniel heard were all the messages of hope, all the needs that he could fill, all the possibilities of their working things out.

By simply avoiding this mistake, Sarah could have made it crystal clear to Daniel all at once, without confusing him and making him believe the opposite, that she really did want to break up and that it was really over.

How to avoid making this mistake

None of the mistakes I'm talking about in this chapter are deliberate. None of us decide to subject anyone in our lives to Chinese water torture. What happens—and I've talked to countless men and women who've made this mistake—is that our algolalophobia leads us to kid ourselves and so we never really acknowledge to ourselves what we want to say.

So, to avoid making this mistake, first know the truth you want to convey. Get it clear in your own mind. Write it down on paper, and ask yourself if this is the whole story or if there is going to be more and then more and then more. Once you're clear about what the truth you want to tell is, so there is no "more," you've done the most important thing you can do to prevent this mistake. You'll have spared yourself and the other person the craziness that always results when you parcel out the truth.

The "Happy Birthday, and, Uh, by the Way . . ." Disaster

If I hadn't done research on this, I wouldn't have realized how often this mistake comes up. You'd be amazed at how often people wait for a happy occasion as a good time to slip in their bad news or any other truth they find difficult to say. But instead of the occasion cushioning their news like the candy coating around a bitter pill, the occasion's ruined. Now you've got the mess from what you've said and a messed-up occasion to boot.

Why doesn't this work as well as we keep hoping it will work? It's because we make a fundamental psychological error. We confuse "the right time to tell" with a happy occasion.

How to avoid making this mistake

It's simple. Never tell a difficult truth on a happy occasion. Realize that happy occasions have a strange way of beckoning you to spill your beans. But although we say, "Let a smile be your umbrella," we should keep in mind that just because someone has a smile doesn't mean he has an umbrella. In fact, a happy occasion might be a time of particular vulnerability. If that's when you choose to tell your truth, you might be sowing seeds of resentment. Don't do it.

A Look Ahead

I don't know about you, but I like learning about the mistakes to avoid. It makes me feel hopeful. It's a lot easier to stop doing some little thing you already do than to start doing a whole big new thing. And these mistakes you've just learned about should make you feel hopeful too. Not only do they make a huge difference between making your social world a disaster and your social world a place that's safe for the truth, but they're easy to avoid.

The mistakes we've just dealt with are one kind of mistake. When you go dancing, you can step on your partner's feet. But you can also trip over your own feet, and that's the kind of mistake we'll deal with in the next chapter. When it comes to saying things that are hard to say, it's often the ways we hurt ourselves that make the most trouble. But once you see what they are, they too are easy to avoid. And they too make a huge difference.

13 Getting Out of Your Own Way

IF YOU'VE EVER SUCCESSFULLY LOST SOME WEIGHT and kept it off for more than a brief period, then you know that you couldn't have accomplished what you did without cluing in to how you screw yourself up when you try to diet. One person is fine except that she can't stop snacking and nibbling whenever she's in the kitchen. Another guy has to eat large portions if he eats anything. One woman likes to buy herself "treats" whenever she's out running errands. I myself can diet all day and then gain back what I've lost by eating after dark.

These are the little, unique ways each of us finds to be our own worst enemy. When you've decided to get serious about changing, it's crucial that you identify and root out these self-mistakes.

For poor communicators, telling the truth is a performance, an exercise in self-expression. Or perhaps I should say an *exorcise* in self-expression, because that's typically how it functions: as a way of discharging pent-up evil spirits. You know—getting something off your chest. Well, that may be therapeutic, as it would be if you heaved a huge rock off your chest, but if it hits the other person in the head, then you have the same kind of interpersonal mess that caused your algolalophobia in the first place. You feel better in the short run, but the other person feels worse and the climate for truth telling is just that much more dismal.

So if you want to "perform" the truth, save it for your therapist or someone who won't be personally affected by what you have to say. But if you want to communicate your truth, then watch out for these self-mistakes that can cause the London Bridge of communication to fall down.

When Your Fears Become Your Focus

You can make progress toward overcoming your fear by understanding exactly what you're afraid of. Most people who fall victim to algolalophobia are suffering from a kind of nameless dread. They just know that the other person will get "upset." They just know that the whole experience will be a "mess."

But I've seen something amazing in my work with people who hate conflict. Telling the truth becomes a lot easier when you can specify what you're afraid of, and here are three things you can do to get past your specific fears.

One is to know that everything you've learned about telling the truth effectively, everything you do to meet the other person's needs, will prevent the reactions you're afraid of.

Another thing you can do is ask yourself why the other person would respond in the particular way you're afraid of. Why would he get angry? Why would she humiliate you? *The other person reacts in a way you're afraid of because of an unmet need. Use your specific fear to identify this unmet need of theirs and then try to meet it.*

One more thing you can do is ask yourself what you need. If you can say exactly what you're afraid of, you can think of something you need that, if you got it, would protect you against the reaction you're afraid of. And the most direct thing you can do is ask to get what you need. That's why people always say, "If I tell you something, will you promise not to get angry?" You can do that with whatever you're afraid of. It works.

The last thing you can do is accept the amazing power that naming a fear has to overcome that fear. It's hard to reassure a child who's afraid of "the dark." It's much easier to reassure a child who can understand that he's afraid of monsters lurking in the dark. Then you can turn on the light and do other things to try to show him there are no monsters. In the same way, knowing exactly what you're afraid of, instead of being a victim of nameless dread, can make it much easier for you to reassure yourself.

So as you read through the following list of fears, ask yourself, "Is this what I was afraid of?" Then say, "Oh, I can deal with that," and ask yourself, "Why would the other person act that way and what can I do to prevent it?"

Anger

Probably the most common reaction we're afraid of when we have something that's hard for us to say is the other person's anger. If you ask for *this,* if you tell them *this,* they'll just blow up. They'll yell at you. They'll call you names. They'll threaten you. Fear of anger is so basic that we typically measure how difficult it is to speak a truth by the degree of anger we anticipate in the other person. And it usually takes very little expected anger for us to shut up and find ourselves hiding our truth. Every husband who hides something from his wife (like me), every employee who hides something from her boss, is typically afraid of the other person's anger.

What deepens our fear is that we can't be sure that the other person's anger will just take the form of words, although words are bad enough. That's why so many of the things we do when we have something that's difficult to say are attempts to manage the other's anger. Silence, of course, seems perfect, if we could only keep it up. More commonly, we do such things as take someone to a restaurant to fire him or break up with him because we know it will be harder for him to blow up in a public place. But we're afraid anyway because we realize that if he does blow up in a public place, it will be even worse. Or we try to manage other people's anger by trying to make them feel responsible for what we're telling them, so that if they do get angry, they'll have to address their anger at themselves.

But none of these tactics work very well. All they do is delay the moment when you'll have to deal with the other person's anger. The solution is to tell your truth in such a way that it doesn't make the other person angry in the first place. And that's what "Tell the truth but meet the need" and everything else you learn in this book are all about. Just trying to meet the other person's needs, just acknowledging those needs, goes a long way toward preventing anger.

Humiliation and Shame

There's good reason for calling it the "naked" truth: when you've spoken it in the past, you've stripped yourself naked and told a truth that was deeply unflattering. Now you're afraid, whenever you tell the truth, that it will reveal that you're weaker and smaller and more flawed than you ever wanted to be seen as.

In many cases the humiliation we're afraid of is obvious. If someone gave you $500 of his to hold on to while he went to the gym and you lost it, confessing that you'd lost it would mean showing yourself as someone who at the very least is incredibly careless, if he didn't end up thinking you are a thief. That's why to avoid being humiliated in his eyes you might silently kick in $500 of your own so he'd never know you lost his money.

But the important thing about humiliation and shame is the way fear of it lurks within most of the situations where we have something difficult to say. Asking for help can provoke a response that makes us feel humiliated. Criticizing someone can provoke him into criticizing you back in a most humiliating way. Even something as potentially wonderful as telling someone you love her can stimulate a fear of humiliation. What if she doesn't say "I love you" back? What if she does say "I love you" back but in a much cooler way? What if she feels she has to give you a list of reasons for why she can't love you?

And how many times, to avoid humiliation, have we kept silent about the truth of our feelings or distorted that truth as we told it?

Disempowerment

If someone knows how we feel or what we want or who we are or what we've done, he has power over us in endless ways, most of which are hard for us to identify. Think back to when you were a kid. Lesson #1 of Kid Lore is that the more stuff grown-ups know about you, the more ways they have to control you. Kids who don't feel completely safe with their parents are reluctant to tell them even what their favorite TV show is because that's the show their parents won't let them watch when they punish them.

We carry this instinctive fear into our lives as adults. Think about telling someone important to you that you're sick. With most serious conditions the power balance shifts. If you tell your spouse you've got ulcers, she can start telling you what you can eat. If you tell your boss you're going through menopause (not an illness, of course, but certainly a physiological change with profound effects), he can take you off key assignments. If you tell your grown-up kids you've got a problem with your heart, they can start telling you where, and how, to live. If you tell people you've got AIDS, they can threaten to take everything away from you.

Abandonment and Rejection

In one way or another, most of us are afraid of being left: left out, left in the lurch, left behind. We're afraid of being let go. We're afraid of being dropped, dismissed, cut loose. We're afraid of being alone. We're afraid of not being liked, which is so often the prelude to being abandoned.

Now think about how you relate to other people in your life. You like being with people who bring you good news and who say positive things. You keep distant people who bring you bad news and who say negative things.

We all understand how negativity puts people off, which is why we're afraid of rejection when we say a difficult truth. We're afraid that needy people are rejected, which is why we might be afraid to keep calling someone to ask for advice. We're afraid that critical people are rejected, which is why we might be afraid to tell a friend we're tired of her being late all the time. We're afraid that people who reveal their true feelings and make things awkward and complicated are rejected, which is why we don't want to tell a friend we're sick of the way she bosses us around.

But I want to make it clear that it's not just the big, hot revelations that stimulate our fear of rejection and abandonment. When people hear anything they don't like, there's a risk they'll go away. Telling difficult truths effectively *means* understanding how we're afraid that *this* truth might lead *this* person to reject us for *this* reason and then knowing exactly what to say to prevent that rejection.

Algolalophobics get into trouble because they think they can ward off rejection by simply not saying difficult things. But the truth they've held back will eventually pop out. And the very fears that prevented them from thinking about how to say it effectively will create the rejection they could have warded off if they'd acknowledged what they were afraid of in the first place and done something to prevent it from coming true.

Exposure

Sometimes we need to preserve our privacy to feel safe. Even with the people who are closest to us, from whom we'd like to think we have no secrets, we need pockets of privacy, whether our secret is a recurrent sexual fantasy we know they'll find disturbing or a junky food we snack on when no one is around.

The words we find so hard to say are always a kind of window on some previously hidden area. What makes it so scary is the risk of being exposed in unexpected ways or of being surprised by the way the other person responds to what we've suddenly revealed.

For example, Brian told his coworkers the truth about why he'd taken so many sick days: he had lymphoma but there was a good chance he wouldn't die and probably wouldn't even become very sick. Unfortunately Brian revealed his condition during a stressful transition when half the staff was turning over and everyone felt deprived and suspicious. And he told them his bad news coldly, without giving them any opportunity to talk to him about it.

They jumped to the conclusion that Brian was lying and that he was really dying of AIDS. People who had trouble dealing with someone who had AIDS treated Brian with disdain. Other people who might have been supportive were furious with him for what they thought of as his lie and yet didn't feel they could confront him with it. Brian's story reveals this basic fear we have of telling a difficult truth: people will jump to some conclusion about us that we can neither predict nor control.

Conflict

I talk a lot about fear of conflict in a general way as what algolalophobics are afraid of, but fear of conflict really has a more specific meaning. It's related to the fear of anger, but they're quite different. At root, fear of anger is fear of what the other person will do. Fear of conflict is fear of what you'll be forced to do and what you'll be faced with losing. In other words, this deep fear that fills so many of us when we have something that's hard for us to say is really the fear of opening a painful and difficult struggle in which we'll be forced to fight (which feels uncomfortable enough) and might end up losing a great deal.

For example, suppose you and your partner have always done the same kind of thing when you go on vacation. What's hard for you to say is that you're bored to death with spending half the day lying on the beach and the other half of the day playing golf. You'd much rather walk through the cities of Europe from one museum to another.

But do you really need the incredible hassle you're going to have to go through if you open your mouth? You're afraid of what it's going to take to get your partner to go on the kind of vacation you want. Think of the conflict that will arise when you say how much you've grown to hate the vacations you used to love, because by your words you'll be destroying the sense your partner had that the two of you felt the same way. Think of the battle you will have to wage to get what you want, including possibly finding yourself forced to demand separate vacations.

Talk about fear of conflict! You know how your partner will keep the argument going in bed when you should be falling asleep and over the weekend and every time you go out together. You know the concessions your partner will start demanding from you as a price for even considering what you want, much less agreeing to it.

All you wanted was to speak the truth of how you felt, and just look at the battles you got drawn into.

We all remember conflicts like this growing out of experiences where we shared what was in our hearts and immediately found ourselves locked in a cold or not-so-cold war with the other person. If losing weren't scary enough, the thought of fighting on and on is at least as scary.

Overcoming Your Fears Right Now

Here's something you can do right now to deal with your fears directly. Ask yourself, *Where have I experienced this outcome before?* If, for example, you're afraid the other person will start yelling at you, think about the last time you said something that was hard for you to say and the other person really did yell at you. It might've been in your childhood. But don't forget your more recent past: people often overlook that the experiences that made them afraid of saying something difficult might have come from their adult years.

The important thing isn't when it happened but what impact it had on you. Sometimes people's reactions when we speak the truth serve as a kind of permanent posthypnotic suggestion. For example, a person who was deeply frightened by one snarling, barking dog as a kid learned a lesson that got generalized to all dogs. Now every time any dog gets near, he acts the way he did when he was first confronted by that scary dog. In the same way, because you were yelled at once when you told a difficult truth, you're virtually hypnotized into expecting to be yelled at every time.

Steven's story

The same kind of thing has happened to most of us who feel uncomfortable saying difficult things, even if you have no memory of it. Steven, for example, hadn't thought he'd had any bad experiences telling the truth while growing up. He was convinced that his was one of those happy families where you could say whatever you wanted. But I challenged him on this because he was a young man who found some things hard to say indeed. Are you sure, I asked him, that all your experiences saying things were equally easy and made you feel equally comfortable?

Naming the fear

It turns out they weren't. As Steven thought about it, he realized that there'd been a taboo so powerful it was virtually invisible. The truths he was not allowed to speak were criticisms of his parents. It's not that he was directly punished for criticizing them, but if he said anything negative about his mother or father, they'd respond with coldness or hurt feelings. For example, if he said anything critical about his father at all, his mother would say, with a scary chill in her voice, that she didn't like to hear Steven saying that kind of thing. If he criticized his mother, his father would say something to make him feel like a jerk or a monster, like a boy who'd hit his mother.

That Steven was unable to give feedback without feeling that it was dangerous had a devastating impact on his life. Because he couldn't tell people they weren't doing their job properly, it was difficult for him to be an effective boss or coworker. It meant he had to work alone on low-level assignments.

His inability to give feedback also damaged his personal relationships. He went through three marriages. In each one he had legitimate criticisms his wife needed to hear that he was unable to voice. Instead of his wives benefiting from knowing what he liked and what he didn't like so they'd have the opportunity to do things differently, they would think everything was all right until Steven did something to end the marriage, such as getting caught having an affair. He was willing to lose a woman he loved and blame himself for this loss, just to avoid having to give her feedback.

But it made a big difference when Steven finally realized where he'd developed his fear of criticizing anyone. Steven could see that was then and things are different now. His experience with his parents, not something about giving feedback itself, had made him fearful. By understanding where his fear came from, Steven could separate the *origin* of his fear from whether there was a legitimate *cause* for his fear. Origin, yes; legitimate cause, no.

Steven had an insight: "Well, those two people had a big problem with criticism. But maybe most people aren't like them. Maybe there are lots of people who welcome constructive criticism and lots of people who can hear criticism without getting upset if you can say it halfway effectively." This didn't immediately eliminate his fear. But it made it possible for him to learn how to give feedback because he was liberated from thinking his difficulty could not be overcome.

It might have happened yesterday

The experiences that provide a posthypnotic suggestion about the difficulty of saying certain kinds of things don't have to come only from one's childhood. It might be, for example, that a couple of times on a couple of jobs fairly early in your career you asked a boss or coworker for help, and instead of their seeming eager to help you, they responded as if you'd shown weakness or violated some rule of professional behavior. So of course you're suddenly filled with the sense of how dangerous it is to ask people for help. So next time you want to ask someone for help, it feels difficult for you to say what you want.

How do you put experience like this in perspective? The easiest way is to talk to friends. Steven could have asked his friends, for example, if it was a big deal for them if they criticized their parents. Just as your pals might tell you they've had no trouble with dogs, shedding a new light on that one bad experience from your childhood, they also might tell you that it was generally no big deal if they criticized their parents, as long as they did it without seeming hostile or using bad language. Colleagues might tell you that they ask for help at work all the time, particularly on critical projects.

Seeing that you can separate your experience from the experience most people have can be incredibly liberating. The problem isn't that some things can't be said, it's that you're missing some knowledge, some tool, that will enable you to say the difficult truth you're afraid of saying.

Your fear is a real feeling. But it's not a statement about an objective danger out there, no matter how many scary experiences you've actually had. Your fear is only a signal that something's missing from your bag of tricks. And you can always pick up new tricks.

DANCING IN THE DARK WITH YOURSELF

To get right down to it, we always screw up the same way over and over. There aren't a million different ways that you fall into traps when you tell someone the truth. There's usually only one or two things you do—but you do them over and over—and they keep getting you into trouble.

Some people will grow old and die before they're ready to think about the impact their words and style of communicating have. But if you can accept that it takes discipline to build a bridge—whether it's a bridge of steel or a bridge of words—then you're ready to look at the things you do that keep getting you into trouble. Just go through the following list of mistakes and ask yourself which ones you commit. Help for *how* to avoid each mistake follows a brief description of the mistake.

Minimizing

You minimize when you understate the truth or downplay the impact of your truth. If your truth were a number, let's say ninety-seven, you'd be minimizing if when you actually speak your truth you say, "Fifty-two." Then as the discussion proceeds, the next thing you're saying is "Sixty-three" and then "Seventy-four." In other words, you do what I did when I made my little confession to my wife: you downplay your story at first. If you wanted to borrow $10,000 from your father, you'd ask for $5,000 now, and then when you got it, you'd ask for another $5,000. If you wanted to tell your husband you wanted a divorce, you'd say you were thinking of a trial separation.

Solution: *Don't minimize.* Whatever it is that you have to say to the other person, there's a whole, real, complete way of saying what that is. If something really bothers you, it doesn't "sort of" bother you. If you cheated on someone, you didn't just commit an "indiscretion." If you want to postpone your wedding for nine months, you don't simply want to express the feeling that maybe things are going too quickly. Telling the truth means telling the whole truth. If you only knew the anger and mistrust you generate when you begin by minimizing what it is you have to say, you'd never minimize again.

Histrionics

You make this mistake when you can't tell the truth without making it a scene from an Italian opera. If you wanted to postpone your wedding, your opening move would be to talk about how completely terrified you are of marriage altogether and then start passionately attacking your fiancé for whatever flaws you can think of. People who hate confrontations and therefore seem timid and shy often surprisingly end up falling into histrionics.

It's almost as if without pain and passion they could neither motivate themselves nor feel entitled to speak the truth.

Solution: *Don't let passion hide your truth and don't feel that you need passion as a passport to the truth.* There's nothing wrong with histrionics. If you want to be intense, be intense. But emotional intensity is like the volume control on a radio. If it's turned down too low, you can't hear the music. If it's turned up to a certain level, you get the point that the music is really there—the music dominates. But if you turn it up too high, it just seems like noise, and instead of the other person's hearing your music, she has to cover her ears. So don't turn up the emotional volume beyond the point where intensity is all that's heard. If you're at all unclear on this, just ask yourself whether you'd be able to hear this truth spoken in such a revved-up way as you'd been thinking of speaking it.

Vagueness

You make this mistake when the other person can't tell what the truth is that you're telling. I'm continually surprised as a clinician that people of considerable intelligence and worldly accomplishment talk about personal issues in a way that no one knows what the hell they're talking about. "I need your support." "You're not passionate enough." "You're too selfish." These are shorthand versions of usually long speeches in which a soul is bared and yet no truth is revealed. It's the interpersonal equivalent of going into a restaurant and telling the waiter you'd like something, you know, *good.* What can the waiter do with *that?*

Solution: *Know exactly what you want to get.* You don't order food in a restaurant to hear yourself talk. You order it to have the waiter bring you something specific on a plate. It's the same thing when you tell the truth, even when your truth is something as personal as a feeling or a guilty secret. If you tell someone you "feel sad," in the end a lot of words and feelings and thoughts will be exchanged, but are you going to get exactly what you want?

If you don't care what you get, fine. But if you do care what happens, then you have to identify exactly what you want to get as a result of speaking the truth. It doesn't matter what that is: it could be not feeling alone, it could be being heard, it could be getting advice, it could be anything you want. But it has to be the exact thing you want. Otherwise you'll never shake the nagging feeling that telling the truth is too much trouble.

Being Closed

Some people are so nervous about telling a difficult truth that they try to micromanage the entire process. If they're going to give you feedback, then you have to listen in a certain way and respond in a certain way. If you start deviating from the narrow path they're trying to keep you on, then they put all their effort into shutting down your responses, instead of into making sure their truth is heard.

Solution: *Let the other person have his responses.* People aren't predictable and our expectations are usually too narrow. Knowing where you want to go means you can let go of fussing over how you get there. Let the other person say what she wants, do what she wants, feel what she wants, ask for what she wants. What do you care as long as you keep your eye on what you were hoping to get as a result of telling the truth? For example, you decided that your truth fell into the category of guilty secrets because you realized that what you wanted to get was forgiveness, which includes giving the other person what she needs to be able to forgive you. Fine. So what do you care what she makes happen as long as you're aware of trying to move things toward getting your forgiveness?

Lack of Focus

Some people find it's so hard to gear themselves up to reveal a difficult truth that when they finally speak, they say a whole bunch of things, each of which may be valid. But for the person on the receiving end, it's impossible to tell what truth is actually being revealed. By making too many points, you end up actually communicating no point.

Here's an example. Suppose you were thinking about postponing your wedding and you said something like this: "I don't know—this whole thing is moving way too fast—and I'm not happy with the arrangements, and, I don't know, am I even ready to get married? And part of me thinks it would be so nice to have a breathing spell—but you and your mother seem so gung ho on this. It's just that there are things that I wish that I could say to you but there's never a good time and—I love you but sometimes I'm not sure I'm really happy with you—you've been getting so bossy about this wedding. I don't know—I do know that I'm going to make sure that Bobby and Tommy treat me to a really good bachelor party—so, uh, I guess we're really getting married."

What the hell is *that?* Actually it's a transcription of words taped during a therapy session, but what it adds up to is anyone's guess. The *effect* of these words was the same as any confusing but rich and emotionally charged communication: they launched his fiancée into a dozen just as confused but equally emotionally charged directions. Feelings were flying around the room, but people heard only what they wanted to hear or what scared them most. This messy truth created a mess in their relationship.

Solution: *One thing at a time.* I've found, after years of experience, that one of the most important secrets of successful communication is the one-thing rule. Whenever you have something to say, try to have only one thing to say. When I do therapy, I try to focus on and accomplish only one thing per session. When I call someone on the phone for business or professional reasons, I try to have only one item on my agenda. Sometimes that's impossible, but every time I put more items on the agenda, I'm less effective and the experience is less satisfying.

It's like trying to combine a honeymoon with an important business trip: neither one will work out well. So when it comes to telling someone a truth that's important to you, let that truth be one thing at a time and you'll end up much happier.

14 Telling without Telling

Wʜᴀᴛ ᴅᴏ ʏᴏᴜ ᴅᴏ ᴡʜᴇɴ ʏᴏᴜ ɴᴇᴇᴅ ᴛᴏ ᴛᴇʟʟ ᴛʜᴇ ᴛʀᴜᴛʜ but that truth is too hot to handle?

There is an answer.

Let's say you're happily married with two children. You were at your twentieth high school reunion. You were dancing with someone you always liked but who was not an old girlfriend. While you were dancing, you found that you were getting incredibly sexually aroused. You mentioned leaving together to "go get a drink." You really don't know what you were thinking of, but having sex was in the picture. The other person said no, and that was that.

You come home and your spouse asks how your reunion went. What do you say?

Here's another vignette. Let's say that on your job you're feeling overwhelmed by hard work and pressure and conflicting responsibilities. The truth is that you can barely cope and you feel close to the breaking point. You want to tell your boss how you feel or give him feedback about what he's doing or ask to be given fewer assignments.

But then when you have a meeting with him to discuss your performance, he says that you're not quite performing at the top level and hints at possible cutbacks in your division. What do you say?

Then there's the old postpone-the-wedding example. You want to postpone the wedding, but the plans are rapidly getting set in stone. You start to be afraid that saying what you want will break your fiancé's heart, turn your in-laws into mortal enemies, and make everyone think you're a jerk.

Then one day your fiancé mentions being nervous at the thought of married life. What do you say?

The Truth Dilemma

You tell the truth to make things better. That's the fundamental rule this book is based on. We live in a world of moral principles but not a world of simpleminded moral imperative. The truth is an absolute value but we don't always absolutely have to tell the truth. As we talked about in the chapter on whether to tell or not, there are situations (although they're fewer in number than we confrontation-phobics would like) where, to make things better, it's best not to tell the truth.

But then what? Is the only alternative total silence? If you don't tell the whole truth, do you say nothing at all?

That's how most people live: trapped between two stark alternatives. They either tell the whole story, with all the painful details, or they clam up, hiding those details but also hiding real problems that might well be spoken about.

That's what I call the truth dilemma. It occurs when specific events or situations seem to be tangled up with needs and problems as inextricably as a yolk and white in a scrambled egg. And everyone knows that you can't un-scramble an egg. So you sit there with your secret and your feelings and your needs and all the details of your specific situation, and you feel incredibly torn between your need to spill the beans and your fear of making a mess.

I know what most of us do in the face of this dilemma because I have to deal with the aftermath in my office every day. Either it's an aftermath of a bloody mess because the guy in the vignette told his wife that he got an erection while dancing with some woman at his high school reunion and his wife got so upset they had a terrible fight and she ended by throwing him out of the house. Or it's an aftermath in which the other guy completely screws up on the job and has a nervous breakdown to boot because like the sorcerer's apprentice in Disney's *Fantasia* he just can't cope with the pressure and overwork he said nothing about. In other words, you either say too much or you wish you'd said more.

Feeling Conflicted about the Truth

I think we fall into the truth dilemma because of our complex feelings about telling the truth. As confirmed conflict-phobes, we feel so much safer saying nothing. And the part of us that likes to see ourselves as savvy constantly reminds us of the wisdom of keeping our mouth shut. But at the same time, we worship the truth, and we hate ourselves for not serving the truth. If we stay silent, the pressure builds until a moment's agitation causes the truth to spill out.

But if there's one thing most of us are clear about when it comes to the truth, it's that manipulation is evil. If you want to stay silent, fine—you're not a chicken, you're a wise owl. If you want to speak up, fine—you're just being honest, and let the chips fall where they may. But to thread your way between the two means to speak with a forked tongue, and only snakes do that.

And so we deprive ourselves of an important resource. Because we think that the truth is an unscramblable egg, we're stuck between all or nothing.

Information hunger

A truth about human relationships is that they're more hungry for important information than anything else.

This becomes clearest if you think about being a parent, for example. To parent effectively, you have to know what's going on with your kid. If he's not doing well with his schoolwork or he's not getting along with other kids or he's throwing up every day after lunch, you need to know that. If you don't, then the next thing you know, what started as a minor problem has become a major problem that's much harder to solve. On the other

hand, as every parent knows who's been called on to step into a fight between siblings that started because one kid was "looking" at another, there's
information that's really not important. It's just an upsetting distraction. It's
like stuff you see on the news that grabs your attention but really has nothing to do with your life.

Providing information

What we have to do as we contemplate the bombshells of truth we carry inside us is recognize that nothing will work well in our lives unless we provide the people who matter to us with the important information they need
if we're going to prevent terrible problems from developing.

The guy in the vignette who got an erection dancing with a woman at
his high school reunion might just be a victim of meaningless, transitory
horniness. But he might also be expressing with his body something missing
in his sexual relationship with his wife. And that "something missing" might
be incredibly important information that could prevent deep and drastic
distances from opening up between the two of them. Something between
the naked truth of "I got horny for this woman" and total silence might save
their marriage.

He doesn't have to tell her that he got an erection while dancing with a
woman. That would just launch his wife into an orbit of jealousy and insecu-
rity that would cause her to become obsessed with information that's actually unimportant. But he does have to tell her *something*.

And the guy in the other vignette who's overwhelmed on his job is probably smart to avoid making his boss think he "can't handle it," because guys
who can't handle it get replaced. But something between "I can't cut it anymore" and total silence might save his job and career and even his life. And
the fact is, he doesn't have to tell his boss anything that would make him
seem like someone who can't handle it. That would just saddle him with a
negative halo, possibly for years. But he does have to tell him *something*.

Virtual Telling

The answer is what I call *virtual telling*. It's like those virtual-reality devices
you put on your head that make you feel as though you're experiencing

something real, but it's not really real. With virtual telling, you tell *a* truth but you don't tell *the* truth. The person you're telling it to hears something real, but it's not really real. What you're doing is conveying the important information without putting in the bits that will make a mess. You're solving problems without creating new problems. You're releasing the terrible pressure that's building up inside you without detonating a destructive bombshell.

How do you do this? It's really the same old principle: tell the truth but meet the need. The only difference is that this time you lead with the need and leave out the parts of the truth that the "To Tell or Not to Tell?" chapter would tell you to leave out. In other words, you leave out the details that would only create pain and no light.

Suppose you're the guy wondering whether to tell his wife about the erection he got dancing with a woman at his high school reunion. You've always been honest with each other, but this little detail will freak her out. Yet there is still a truth that should be told. How do you find that truth? *You ask yourself what need is pointed out by the real truth you cannot tell.* What you'd have to do if you were this guy is think about what need your erection pointed to, so to speak. What are you wanting and missing that you'd get so aroused dancing with a woman you barely care about? Maybe you don't know, but you are aware that something's wrong.

So you come back from your reunion with a story to tell, one that's vitally important, but you don't tell the literal truth. You only engage in virtual telling.

Virtual Telling in Action

For example, you might say to your wife after you've set aside some time to talk, "Honey, there's something I have to tell you. You know, when I was at my reunion, I thought about all kinds of things. I remembered what it was like to be in love when you're in high school—you know, that kind of crazy passion. And I saw a lot of people in my class who'd already gotten divorced. And I'd like to ask you for something. I think we've been taking each other for granted and things aren't so romantic between us as they used to be. Unless you disagree with that, I'd like to ask you to kind of talk with me and work with me about what we can do to bring back the romance a little. It's not something I'm so good at. And I'm not saying it's your responsibility, but maybe together we can heat things up a little. I just don't want us to lose what we once had. Are you willing to talk to me about this so we can maybe do something about it?"

Knowing the Response You Want

Notice that when you use virtual telling, you still have to decide what category your truth falls into, and this guy decided his truth fell into the category of a request. As long as he was clear about it, he could have told his wife his feelings or given her feedback or made a personal disclosure. It all depended on what response he wanted from her: "I'll do what you want" (a request), "I hear how you feel" (sharing his feelings), or "I'll try to change" (giving feedback).

Look at what he's accomplished. He's made a clear statement that their relationship is a place where people tell the truth without unnecessary pain. Instead of making her crazy by telling her something she'd have no idea what to do with, he's given her something specific to deal with. And instead of adding that one (admittedly true) detail that would have caused her pain and completely distracted her, he told her truths that were real and got to the heart of the important information he needed to focus on.

The truth he told was about the need that the truth he couldn't tell her pointed to, and that's what virtual telling is all about.

Virtual telling at work

Let's go to our other example, the guy whose boss overwhelmed him with work. He can't tell the truth that he just can't cut it and is about to collapse. But the first thing he can do is ask himself what need is pointed to by the truth he can't tell. "What do I need?" This is one of the most difficult questions we ever have to ask ourselves. The pain can be so obvious, but the thing we need that will remove the pain seems completely elusive.

To find the need you just have to work patiently, like a detective. If you were this guy, the truth you couldn't tell, the real truth, would be that you couldn't take all the work that was being piled on you. So, at least as a first step, your need is to have less work. But of course you can't go to your boss and say, hey, I'd like to work less. That's why you're engaged in virtual telling to begin with.

So what you need is something that will get you less work. And what will that be? What, if you had it, would mean you could work less instead of working yourself into a nervous breakdown? Is a personal assistant the answer? Do you guys need to take on more people in your department? Is there some organizational restructuring that would make a big difference, such as dumping off one whole area of responsibility to another department (for efficiency's sake, of course)?

Maybe what you need is more drastic, like a transfer. Maybe, because of the kind of nut your boss is, the only solution is a new job, and what you need from him is a good recommendation when the time comes.

I don't know what you need. But you need to know what you need, and if that means talking to a friend or a counselor, then you've got to do that. But if your truth is connected to any need at all (and if it is not, then you shouldn't waste your time with virtual telling or any other kind of telling), you've got to discover that need and do something about it.

I've talked about how hearing the real truth can be a problem for other people because it creates in them an explosion of unmet needs. Well, your own real truth is creating an explosion of unmet needs in you. And that's why you have to identify the most important of these needs. And that's why you have to deal with your need through virtual telling, so you don't create a completely new and yet utterly distracting set of needs.

So how do you go from telling a real truth to virtual telling? Ask yourself what need is pointed out by the real truth you cannot tell. Now let's go through the six categories, where I can give you some more detailed help.

Sharing Feelings

How do I love thee? Let me count the ways. How do you disgust me? Let me say nothing about it.

That's the problem with certain feelings: they make other people upset. And why would you want to create such a bad response that you'll spend all your time and energy dealing with the other person's feelings about your feelings? And this is especially important because, if you remember, a truth falls into the category of sharing feelings because the response you want is "I hear how you feel," not "I hear how *I* feel given how you feel."

In other words, when it comes to communicating feelings, the trick is to communicate a focus and intensity that allows your feelings to get through but doesn't create a response that's so intense that it *prevents* your feelings from getting through. But if you say nothing because you want to avoid that intense response, then you yourself have prevented your feelings from getting through.

Suppose you have a close friend and the two of you have really good times together. But when she's not with you, she's increasingly been sleeping with men who give her money so that . . . well, she's turned into a whore. You can barely believe it yourself, but the facts are there. This story might sound incredible, but it's based on a true case and it reflects a common pattern where people who are important to us do things we can't stand.

But the problem is that you sense something must be going on with your friend's self-esteem, so that if you tell her how disgusted you are, it'll be even harder for her to hear than if she were feeling okay about herself. So you can't say how you feel but you have to say something.

So you go to the principle. You ask yourself what need is pointed out by the real truth you cannot tell. You certainly don't have a *need* to tell your friend how disgusted you feel with her. In a sense you need her to turn her life around and stop being such a slut, but on the other hand it's her life. Well, as you think about it, you realize that the other thing you feel besides disgust is fear. You're afraid about what your friend's doing and what it will lead to. And you're afraid because you care about her.

Fear and caring are feelings you can share with your friend. Sharing those feelings is a form of virtual telling about the feeling you can't share, your disgust. You're not lying: you really do feel fear and caring. And why pour out your disgust when if you talk about your fear and caring, your message will get through without your relationship being placed in jeopardy?

Giving Feedback

Let's say you're aching to give your boss some feedback, like with a two-by-four upside the head. The feedback is simple: "You're too bossy. You over-control and micromanage. You're so busy telling me what to do and how to do it that I never have time to actually go and do it."

But you can't give your boss that feedback. He won't promise to change. Instead, he'll give you a big lecture about how he *is* the boss and you're the one with problems about taking direction. Besides, he'll say, you're slow to learn. And before you know it, a discussion where you were going to give feedback has turned into a discussion where you get feedback. Instead of his changing he's yelled at you.

This situation cries out for virtual telling. You're going to explode if you don't tell at least some truth and get your boss to agree to make some kind of change. Maybe it won't be exactly what you want, but if it's close enough, your life will be a lot better.

So what need of yours does the truth you can't say point to? The truth is that your boss is too bossy. The need you have is for him to let you the hell alone. But you can't tell him that he's too bossy.

Meredith's story

Here's a solution one person came up with. If you can't say your truth, there's always something else you can say that will serve the same purpose. Meredith's boss was all business and rarely took things personally. Following her intuition, Meredith told her boss that she thought he didn't like her and that he was trying to make it hard for her to like him. She added that she understood that this wasn't junior high school and their jobs weren't about people liking each other, but still it was too bad.

As Meredith had guessed would happen, her feedback threw her boss for a loop. She wasn't trying to tell him how to do his job, but he was just sensitive enough about workplace relationships to know that people not liking each other is a problem. Although he was tempted to dismiss what she said, what he actually said was, "Well, I'd like you to think I like you and I don't want to make it hard for you to like me. I don't know what I'm doing to make you feel this way, but if I can change, then I'd like to change."

So Meredith said, "Well, gee, I don't know, but the way you're always criticizing and controlling every little thing I do is what most makes me feel that you don't like me. Maybe you think that if you didn't like me, you'd just leave me alone. But I'd be feeling a lot more liked by you if you weren't always after me." Amazingly, this worked. Meredith's virtual telling accomplished everything that telling the real truth would've accomplished, but it tapped into an area that made her boss feel concerned, not justified.

The point isn't for you to use the exact strategy Meredith used. But there's always some less troublemaking way of giving feedback that focuses on an area where another person will want to change and where that change will give you much of what you wanted in the first place. What's interesting about Meredith's virtual feedback is that it was something that you might've thought was hard to say—"I don't think you like me"—that was actually easier to say than the real feedback it replaced.

Asking for Something Difficult

Sometimes there's nothing harder to ask for than information. "Do you love me?" "What do you really think of me?" "Are you planning to let me go?" "Can I get more from you than you're offering?" "What are you going to do?"

These questions might be innocuous in some contexts, but lots of times asking for information will either annoy the hell out of the other person or cause him to go into hiding or make you doubt the value of what he's saying precisely because you asked. And few bits of information are harder to ask for, if you happen to be a woman, than just what some guy you're going out with has in mind for the two of you. It's not that you aren't a tough, smart woman. It's that you're afraid that if you put on pressure or seem needy, the guy will panic and bolt. Besides, you'd like him to tell you he wants to marry you, for example, without your having to prompt him.

So what you're asking for is information: "Is marrying me something you're thinking about or is it something you'd never consider?" But you can't ask that. But that request is your truth, and you've got to ask something.

Ivy's story

Here's where virtual asking comes in. Ivy had been staying at Rick's almost all the time for six months, but she kept paying the rent on her own apartment, where she spent an occasional weekend. To Ivy, the two of them seemed highly compatible, and Rick seemed genuinely fond of her.

But she was twenty-nine and Rick was twenty-seven. In Ivy's view, thirty was just around the corner, and the time when her biological clock would stop ticking was just around the corner from that. She frankly admitted (but only to me and her close friends) that she was getting a case of marriage panic.

Rick, while a good, responsible guy, was romantically inexperienced for his age. He'd simply worked too hard to have the time to date many women. Ivy thought Rick, in his own sweet, shy way, would run screaming from the room (so to speak) if she brought up marriage. Or, perhaps worse, he'd go along with their getting married because he wouldn't know how to stop it, but his heart wouldn't be in it.

The question technique

Ivy wanted to know if he'd marry her. She didn't think she could ask him that, but her more general need was to know more about how he worked and what he looked forward to and planned for himself. So Ivy decided to go on a campaign of asking Rick questions about all kinds of things, "just to get to know you better." She asked him how he felt about married guys having affairs. She asked him how old his father was when he got married. She asked him if he wanted to have sex with a whole bunch of different women: "I mean, like, are you a variety freak?" She asked him how he felt his parents' divorce affected him. She asked him if he thought he'd be a good father, if he even wanted to be a father.

Ivy asked Rick these questions and many others like them over a long time so that at no point would he start feeling grilled. And she was careful to be positive and accepting about every answer he gave so that he wouldn't start feeling he would get in trouble for giving the "wrong" answer. They were all virtual questions. At no point did she ask directly about the one thing she wanted to know because she felt it would put too much pressure on Rick and either she wouldn't find out anything or she'd push him away.

Of course, information is only one of the endless things we want to ask for from the people in our lives. But what Ivy shows is that if for some reason you can't directly ask for one thing, you can always use virtual asking to get other things that go most of the way toward meeting your needs. And that's far better than sheer silence, which leaves you frustrated and resentful, or taking the risk of asking for something you strongly suspect it's a mistake to ask for.

Confessing a Guilty Secret

Virtual telling is never more useful than when it comes to confessing a guilty secret. When I think about my stupid little involvement with that other woman and how I confessed it to my wife, I often think I would've been better off confessing something that would've done the job as far as pointing to issues in our relationship but that wouldn't have been so devastating.

Let's face it, there are three main reasons why we confess a guilty secret.

One is that the other person will find out anyway. So you confess so you can at least get credit for honesty. Here virtual telling can't help you.

The second reason for confessing is that there's a real problem in your relationship that your guilty secret points to, and confessing is a way of highlighting that problem. But if that's the case, the question is whether there's a better way to highlight the problem than making that specific confession.

The third reason for confessing is that you feel guilty and want forgiveness. But that's not necessarily a reason for confessing to the person you've wronged. If she doesn't know what you did, then by confessing, you're adding painful knowledge to your original transgression. In the moment of asking forgiveness you're increasing what there is to be forgiven.

To virtually tell or not to virtually tell

In the "To Tell or Not to Tell?" chapter I tried to make clear the specific circumstances when not telling is better. And I also tried to make a case for why in general we all need and deserve more truth. So I don't want this discussion of virtual confessing to seem like an invitation to hide. There's one other reason for confessing that I haven't mentioned, but it's really a reason for telling any of the categories of truth. It's that in general we all want and need more truth in our lives. More truth is healing.

But we tell the truth to make things better. If the content of your guilty secret will make things worse, everyone will be grateful for your using virtual confessing. Suppose I'd used it when it came to my own situation with my wife. What could I have confessed that would've been a big enough deal to have got my wife's attention and made her see that we were drifting apart and that things were getting serious, but that wouldn't have pressed all her buttons?

How about this. Suppose I'd confessed that, instead of getting actually but nonsexually involved with another woman, I was having sexual fantasies about another woman but wasn't actually involved with her. My wife certainly knew that you can't control the mind, and she certainly believed that there's a big difference between thinking about something and acting on it. Saying that I was thinking about sleeping with another woman whom I wasn't involved with would've seemed serious to her without making her insecure. After all, my confession was a sign that she could trust me.

The trick with a virtual confession is that it's got to be a lie that tells the truth (which was Picasso's definition of art). It's not a weaselly lie that gets you off the hook. Instead it's a well-intentioned lie that points to important issues that will get lost if you tell the real truth.

Revealing Explosive Personal Information

I think most of us have had the experience of entering into some kind of business or personal relationship and having some bit of information we know we should reveal but we're reluctant to bring out. There never seems to be a good time to reveal it, and as the weeks and months go by, it both seems less relevant and yet you seem more guilty for not having revealed it, so there's all the more reason to keep quiet. The only problem is that you feel guilty, and besides, there's some good reason why the other person should know this fact.

Jessica's story

Jessica was a young psychiatrist who came to see me with a number of different problems. One problem was a recurrence of the kind of paranoid thoughts that had ended up putting her in a private mental hospital for many months back when she was in college. But the other problem was that the people at the HMO where she'd recently been hired didn't know that she had a history of mental illness. She felt she had all kinds of ethical and professional reasons for telling them the truth about her past mental illness. However, she felt that this might ruin her career, and based on solid evidence that I knew, Jessica was an unusually sensitive and talented clinician and the world would be a worse place for losing her potential contribution.

Jessica came up with the solution herself. Patients need to be protected from impaired physicians, but that applies only to current impairments. Jessica decided to tell her supervisor that she was currently in therapy for stress-related problems. She told her supervisor he could call me and told me that I could tell her supervisor anything about her I wanted to except that she'd previously been hospitalized. She also asked me not to scare her boss about her, but that if I felt that she was currently impaired in such a way as to affect her performance as a clinician, I should tell him. Jessica's virtual telling consisted of revealing pertinent information about her present circumstances while keeping silent about her probably irrelevant past hospitalization.

Something interesting happened with this. The minute Jessica found a solution to her what-to-reveal problem, she felt a lot less stress. That stress reduction alone seemed to cause a marked reduction in the paranoid thoughts that had brought her into treatment with me in the first place. As I worked with Jessica to find ways to further reduce on-the-job stress, her entire mental status continued to improve.

Bringing Bad News

Obviously, in plenty of situations it's simply impossible to bring "virtual bad news." You can't virtually fire someone. If someone's dog got run over when you were house-sitting for him, you can't do anything but tell him his dog got run over.

But in many situations the actual bad news isn't such a simple, unavoidable fact, and it's possible to take different views of what actually happened and to select what the best thing is to say.

Back to Ron

If you remember Ron at the beginning of the book, he had to give his wife the bad news that he was no longer on the fast track at the company where he was an executive. Ron, of course, blurted out his news in a painful and destructive way. He could've told the truth in a much more effective way by meeting his wife's needs about this truth.

But it's possible that Ron knew things about his wife and his life with her that would have made virtual telling a smarter idea. In other words, he could've begun by asking himself what his own needs were. Was his need for his wife to stop bugging him about promotions that weren't going to happen? Was it for her to not run up debts they wouldn't be able to pay off? Was it for her to stop living vicariously through his career? Was it for her to think highly of him regardless of the vicissitudes of fortune?

I unfortunately didn't see Ron until after the damage had been done by his blurting out his bad news in an unthinking way. Based on what I learned about their relationship, I think there's a fifty-fifty chance Ron could have found a way to tell the truth and meet his wife's needs. But I also learned that Ron's biggest concern had been his fear that his wife wouldn't think highly of him. All he'd wanted was her respect. And he hadn't been able to face the possibility that her respect was based on his promotions. Only one guy gets the top job anyway. Why even get going in that game of promotion-based respect?

In our work together, Ron realized the difference it made that he was a lawyer, a professional, someone of stature and accomplishments who did worthwhile things regardless of the power he had. You don't become a lawyer to get promotions. So Ron saw that instead of telling his wife the truth, he could have engaged in virtual telling and let her know that he'd been put on special, important projects. What difference would it have made that those projects were off the fast track? They were for him important and interesting in themselves.

Not only could Ron have told his wife his bad news in a less harmful way, but he could have revealed what was going on without telling her the bad news at all. It was only bad news from the point of view of losing out on the possibility of big bucks much further down the line.

What This Means for You

I'm not advocating virtual telling. I'm advocating truth telling. But our largest goal isn't truth in and of itself but the information and healing that comes with communicating the truth.

Think of the truth as a kind of healthful herb. Most of the time it works its magic all by itself. But some herbs with incredible healing properties are also highly toxic under certain conditions. You can't take them straight. And that's the way it is with the truth sometimes. You can extract the essence of what you're trying to accomplish while eliminating the harmful properties that would make you sorry afterward that you told the truth.

So if you have some bombshell to reveal to someone, gauge whether it's best to reveal the whole truth. If you sincerely determine that the world will be a better place if you reveal only part of the truth or only a shaded version of it, then virtual telling is your answer.

15 Preparing for What Will Happen after You Tell

Wʜᴇɴ ʏᴏᴜ ᴛᴇʟʟ sᴏᴍᴇᴏɴᴇ ᴛʜᴇ ᴛʀᴜᴛʜ, what you want, of course, is that instead of responding like a nut, the other person won't get upset, won't emotionally disconnect from you or physically walk out on you, won't start a fight, won't make you crazy by changing the subject or bringing in extraneous issues, won't be blind to your needs. In other words, you want the other person to respond to your truth as if it were simply information and not a red flag to a bull.

You now realize that the most important way to prevent him from going nuts is to meet whatever needs he's going to have when he hears your truth. Still, for each of us some potential responses from the other person are particularly frightening: being insulted or rejected or threatened, or being met with silence or tears, or any of the other responses.

Whatever your biggest fear, that's the response it's most important for you to prepare for. And the best way to prepare is to prevent it by the very way you tell your truth. Here are some of the responses people have the most trouble with, and here are ways to head off these responses.

Will the Other Person Feel Blamed or Attacked?

Someone feels blamed by you when, no matter what your words are, he hears you saying to him, "Because you're bad in this way, it's your fault that . . ." And you know someone feels blamed by you when he attacks you back or starts explaining himself or starts arguing with how you see things. Because people hate so much to feel blamed, they'll put all their energy into dealing with their sense of blame—so much so that they might not hear one single word of the truth you're trying to communicate.

For example, suppose that all you want to do is postpone your wedding. But in your attempt to justify what you want, you criticize your fiancée. You make it sound as though the reason you want to postpone it is that there's something wrong with her. Instead of the truth of the postponement issue lying there on the table for the two of you to deal with, you'll end up arguing about all the things she does that she thinks you think are bad and whether she does them at all and how bad they really are. And what about all the bad things about you! If you'd only done this or that, your fiancée will argue, the two of you wouldn't be in this fix in the first place.

But you could have prevented her response from being all about her feeling blamed or attacked by taking out of the truth you had to tell anything that sounded like criticism. That's not to say that she couldn't still go on to feel blamed. But at least then you could consistently point to how you'd done and said nothing to indicate blame. In other words, you want to be able to say, "It's not you; it's me." But you can't do that if you've been saying, "It's you."

Confrontation-phobics beware

Confrontation-phobics often make a huge mistake here. They do everything they can to stay as far away as possible from the response they're most dreading. If they're afraid of the other person's feeling attacked, instead of preventing the other person from feeling blamed by making it clear why the other person shouldn't feel blamed, they say nothing at all. Why bring up the very thing they find it most hard to deal with?

But this is like not taking an umbrella to work on a day when you're afraid it will rain because you think that taking the umbrella will make it rain. It's like not buying life insurance because you're afraid that it will bring about your death. It's like not clearing a project with your boss in advance because you're afraid he'll say no to it. It's understandable. But it's stupid. A good salesman or lawyer knows that if a difficulty already exists in the mind of the person who has to make the decision, silence doesn't make that difficulty go away. Instead you bring it up yourself to take away its power.

People can feel blame no matter what your truth is, for example when you make a request. They might feel blamed for putting you in the position of having to make the request in the first place or for not having given you whatever it is you want without your having to ask. Or they might feel unable to meet your request and feel blamed for whatever is wrong with them that they can't meet your request.

And if people feel blamed for everything, imagine how they feel when you're criticizing them. As a clinician for families and individuals and as a consultant to organizations, I sometimes feel it's a miracle that any feedback ever gets through at all because of the degree to which feedback stimulates a sense of feeling blamed. You might think that all you're saying is do more of this or do this differently, but the other person hears you saying that he's just no damn good.

It's up to you. If when you tell your truth you want to talk only about it, then you've got to prevent the blame monster from appearing and eating up the truth you're trying to convey.

Solutions

Here's how to do it. Make sure that as you tell your truth, you say clearly and directly, "I'm not blaming you." Don't say, "I'm not blaming you but here's why it's your fault." Instead say, "I'm not blaming you," and offer praise and hope. You prevent blame from appearing by preempting it with praise and hope. You think about how the other person would feel blamed and you praise him in a way that prevents that sense of blame. You convey hope in a way that prevents a sense of blame.

Instead of saying flatly, for example, that you want to postpone the wedding, you talk about how wonderful your fiancé is and what you value about him and how much you're looking forward to a life with him. You say all this before you talk about the postponement, and you say it again afterward.

If you want to do something as simple as telling a friend or a loved one that they need to lose weight (assuming that you've decided that that's a wise thing to do), then you've got to preempt the sense of blame everyone feels when someone calls them fat—the sense that if they're fat, it's because they're weak and self-indulgent and self-loathing and defective in a dozen other ways. You could say something like "I'm only telling you this because I know you can handle hearing it and can respond appropriately, but I've noticed that you've been putting on weight recently and I'm worried about you. But you've got three months before your speech to the convention, and that's plenty of time to get down to the weight you want without killing yourself."

Extra help

But what do you do if, in spite of your efforts, the other person responds as if you're blaming or attacking him? You simply repeat over and over if necessary that you're not blaming them or criticizing them or putting them down in any way. Even if your truth is a criticism, you can make it clear that other than this specific piece of feedback, which you're hopeful about their being able to change, you don't feel any blame toward them.

If they continue to act as though you're attacking, you can say explicitly, "What do you need not to feel blamed here? What can I do so that you won't feel blamed?" Then the ball's in their court. Then you're basically saying that either there's a problem you can solve or they're a nut. And if someone insists on feeling blamed in spite of your making it clear that you'll do everything necessary to take the blame out of what you're saying, then the best thing to do is just assume that they've got to go through a period of feeling blamed as a way of digesting your truth.

Defensiveness is like an infection. You'd be surprised at how rarely it comes up when efforts are taken to prevent it. If it's still there in spite of your best efforts, you can always respond as if the other person is simply telling you the truth of her feelings and say, "I hear how you feel. I'm sorry you feel that way. Is there anything I can do?"

Will the Other Person Reject What You're Putting Out about Who You Really Are to Each Other?

I need to explain a bit what I mean by this. You are your parents' child, your child's parent, your spouse's spouse, your boss's employee, your subordinate's boss, your doctor's patient, your car mechanic's customer . . . You see, that's the problem. You may see yourself as your mechanic's customer, and if the customer's always right, then you're the boss. But your car mechanic may see himself as your adviser, and people are always supposed to listen to their advisers, which makes him the boss.

Here's another example of how who you are to someone can get confused. When you were little, it was clear what it meant for you to be your parents' child, but when you became a teen, the issue of figuring out who you were to each other became a battleground. Could they continue to treat you like a little kid? Or should they treat you like an adult?

When your truth alters your relationship

There's always the potential for who you are to someone to turn into a battleground. And difficult truths have a way of bringing out potential sources of conflict about who you are to the other person.

Just look at the postponing-the-wedding example. While you're engaged, you're supposed to be committed to each other. By suggesting a postponement, you're saying that your bond is less clear and less tight than the other person had thought it was. You're also supposed to be equal partners. After all, you jointly made the decision to get married. If you're saying you want a postponement, you're saying you can make decisions about the nature of your relationship without consulting the other person. Well, who died and made you king?

And if you criticize someone, who are you to be criticizing her? And if you ask for something, who are you to feel you have a right to ask for it and to get it? And when I made my confession to my wife, she saw me as changing the nature of our relationship from committed and exclusive to less committed and only semi-exclusive, and she also felt as if I was saying that I could make those changes and she couldn't. Well, she wouldn't sit still for that. No, no, no, she said—because of what you did, if anyone has the right to say who we are to each other, it's me.

You have to choose

So you have to be careful with this issue. You can tell someone the truth. Or you can try to change your relationship with someone. But if you try to do both at the same time, you're going to get into trouble. So if you were coming out to your parents, for example, telling them you're gay gets through more easily if at the same time you grant their wish for how the relationship is defined. In other words, "I'm gay and I'm a grown-up and you can't tell me what to do" is a much tougher sell than "I'm your son and I'll always love you and respect you, but because I'm your son, I think you're entitled to know the truth about me, which is that I'm gay."

Lots of people have trouble coming out to their parents precisely because they've battled so hard and so unsuccessfully to be seen as adults who can do what they want that they're unwilling to *ask* for acceptance as gays, particularly when this asking is in the relationship of child to parent.

Solutions

The way to avoid the problem of there being a big fight about who you are to each other, if it's possible to avoid it at all, is to ask yourself, first of all, who you *actually* are to each other, not who you'd like to be to each other. Second, you have to ask yourself who the other person *thinks* you are to each other. Third, you have to let go of what you'd *like* the two of you to be to each other.

With my wife, that's who we actually were to each other: husband and wife, and not in the sixties-style, open-marriage sense, but in the more traditional 100 percent monogamous sense. Who my wife thought we were was people who respected each other's wishes. So this was definitely not the time for me to make a bid for us to be two people who went off and did whatever they wanted, although that's exactly how my confession came across.

What I should have done instead and what you should do is *reinforce the other person's definition of who you are to each other* as you tell your truth. Often it will seem as if it's against your interest to do this. Why would I have reinforced that we were supposed to be special to each other and respect each other's wishes when the very thing I was confessing was violating that?

Suppose you have an employee with whom you've had a buddy-buddy relationship, and now you need to give him feedback about what a lousy job he's been doing. This is just when you'd feel like reasserting your role as boss, and it would feel stupid to underline your role as friend if that's exactly what makes it hard for you to come on as boss.

But here's what I'm suggesting you do. You don't have to surrender your sense of who you are to each other. But as part of telling your truth you have to openly acknowledge that you understand the other person's sense of who you are to each other. Like this: "I know we've had a very friendly working relationship, more like two pals than boss-employee, so I understand that that makes it hard for you to hear what I have to say, but . . . ," and then you give your feedback.

If you think there's going to be a problem about who the two of you think you are to each other, then you have to openly and directly acknowledge the other person's sense of your relationship so that he's quieted down to the point where he can hear your truth.

Will the Other Person Feel You're Pushing Him Too Far or Making Too Many Demands?

You want to tell your fiancé that you'd like to postpone the wedding. But suppose the two of you have been struggling over the past month and a half about a seemingly endless series of details not only having to do with your wedding but with what kind of a life the two of you are going to have together. Your fiancé sees you as having been pushing and demanding.

How do you think he'll hear your saying you want to postpone the wedding?

It'll feel like, "While you're up anyway, would you mind going to the kitchen and getting me a beer, and while you've got the fridge open, would you mind taking out the salad fixings, and while you've got the salad fixings out on the table, would you mind making the salad, and since you're making a salad anyway, wouldn't some lasagna go well with it?" This is an exaggeration, but it's actually realistic as an illustration of how your truth often makes other people feel.

With my wife and me, we'd been growing apart precisely because, among other things, I'd started making decisions about things husbands and wives usually discuss, like spending money or disciplining the kids. Then I come mentioning this "other woman," even though it's a confession, and my wife hears it as just one more demand, particularly when I refuse to do what my wife wants about not seeing this woman anymore.

The straw that broke the camel's back

What often happens when you criticize people? Don't they act as if they've been on the receiving end of an endless stream of criticism, *and now this?* What often happens when people come out to their parents? Don't their parents often act as though there's been a long stream of difficulties and disappointment, *and now this?* In a way this reaction makes sense. A difficult truth *is* a burden. It *does* make demands. That's why it's difficult.

Solutions

You minimize the problems this issue causes by making sure that when you tell your truth, you take away some of the demands that might seem to come with it. And here's how you do this.

First, to the extent that what you're revealing places a demand that cannot be escaped, *you freely acknowledge the full extent of the demand*. If you wanted to postpone the wedding, for example, you could say, "I know you've already made a ton of concessions about our life together after we're married, so I know it's not fair of me to ask you to make a still bigger concession, but . . . ," and then you talk about the postponement. The reason you do this is that by *your* talking about the demands, the other person doesn't have to.

Second, *indicate all the ways you're not making demands*. Suppose you had to confess that you'd actually had an affair. A confession is satisfying to you if the other person says, "I forgive you." But if you indicate that you're willing to do what the other person wants you to do to earn her forgiveness, then that's a lot better than your demanding forgiveness in exchange for nothing at all. And if you indicate that you're hoping your partner forgives you but you understand if she's extremely upset, then you're saying that on top of forgiveness you're not also demanding that she swallow her feelings and pretend nothing happened.

Now you see why people who come out to their parents do better when they ask their parents to love and accept them but don't make the additional demand that their parents change the way they feel in general about a "homosexual lifestyle."

Inexperienced or unrealistic people expect they'll get what they want when they tell the truth. Discouraged people are willing to settle for whatever they get when they tell the truth. But wise people know they should pay attention to what they want and try to get it, but that they should also accept what's realistic for them to get. Telling the truth is a big deal. If you include too many implicit demands along with it, you'll just overload the other person.

Will the Other Person Feel You're Pulling the Rug Out from under Him So He No Longer Knows What's Real?

It makes a lot of people crazy when they're no longer sure that what they thought was true really is true. This is why if you tell someone you want to postpone your wedding, for example, she's likely to say, "Well, screw you. First you didn't want to get married, but then you were all gung ho about this wedding and talked about how we'll love each other forever, and now you want to postpone it, and tomorrow you'll want to elope or you'll want to marry someone else or you'll want to move to Timbuktu or you'll tell me you're a woman trapped in a man's body or who knows what. Why don't we have nothing to do with each other until you can make up your mind about what's what?"

Again, a difficult truth is radical news. It's the kind of truth that rocks someone's sense that he knows what his world is like. That's why when you criticize a coworker, he's likely to say, "But you told me you liked what I do."

Or you come out to your parents and they start telling you about all the people of the opposite sex they remember you dating.

Or you ask someone for a loan and he suddenly isn't sure whether you're trustworthy or solvent or responsible anymore or whether your relationship is based on friendship or cash—nothing is what it seemed.

Or you tell someone you feel bored by a project the two of you are working on and he doesn't know if you're committed to it anymore.

In all these cases, you've shifted reality around so that the other person has to struggle to reorient himself. No wonder so many difficult truths put such a strain on relationships. We feel comfortable with someone because we know what's real. Undermine that confidence in what's real, and the relationship suddenly becomes less desirable.

Solutions

Here's how you deal with this when you come to tell your difficult truth. *You acknowledge the discrepancy between the new version of reality and the old version.* You say words to the effect, "I know I was acting as if one thing were the case, so I understand how it's hard for you to accept what I'm telling you now."

For example, you might say, "I know I've been going along with our wedding plans as if everything were fine, and now I'm talking about a postponement as if when I was going along with everything, I was really living a lie, so I can see how you'd feel confused and suspicious, but I wasn't even clear about what was real for me for a long time, and then once I saw how I felt, I wanted to make sure I meant it before I said anything. And that's why I waited to speak until now."

In the same way, with my wife I should've acknowledged the way I had not told her about my friendship with the other woman when it was first starting, and that therefore for a period of many months I had been lying and cheating about what was really going on.

In other words, if someone's confused about what's real, you don't make things better by denying that something's making him confused. If you think the other person might get confused about what's real because of the truth you're telling, then acknowledge that reality has shifted and you can understand how the other person might find this confusing.

Will the Other Person Feel Tremendously Disappointed?

It's one thing to criticize a person, for example, but it's another thing to criticize him when he's expecting to be told how terrific he is. It's one thing to ask your father for money, but it's another thing to ask your father for money when after much difficulty he finally thinks you've gotten launched in life. It's one thing to speak from your heart and say that your preference would be to set a date for the wedding many, many months in the future, but it's another thing to talk about postponing the wedding after the date's been set.

As hard as it is to hear some things, specific expectations often add greater difficulty. In a sense this is a version of "Tell the truth but meet the need." Needs grow out of expectations. Anytime you can identify an expectation, you'll have gone far toward meeting the other person's need.

Uncovering expectations

There's no magic formula for uncovering what someone's expectations might be. The secret lies in knowing the other person. You don't have to be intimate with her, but you do need to get a sense of her life so you can make a good guess about her expectations. People who report a successful experience telling their parents they're gay, for example, are usually sensitive to the ways their parents have been expecting to become grandparents. You don't have to be a genius to do this. You just have to remember to ask yourself, "If I say this to this person, what expectations will my words be flying in the teeth of?"

Of course, many expectations are predictable. The wedding-postponement example is all about disappointed expectations. If you've ever had to fire someone, you know exactly what expectations you're confronting: not being fired.

But it's often vital to dig deeper. The most powerful expectations can lie below the surface. People have hidden agendas. People have stories they tell themselves about what will happen and what it means.

Will's story

An actor friend of mine had a difficult time making it, as most actors do, but Will finally reached a certain level of visibility and desirability in the New York theater world. He understood how competitive the business was, and when his agent called him to tell him he didn't get a specific role, my friend wasn't particularly devastated.

But when his agent called about a smallish role he was up for and told him the producers wanted him to audition, my friend was so devastated he threatened to quit the business. He'd gotten it into his head that he'd reached the level where people knew his work well enough so he wouldn't have to audition like some kid starting out. When his agent said Will was going to have to audition for the role, my friend heard it as, "You're a no-body in this business and you always will be."

I don't know about you, but I think it's reasonable to think that the agent could have told my friend about the audition in a way that was sensitive to his expectations and helped him understand what it meant.

Finding clues

Here are some questions you can ask yourself that will help you clue into the other person's expectations:

- What hopes or dreams has the other person had in this area?
- Is there some special way the other person's felt particularly safe?
- Is there something here the other person feels particularly proud of?
- Has the other person made plans that will be intercepted by your truth?
- Has the other person formed an image of you or your relationship that she cherishes?

Here, too, "Tell the truth but meet the need" is the beacon by which you should navigate. A disappointed expectation is just a particular kind of need.

Solutions

Here's what you can do.

If appropriate, you can tell the other person that in spite of how it seems, *her expectations haven't been disappointed at all.* For example, once my friend's agent learned Will was so disappointed he was thinking of leaving show business, the agent told him stories of huge stars who still had to audition for roles. Often lesbians and gay men who come out to their parents can talk about their plans for having children and make it clear that their parents will become grandparents after all. The person who's asking to postpone the wedding can make his commitment to going through with the wedding absolutely clear.

I could've done this with my wife. I could've acknowledged that my being interested in another woman made it look as though her expectation that we'd be special to each other was unrealistic, but in fact nothing had changed for me. I might be stupid and angry, I might feel rejected, but in spite of the fact that we were going through a bad patch, I would do nothing to violate our commitment to each other. That I was confessing something I didn't need to confess was proof of this. I could have made all of this clear if only I'd thought about her disappointed expectations.

Then it's often possible to show that *different expectations are just as reasonable and as good.* People who break up with someone by saying "Let's be friends" are attempting to do this. This has become a cliché, but in some cases when the feelings are real and the possibility is realistic, being good friends is better than being bad lovers.

My friend the actor tells me that a lot of young actors go out to Hollywood hoping to become romantic leads—the newest Sharon Stone or Harrison Ford. The only problem is that these hopes too often don't come true. Wise agents sometimes break the bad news by helping their clients become character actors, where there's less glamour but the work is a lot steadier.

So if your truth means that one of the other person's expectations are dashed, then identifying other expectations that are just as important to him but much more realistic will go far toward preventing him from going nuts when he hears your truth. People don't like being criticized, for example, because among other things it means that they feel less respected. But if when you criticize you talk about how your relationship has moved on to a new level of honesty and openness, then the other person can feel new hope.

Another way you can help someone come to terms with disappointed expectations is by *offering some kind of compensation*. Compensation, at heart, is a kind of gift. The cheapest form of compensation, and yet a surprisingly effective one, is an apology. You say you want to postpone the wedding and you say you're sorry for the postponement. This might sound obvious, but it was something I didn't do when I told my wife my guilty secret. I was afraid that if I apologized for getting close to another woman, I'd be indicating that something bad was going on for which an apology was necessary. No apology, no crime. What I didn't realize was that a sincere apology is a form of payment for loss.

But of course an apology is made up of words. Words are important, but sometimes words are not enough. Remember, the point of this is to find a way to prevent the other person from going nuts when you tell her the truth. So it's vitally important that you ask yourself if there's anything you can do for the other person, anything you can give him, that will take away the sting of his disappointed expectations.

Will the Other Person Feel a Sense of Guilt?

When you make people feel guilty, they are apt to pull away from you or attack you. That's why guilt is so toxic in relationships. Anything you can do to prevent guilty feelings will prevent damage to your relationship. But we're often unaware of how the simple truths we speak make other people feel guilty.

My dog's story

About a year ago I had to bring my old, sick, and failing dog to the vet. I was hoping something could be done, but I was afraid it was all over. After examining him the vet said that little could be done and that given his age she didn't feel it was fair to him to subject him to the anxiety and discomfort of treatment. She recommended putting him to sleep.

I know that these are not words that vets like to say. But this particular vet had an instinctive understanding of just what my loss was. It wasn't so much having my dog die on me. He was old. She must have figured I'd been anticipating his death. Instead, what the vet's bad news really cost me was guilt. I know I found her words comforting when she said, "He's had a very good life, and you've obviously done everything possible for him."

Notice what she was doing. She wasn't addressing my grief. She was addressing my guilt. She didn't have to tell me I could get another dog or that I'd get over feeling bad. I've lost pets before. But if I'd felt he hadn't had a good life or I hadn't done everything possible, I'd have felt guilt that would have been much harder to recover from.

Almost anything you tell to anybody could make them feel guilty. Telling someone you want to postpone the wedding might make him feel guilty for possibly having pressured you. Because he hates feeling guilty, he might astound you by debating about how much pressure he'd put on you.

Solutions

You prevent the other person from feeling guilty as directly as possible. Ask yourself what he might think you're blaming him for, then tell him you don't blame him for it. For example, "I don't want you to think that because I'm asking for a postponement that you've done anything wrong. You haven't pressured me or done anything to make me not want to marry you. I just need the extra time to get myself psychologically ready."

Will the Other Person Feel Betrayed?

It's one thing when your truth disappoints someone. It's another thing when *you* disappoint someone. And often the word for that is *betrayal*.

Suppose you have to call an employee into your office to tell him about how he's been doing a bad job. He might go nuts at being criticized because he was expecting to move up in the company, and so he might give you a big argument about how your criticism is misplaced. But he might go nuts because he felt you should have told him much earlier about the problems he was having, before his poor performance started making such a big difference. Instead of defending himself, he might start attacking you.

Suppose you ask a parent for money. He might be disappointed that you still need money from him. But he might feel betrayed because he'd been under the impression that the last sum of money he gave you was enough.

How could you have done this to me?

The hallmark of betrayal is the other person's wondering how you could deliberately have done this to him. And usually the betrayal doesn't lie in the truth itself but in your not having done something to prevent that truth from being a reality. Your fiancée might be disappointed that you want to postpone the wedding, but she feels betrayed because you didn't take care of whatever needs you had before the wedding date was set.

Solutions

When you think about telling any truth to someone, ask yourself how it might be that he'd feel screwed by you. And the most common ways people feel screwed are "Why didn't you tell me this sooner?" and "Why didn't you do something to prevent this?" And let's face it, you probably could have told the other person sooner or done something to prevent it.

Here too acknowledgment is an important tool. You don't make things better by trying to argue the other person out of his sense of betrayal unless you have overwhelming evidence. So the best thing you can do is tell the other person how sorry you are that you didn't tell him sooner or that you didn't do something to prevent this from coming up in the first place.

Often it's our fear of the other person's feeling betrayed that leads us to hide the truth in the first place, so that when we finally blurt it out, the other person feels even more betrayed. Suppose you're in a romantic relationship with someone that's great except for the sex, where you feel your partner's a little blah and perfunctory. But who wants to make trouble? So you don't say anything.

Should you be stupid enough to just blurt out how you feel, you now know that the other person will probably say, "Why did you let me go along with this? How long did you feel this way without saying anything?" But if you begin by saying, "I wish I'd told you this sooner, but I just didn't know how," then chances are you'll diminish his sense of betrayal.

Will the Other Person Feel Trapped?

Two things make us feel trapped: being made to feel there's only one thing we can do or being made to feel there's only one way we can respond. You tell your fiancée you want to postpone the wedding. You present an excellent case for why this is absolutely necessary for you. The result is that your fiancée feels she's got to do what you want her to do and feel the way you want her to feel. She might not do it or feel it, but the sense of being trapped comes from knowing she'll pay a price for not going along with it relatively cheerfully.

Now, you might think that no one's feeling trapped, since other people routinely give us such a hard time. Otherwise why would they feel free to give us a hard time? But what you experience as the other giving you a hard time might be something he experiences as trying to break free of a trap.

So the guy who tries to get his fiancée to agree to postpone the wedding might find she scolds him and tries to make him feel like a jerk. But what it may feel like inside for her is that unless she fights him, he's got her.

Remember when you were a kid and got dragged along to visit some cranky relative? You didn't want to go but you were trapped, and the only way you could preserve your sense of self was to act sullen the whole time. Well, adults do the same thing. That's just how all-pervasive feeling trapped is.

If you don't take steps to prevent the other person from feeling trapped when you speak your truth, what he or she does in response to feeling trapped will harm your relationship. Suppose your truth is something as mild as your telling your boss that you're feeling restless and unsatisfied on your job. Perhaps you're hoping that he'll give you some fresh responsibilities or move you a bit faster toward a promotion. But exactly what you're hoping he'll do is what he might feel trapped into doing. And he might respond to feeling trapped by unconsciously doing things to make you feel you can't handle new responsibilities.

Solutions

The way you prevent people from feeling trapped is by giving them freedom. So you could tell your boss how you feel but indicate you're not sure what the best thing to do about it is. Ask him how fast he thinks you could move up. Ask him what he thinks is the best thing for you to do with the way you feel. In other words, give him *response options*. The more response options he has, the less trapped he'll feel.

Whatever your truth, it works beautifully to give the other person response options to prevent him from feeling trapped. Do you want to postpone your wedding? Give your fiancé a lot of choices. Let him decide how you're going to announce it. Let him decide how long the postponement will be, at least within a given range. But it's also important that he have choices about how he feels. Make this explicit. Let him know, "I can't tell you how you should feel about this. You're entitled to feel however you want."

This is another one of the mistakes I made with my wife. I was so gung ho about minimizing the whole story that I must have made it all too clear that only one response was permissible: a nonchalant, supersophisticated dismissal of the whole thing as unimportant. Any other response would be highly criticizable as all too uncool. Of course she felt trapped by what I was putting out, and she is far too strong a woman to respond meekly to someone's trying to trap her. Whatever she would have felt anyway she felt double just to indicate her freedom to feel any way she wanted.

Helping the other person not feel trapped is particularly important when your truth is a request. It's precisely because you're asking for something specific that he's most likely to feel trapped. Two bad things can happen: either you won't get what you want just so the other person can feel free, or he'll feel trapped into giving you what you want and for that reason resent the hell out of you.

Again, you deal with this by giving him response options. For example, if you want to borrow money and you care about the relationship as well, then you have to give the other person choices about how much to lend you and about how you'll pay it back. You might not get as much money as you wanted, but then again you might get more because the other person feels free to give it to you. But whether or not you get any money at all, the feelings in the relationship will be kept unpolluted because you're giving the other person choices about how to respond.

Will the Other Person Feel That He's Stepped into a Piece of Bad Personal History?

You're going to tell your fiancée you want to postpone the wedding. Imagine three scenarios.

One, your fiancée's parents got divorced in an emotionally scary and devastating way for your fiancée, so that she's incredibly leery of her own marriage ending in disaster.

Two, your fiancée's parents have a storybook marriage, one that's always pointed to as the dream marriage the rest of us can only aspire to, and she's terrified that she can't possibly accomplish the same herself.

And three, your fiancée had a long-standing relationship before the two of you met that ended when out of the clear blue sky the guy dumped her, and that breakup shattered her so that she's paranoid about being dumped again.

Wouldn't it make sense that the way you told her you wanted to postpone the wedding varied depending upon which of these is true? If you're going to meet her needs while you tell the truth, don't you have to focus on the specific fears that her history has created?

Solutions

To do this, make a clear distinction between what's happening now and what happened in the past. If her parents have gotten divorced, then you could say something like, "I know you don't want to go through the same kind of horrible mess yourself that you saw them go through, but for one thing we're not breaking up at all and I don't want us to break up. And for another thing, it's my belief and intention that this postponement will strengthen our relationship and make our breaking up much less likely."

If her parents have a storybook marriage, then you could say something like, "I know how badly you want to have as good a marriage as your parents, so I can see why you'd be disappointed about my asking for a postponement. But I think we have just as good a relationship as they do, and I hope our marriage turns out as well. I certainly want it to. And what I'm aiming at is that this postponement will help us have as good a marriage as they do. It'll just mean that I'm a little more ready when we finally do take our vows."

And if she herself was dumped, then you could say something like, "I know you were really hurt when Sam walked out on you, and I can understand why this postponement makes you think of that, but it's not the same thing at all. Sam couldn't ask for what he needed, but I can. And that means I don't have to walk out if I'm not getting everything I want."

In each case, her personal history was addressed directly and pre-empted, and she was shown exactly how the present was different from the past.

Will the Other Person Feel Helpless?

This might surprise you, but helplessness is really about familiarity. We all know how to deal with things we're familiar with, things we've gone through before. But when someone says something to us and we have the sense that, Toto, we're not in Kansas anymore, then it's the strange new world we face that makes us feel helpless.

It's an essential quality of a difficult truth that it introduces something unfamiliar into the other person's life. Not only do you rock his world, but you shove him into a different world. This is a quite different issue from changing someone's expectations. When someone's been fired, he has to deal with that he's been expecting to keep the old job. But he may feel *helpless* because he's being thrust into a world in which he's got to find a *new* job, and that may be something he hasn't done in a long time or that he's never done at his level of corporate responsibility.

So you can probably guess the difference this makes if, for example, you tell someone you want to postpone your wedding. Of course you've disappointed her expectations, but the new and unfamiliar world that makes her feel helpless might be, for instance, one in which you have to deal with a crazy guy who does things like postponing weddings.

That was one of the problems my wife had with the way I told her about being involved with another woman. She had dealt with all kinds of things in her life, but she'd never dealt with that, and the utter unfamiliarity of it made her feel terribly helpless.

Helplessness is dangerous

The reason this is a problem for you is that nothing makes people go nuts like feeling helpless. They either panic or collapse or they find a way to do both. In their panic they might attack you or abandon you. In their collapse they might act depressed or run for comfort somewhere.

Suppose the truth you tell is something as utterly mild as telling your lover you wish he'd spend more time in foreplay when you have sex. What's the big deal about that? But suppose he doesn't know what to do *in* foreplay.

Suppose he's already doing everything he can think of in the eleven and a half minutes you usually spend in foreplay. Now he hears you asking for a whole half hour of new stuff. So he has a sense of being thrust into a completely unfamiliar world, where he not only doesn't know what to do but somehow feels there's something wrong with asking for directions. And so he feels terribly helpless. He feels so helpless, in fact, that he turns on you and attacks you for God knows what problem in your own sexuality. And then he just stops initiating sex altogether.

You've got to assume that anytime you open your heart to anyone important to you and unburden yourself of some truth you've been holding back that you're going to move the person into an unfamiliar world where he feels helpless. It's not just for his sake but for your sake as well that you must make the unfamiliar familiar to prevent the sense of helplessness and so prevent him from going nuts.

Solutions

Ask yourself what the other person will find to be new territory in what you're saying and then give him a road map. If you want to tell your lover that you want him to spend more time in foreplay, then tell him what you'd like him to do. If he knows exactly what's expected, then you've made the unfamiliar familiar and he won't feel helpless.

I know about one man who failed to do this when he asked his sister if he could borrow a sizable sum of money. In her entire life she'd never imagined anyone, much less her older brother, asking to borrow so much money. The whole thing was so unfamiliar that she panicked and said no in a harsh, abrupt way because she simply didn't know how to negotiate any other solution with him. Their relationship was damaged because he never stopped and thought for a moment about how weird it would be for her to have him ask for money. And so he never did such simple things as give her the opportunity to ask questions or take the time to make up her mind slowly.

If you don't know what the other person's going to find unfamiliar, then when you tell your difficult truth, the first thing to do is acknowledge that you're both in unfamiliar territory and that you want to take as much time as is needed to talk everything over.

Make it clear that the other person doesn't have to deal with what you say all by himself. Any problems he has figuring out what your words mean or what he's supposed to do with them can be brought out into the open. For example, "I know that in your whole life no one's ever told you he wants to postpone your wedding, but we can talk together about this until you get clear about how you want to deal with it. I'm not telling you this just to dump it into your lap, but for us to help each other with it."

Expect that you'll have to keep on doing this as you talk about the truth you've spoken. There's always some new bit of unfamiliar territory just around the corner. And so you have to continually reassert your willingness to help the other person make sense of it.

Will the Other Person Feel the Threat of Loss?

Sometimes this issue is completely obvious. In our postponing-the-wedding example, you'd have to be pretty stupid not to figure out that telling someone you want to postpone the wedding is going to make her feel you might pull out altogether. But even here, it's been my experience that a lot of people are so much in the habit of blurting out the truth that they might very well just come out and say, "Listen, I'm feeling things are going too fast and I need some space for myself, so I'd like to postpone the wedding." And they'd simply forget to mention that they're still 100 percent committed to going ahead with it, just at a later date.

But at least in this situation we can feel pretty confident that if they did consider the other person for a moment, they would think of saying that they weren't pulling out of getting married.

Identifying the loss

Much more difficult are the situations where the loss the other person's threatened with isn't obvious. For example, Lynette and Roslyn were partners in a business where they designed and manufactured women's clothes, just like Calvin Klein or Nicole Miller, but smaller. Lynette was in charge of the business end and Roslyn did the actual designing.

At one point Lynette started feeling they needed to expand their product line, both to generate more revenue and to diversify their offerings in case things slacked off in their main line. On two occasions she suggested Roslyn apply a specific design to new products, in one case handbags, in another case men's ties. But Roslyn had dug in her heels and said it wasn't possible and that things didn't work that way.

But Lynette couldn't let it go. After thinking about it an entire Saturday, she called Roslyn one Sunday morning and said, "Let me just run an idea by you. What if we started a whole new label, where instead of having to be consistent with our designs we took a whole new approach. That way you wouldn't be locked in and you'd feel a lot freer."

Roslyn stunned Lynette with her response: "Let me stop you right here. Let's not talk about designs and product lines. Let's talk about the real issue, which is that maybe I'm not the right partner for you. What I hear you telling me is that you're not going to be happy unless you find one of those people who churn out one new design after another, no matter how tacky or derivative. But I'm not like that, so I think you should get someone else because it doesn't sound like you'll be happy until you do."

When feelings explode

We like to feel we can all have our feelings with people who are close to us and yet everything will eventually be okay. It's what we see in sitcoms, where ruffled feelings don't go on too long before they're soothed. But in real life, even though we think we can let our feelings hang out, clashes too often lead to disaster. That's what almost happened to Lynette and Roslyn. Roslyn meant it when she said Lynette should try to find a new partner. Lynette felt rejected and suspicious after Roslyn talked about breaking off their relationship. In the real world, their relationship was almost destroyed.

Roslyn had grown up in the garment business. She knew all too well how easily partnerships got formed and dissolved. In that business, people left each other all the time. She was terribly afraid of being left herself. With Lynette's pressure to start new product lines, Roslyn could smell the kind of dissatisfaction that she knew led to breakups. If she was threatened with loss, she wouldn't wait for it to happen, she'd make it happen.

What made this tragic was that Lynette wasn't threatening Roslyn with loss at all. All Lynette wanted was to feel free in their relationship to put forward her ideas. If Roslyn couldn't do it or didn't want to do it, fine. But what kind of jail was Lynette in if she couldn't even bring it up? By slamming the door in her face the way she did, Roslyn seemed to be saying to Lynette that Lynette simply couldn't be herself in that relationship. So why would she want to stay? Roslyn's response to a nonexistent threat of loss made real loss a possibility.

Plan ahead

Lynette could have prevented all this if she'd thought about how Roslyn might go nuts if she spoke from the heart. She could have said to herself, "I'm pushing on Roslyn to do something. That means I'm expressing dissatisfaction. When people are dissatisfied, they leave. Won't Roslyn think I'm planning to leave?" Obviously this was something to be taken care of.

The best way to take care of it was directly. Lynette needed to preempt Roslyn's negative response. She could have said something like, "I need to ask you for something that's important to me, but I don't want you to think that because I'm pushing for this that I'm unhappy with you or that it will be a problem for me if you can't do what I ask. I'd like you to go along with it, but the most important thing for me is to feel that I can bring this up at all."

Solutions

You can do the same thing, and if you do, it will make you tremendously effective at being someone who can speak from the heart and yet not undermine her relationships. Just ask yourself, whenever you have something you want to say that's hard for you to say, where the other person might smell out some possible loss he'd feel threatened by.

I think that any of us who have to speak from the heart and say something the other person might find hard to handle would do well to commit the following sentence to memory: "Look, you're probably afraid of [and name some loss], but that's just not in the cards. You don't have to be afraid of it because [and explain why]." The more often we say something like this, the less often the people who are important to us have to leave us to prevent us from leaving them.

I hope you realize how much territory we've just covered. I know that as an algolalophobic you're certainly dreading the other person's response when you finally speak your truth. But there's always something vague about dread. What you now know that you didn't know before are the most common hard-to-deal-with responses that can come up. And what's most important is that you know how to deal with these responses. You know how to prevent them if possible. And you know how to respond if they come up.

WORDS TO ANSWER BACK WITH

Sometimes the responses that are hardest to handle aren't senses of betrayal, loss, or helplessness. Instead they're simply words the other person says that stop you in your tracks. Here are the most common of these challenges that make telling the truth so difficult, and here's how to deal with them.

"Why Didn't You Tell Me Sooner?"

First of all, you should've preempted this by apologizing for not having told sooner and by giving some kind of explanation for why you're telling now. But since you're telling the truth anyway, if someone asks you this, respond with the truth: "I was afraid of how you'd take it and I was too cowardly to say anything sooner. I was waiting until I felt brave enough." Or "I didn't know I felt this way myself." Or "I was hoping you'd change on your own without my saying anything."

The point is that we almost never have a good reason for why we didn't say the truth sooner. It's better to acknowledge that you screwed up than to say something lame to try to get yourself off the hook.

"If You're Telling Me This, Why Should I Believe You Don't Have Other Bombshells to Drop on Me?"

First of all, you have to show you understand why the other person would say this. In fact it isn't a crazy thing to say. But then you have to work at rebuilding trust. What I know from working with people in the most damaged business and personal relationships is that you rebuild trust with people the way you build trust with a wild animal. All you can do is have patience, act in obviously innocent ways, offer something reassuring, and make sure to do absolutely nothing to sow a seed of distrust. It's what you do with a squirrel in the park. So you do the same thing with a friend or a brother or a boss. It helps a lot to acknowledge that you're the one with the responsibility to do what you can to make it reasonable for the other person to trust you again.

"You Must Think I'm Awful to Say That"

The person is just saying that he or she feels attacked or blamed. You must say something like, "On the contrary. The fact that I'm telling you this means that I respect and value you." Be specific. (You can also turn to the section earlier in this chapter where I talk about how to deal with people responding to feeling attacked or blamed.)

"Well, Then Why Should We Have Any Kind of Relationship at All?"

What's happened here is that you must have said something to indicate some kind of problem or difficulty in the relationship. Unless you yourself want to end the relationship (in which case *that* should be the truth you're telling), you need to do two things. You need to talk about what you value in the relationship and why you want to keep it going. And you need to ask the other person to talk to you about whatever problems she has with what you've said. You can say something like, "I don't want us to talk about not having a relationship. I do want to talk about doing whatever you need to feel this relationship works better for you."

"You're Too Much for Me to Deal With"

Apologize for telling your truth in an overwhelming and confusing way. Then say you hope that what you have to say isn't too much to deal with. Then say something like, "Whatever those things are that you find too much to deal with, let's talk about them one at a time until we feel we can deal with them."

"You Say You're Telling Me the Whole Truth about This, but I Think You're Still Lying and Holding Things Back"

This response is particularly common when you confess a guilty secret. But we're back to the trust issue again. All you can do is promise that you have told the whole truth and that there won't be any further revelations. But you had better make sure that you followed my advice and told the whole truth in the first place. (This is why using virtual telling is such a grave decision. Once you've chosen to tell an alternate version of what's real, you can't go back. That's why if the other person can ever find out the real truth, you can't use virtual telling.)

"What Kind of Person Are You to Say Something Like That?"

You have to find out what she means by this. "Tell me how this gives you trouble," you could say. Your job here is to indicate your willingness to hang in there and work out the difficulties that come up from your having spoken the truth.

"I Don't Want to Talk about It"

Don't believe it and don't let him get away with it. Respond as if this were simply a request for time to think about how to deal with your truth. You could say, "What do you need to feel ready to talk about this?" or "When do you think you'll feel ready to talk about this?" Make it clear that you want to hear what he has to say.

"Every Single Thing Between Us Is Different Now"

The other person has just swallowed something huge and hasn't digested it. You have to help her digest it. "Well, what difference is hardest for you?" you might ask. The thing you have to do is indicate a willingness to hang in there and talk about everything that needs to be talked about.

"Let's Fight"

Of course, no one ever says this in so many words. But it's what you're afraid of if you're a confrontation-phobic: being challenged, being yelled at.

The way you deal with this is surprisingly simple. *Say* that you want to avoid a confrontation. You'd be surprised at what you get for yourself when you say something like, "Look, I wanted to tell you this, but I really hate confrontations and what I had to say wasn't easy for me to say, and it probably wasn't so easy for you to hear, but I'd like this whole discussion to go as smoothly as possible." This is powerful. Even people who are primed to make a big deal out of whatever it is you have to say will often feel they have to restrain themselves just because you've said so clearly that you want to avoid a confrontation.

Silence

You probably can't put this response in words. But when we reveal a difficult truth, the other person is often hurt and sad. To put it bluntly, your words have made him depressed. A good thing to say is, "I know this is hard for you. Do you want to talk or do you need for me to leave you alone for a while?" If the other person wants to talk, the most important thing you can do is listen without giving her an argument. But if anything she says reflects a negative or doom-laden version of what you've said, you can give a much more positive reading of what your words meant. If the other person wants you to leave her alone, it's important that you go along with this, but you have to make it clear that you look forward to the two of you talking about it in the not-too-distant future, but only when she's ready.

FINAL THOUGHTS

Dealing with what happens after you tell your truth is all about one thing. You had certain intentions. You were interested in more than just mouthing words. You wanted those words to cross over and produce certain kinds of results in the other person. Your intentions might have been as simple as having the other person say, "I hear how you feel." Or your intentions might have been as complex as having the other person accept you for requesting what you were requesting while at the same time discussing with you what he needs to give you what you were requesting.

The one thing the aftermath is all about is the gap between your intentions and what actually happened. The reason you learn how to tell the truth effectively is so that gap will be small. But this isn't rocket science, and other people can be unpredictable. So there's always some gap. That means there's always some surprise in store for you.

The secret to managing that surprise is to know that you shouldn't be surprised at being surprised. In other words, expect the unexpected. Sure, you *tried* to meet the other person's needs as you thought about how to tell your truth and as you actually told it. But just the way golfers need at least three or four shots to get the ball to progress from tee to hole, you're simply going to have to respond to whatever the other person says that shows a discrepancy between what you intended and what has actually happened.

The most important psychological position to take as you go through this is that it's all about cooperation. And that's perfect for someone who's afraid of confrontation, because cooperation is the exact opposite of confrontation. So you can be the person in the know. You can understand that even the confrontational things the other person is saying are part of an unconscious effort to adjust his response to what you seem to want.

New hope

One of the biggest tragedies I've seen as I've helped people with these issues over the years is the way it seems to us truth tellers as though the other person is somehow intentionally or even maliciously misunderstanding what we're trying to do. We feel so pure in our hearts and yet the other person's response seems so wildly inappropriate. How could that be unless the other person were doing it deliberately? So we feel injured or insulted.

This is a bigger problem the closer the other person is to you. Whether it's a lover or a friend or a close business associate, you think that greater intimacy will bring about better communication. Isn't that what it means to be close: that you have an easier time understanding each other?

In a sense the opposite is true. What I've seen clinically and what my research confirms is that the closer someone is to us, the more we stop thinking about how we're going to say truths that the other person might find difficult. We trust our very closeness to the other person will bridge any gap that our words might create.

In other words, we relax, or perhaps I should say collapse, into intimacy as if that were a place that entitles us to lazy talk. The people we care most about we're most careless with in saying the things that are most important. And then we're shocked, *shocked,* when there's a huge gap between the impact we intended our words to have and the way the other person actually responded.

You should tell the truth to people the way you buy presents for people. The more important someone is to you, the more care you put into buying him or her a present, and so the more care you should put into telling this person the truth that's in your heart. The understanding I've tried so hard to develop through years of work and to present in this book is important everywhere, but nowhere more important than with the people you care most about.

Just keep closing the communications gap

And what you do with this understanding as you actually go through the telling and deal with the aftermath is to stay focused on just what the gap is between how you want to be understood and how you're being understood. Assume that the person who misses your intentions is still your partner in trying to come to an understanding. And if he doesn't "get it," he's still trying to cooperate with you in trying to get it.

Keep your goal in sight

Stay focused on the very goal that enabled you to decide what category your truth fit into. Keep using the phrase "All I want is for you to . . . ," then say, "Hear how I feel" or "Find a way to give me what I want" or "Forgive me" or "Accept what I have to say" or "Agree to try to change." Make it clear that if the other person is having trouble with this, you're there to help him out. It's important not to seem disconcerted by the gap between what you were intending to convey and what seems to have come across. So what if there was a gap? That's all communication is anyway: a process of ironing out misunderstandings. There's no point in getting all tense and upset over a perfectly natural process.

The power of positive persistence

By your hanging in there you make it possible for the other person to hang in there. And that's what we want our relationships to be with the people who are important to us. Not a place where we can blurt out whatever pops into our heads or hearts. It's unrealistic to think you can ever get away with that. What we want is for our relationships to be a place where it's safe to talk about the truth. And you get that when you're respectful and responsible about how you tell the truth to the other person and when you make it clear that you're there to deal with his needs and responses to what you have to say.

The bridge of truth

To tell the truth, you build a bridge. It's a bridge of words. One end of the bridge is anchored by your reason for telling the truth in the first place. The other end is anchored by the needs the person you're telling the truth to will have in hearing your truth and in giving you what you need in response.

By being clear about your intentions and by meeting the other person's needs, your truth gets across that bridge. But afterward, the bridge is still standing. Next time it will be that much easier and it will feel better and it will be more productive for you to tell the truth to that person. The more of these bridges you build, the more harmony you'll have in your life. And the more that harmony will be built on a solid foundation of truth.

ABOUT THE AUTHOR

Charles Foster has been a clinician in private practice for twenty years and is currently the director of The Chestnut Hill Institute and a research associate at the Family and Children's Policy Center of the Heller Graduate School. He has a Ph.D. in Mental Health Policy from the Heller Graduate School for Advanced Studies in Social Welfare at Brandeis University and received his M.B.A. from Boston College. He works both as a psychotherapist and as a management consultant on organizational issues. His previous book, *Parent/Teen Breakthrough*, was chosen as a Parent's Choice Best Book. Dr. Foster has been married for thirty-one years, since the age of nineteen, and has two daughters, ages twenty-eight and twenty-six. He put himself through college playing drums in rock and roll bands. Now he grows roses and plays squash. He lives in Boston.